SEVEN SEAS ENTERTAINMENT PRESENTS

NEW GAME!

story & art by SHOTARO TOKUNO — VOLUME 1

W9-CBL-400

TRANSLATION
Jenny McKeon

ADAPTATION
Jamal Joseph Jr.

LETTERING AND RETOUCH
Courtney Williams

COVER DESIGN
Nicky Lim

PROOFREADER
Danielle King
Dayna Abel

ASSISTANT EDITOR
Jenn Grunigen

PRODUCTION ASSISTANT
CK Russell

PRODUCTION MANAGER
Lissa Pattillo

EDITOR-IN-CHIEF
Adam Arnold

PUBLISHER
Jason DeAngelis

NEW GAME! VOLUME 1
© Shotaro Tokuno 2014
First published in 2014 by Houbunsha Co., LTD. Tokyo, Japan.
English translation rights arranged with Houbunsha Co., TLD.

Seven Seas books may be purchased in bulk for educational, business, or promotional use. For information on bulk purchases, please contact Macmillan Corporate & Premium Sales Department at 1-800-221-7945 (ext 5442) or write specialmarkets@macmillan.com.

Seven Seas and the Seven Seas logo are trademarks of Seven Seas Entertainment, LLC. All rights reserved.

ISBN: 978-1-626927-76-6

Printed in China

Second Printing: September 2021

10 9 8 7 6 5 4 3 2

FOLLOW US ONLINE: www.sevenseasentertainment.com

READING DIRECTIONS

This book reads from *right to left*, Japanese style. If this is your first time reading manga, you start reading from the top right panel on each page and take it from there. If you get lost, just follow the numbered diagram here. It may seem backwards at first, but you'll get the hang of it! Have fun!!

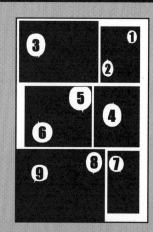

Employment Interview ②

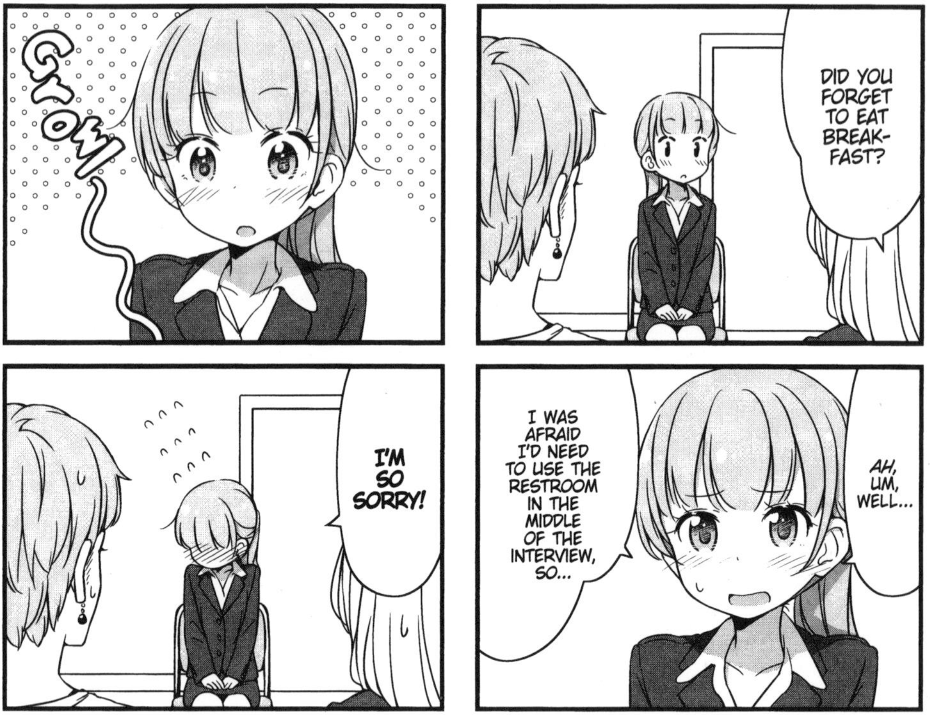

DID YOU FORGET TO EAT BREAK-FAST?
Growl
AH, UM, WELL...
I WAS AFRAID I'D NEED TO USE THE RESTROOM IN THE MIDDLE OF THE INTERVIEW, SO...
I'M SO SORRY!

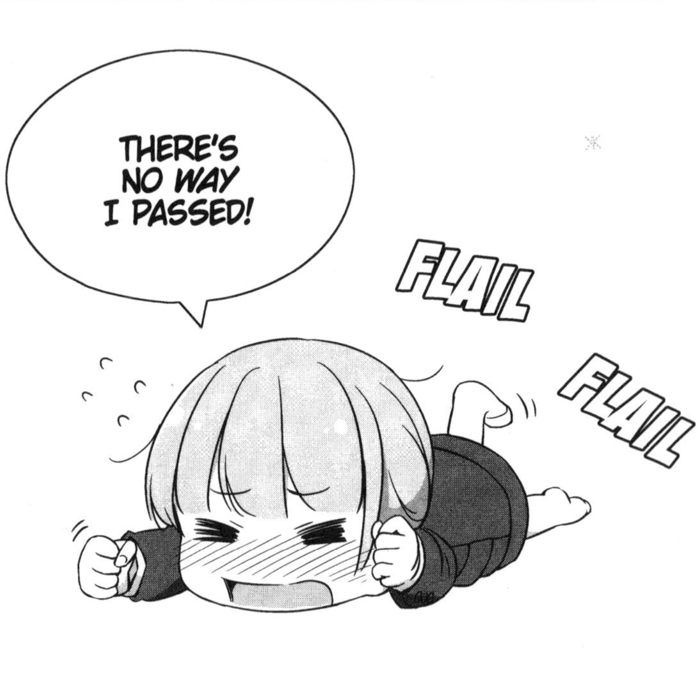

THERE'S NO WAY I PASSED!
FLAIL
FLAIL

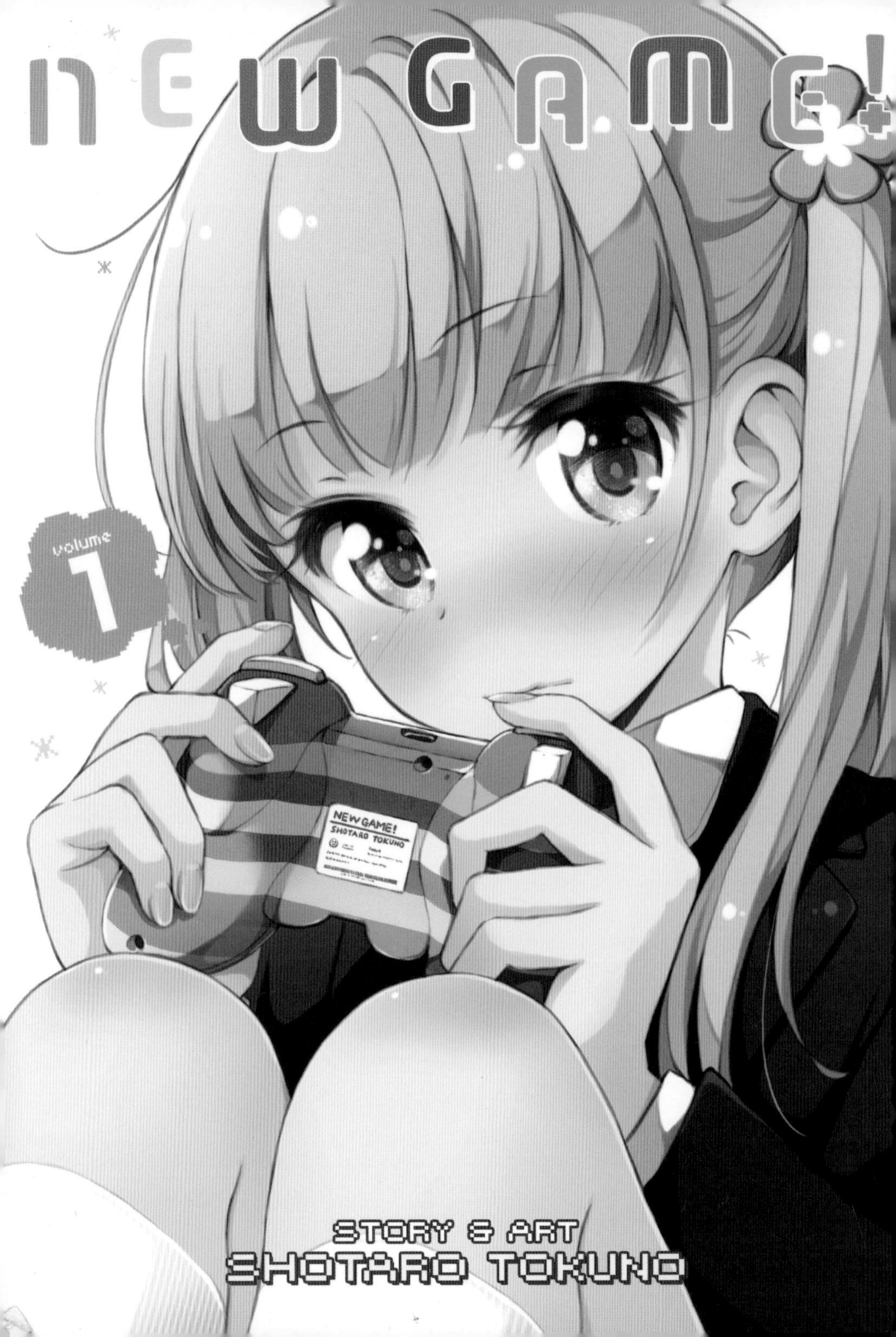
NEW GAME!
volume 1
NEW GAME!
SHOTARO TOKUNO
STORY & ART
SHOTARO TOKUNO

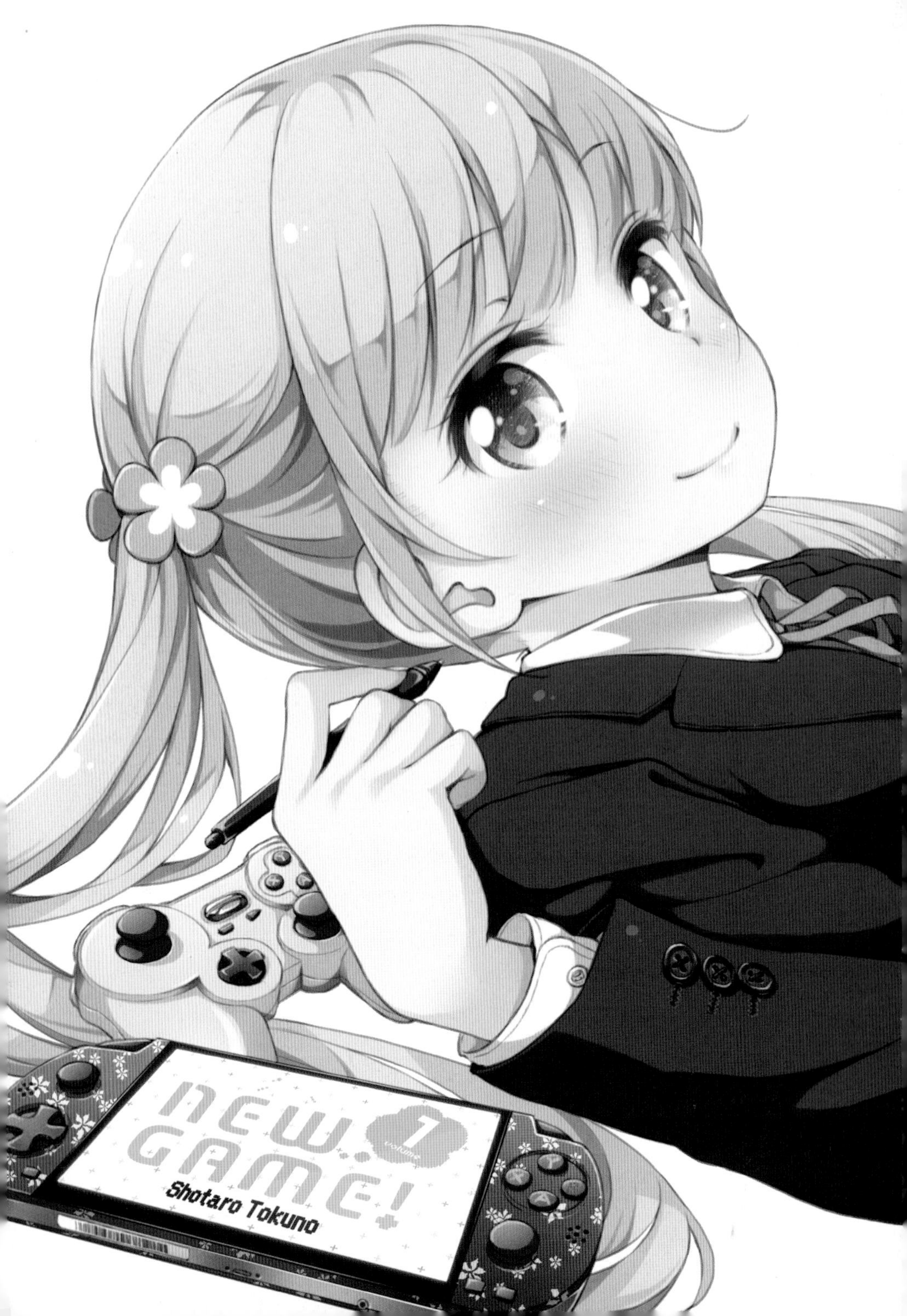
NEW GAME!
volume 1
Shotaro Tokuno

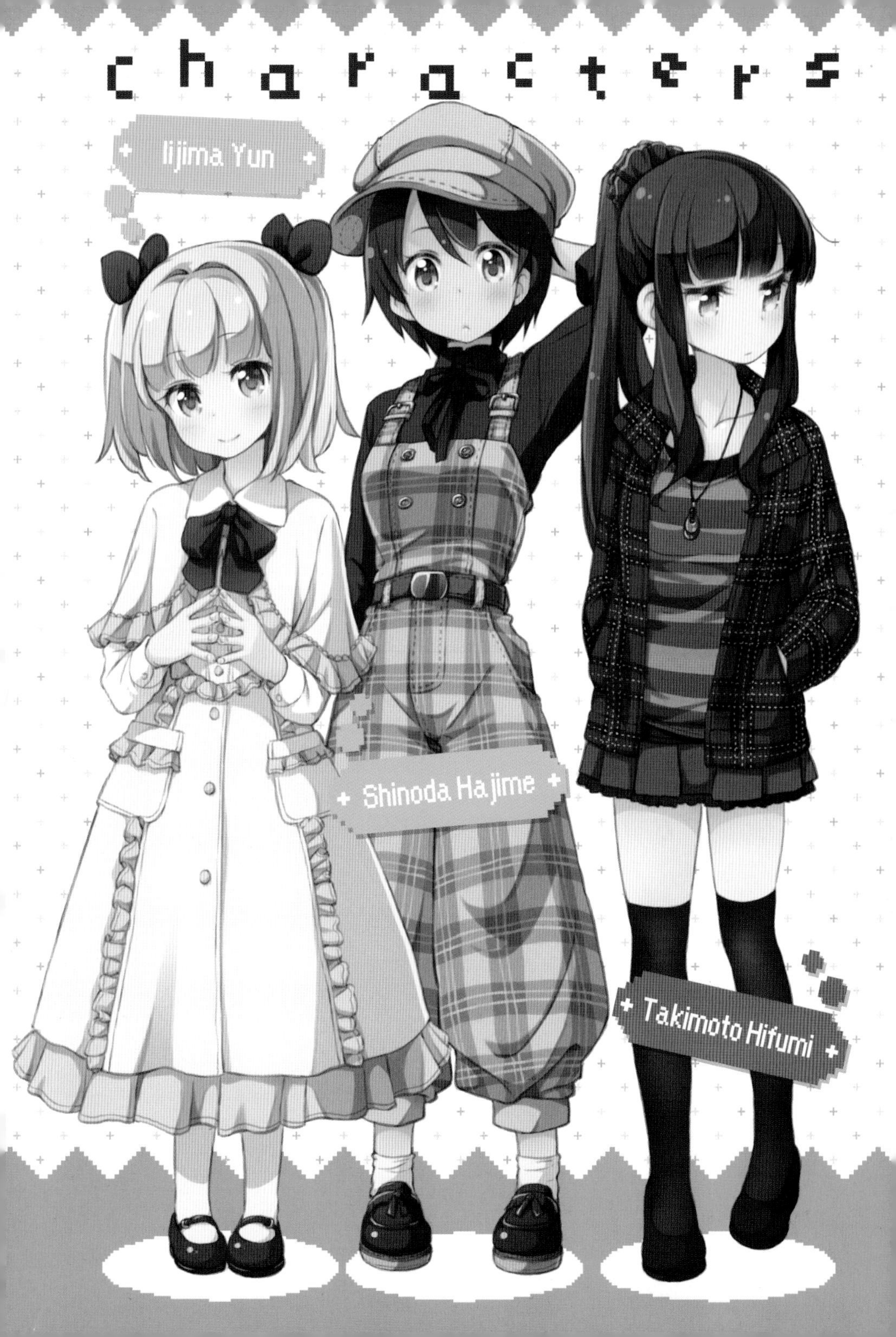
characters
Iijima Yun
Shinoda Hajime
Takimoto Hifumi

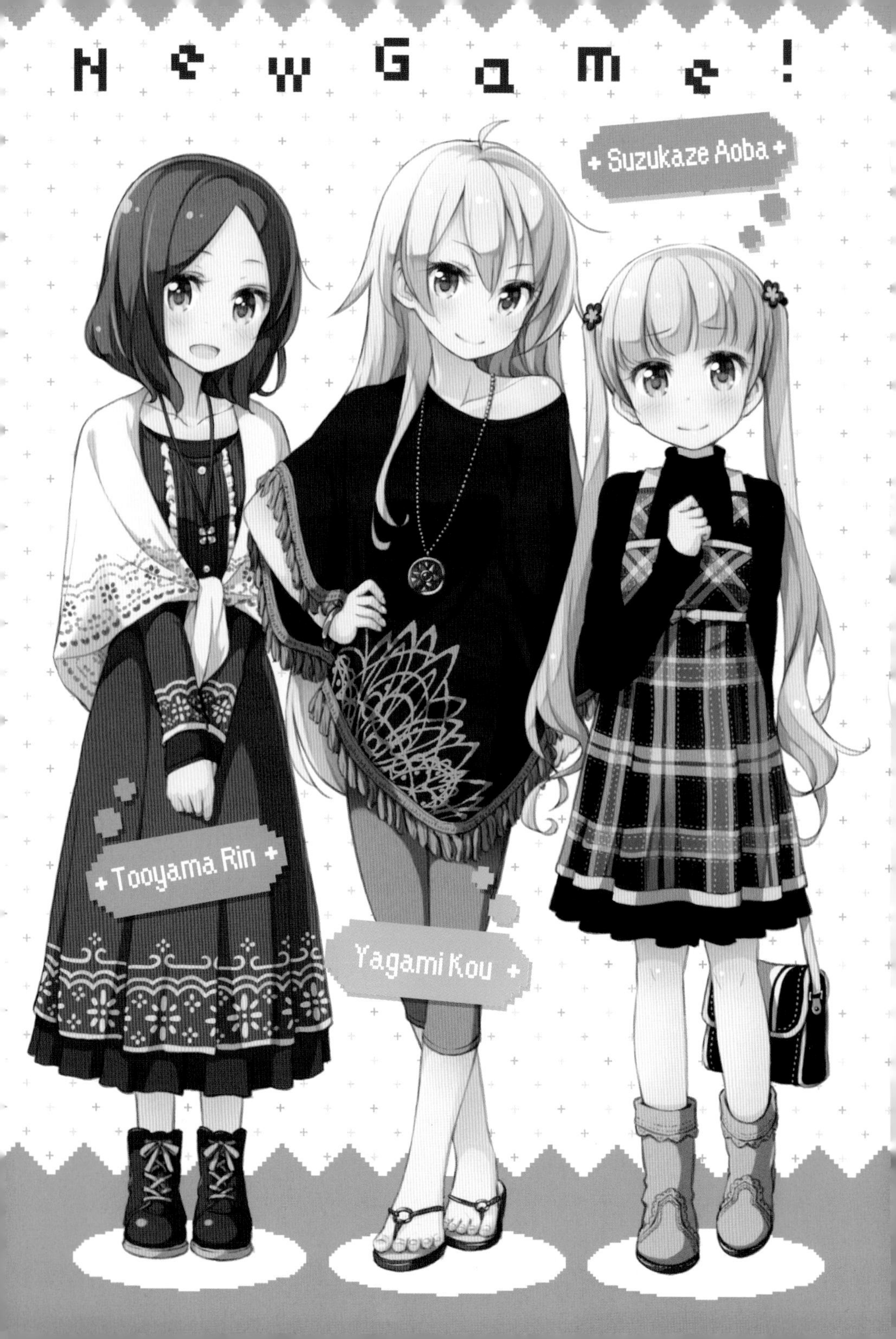
New Game!
Suzukaze Aoba
Tooyama Rin
Yagami Kou

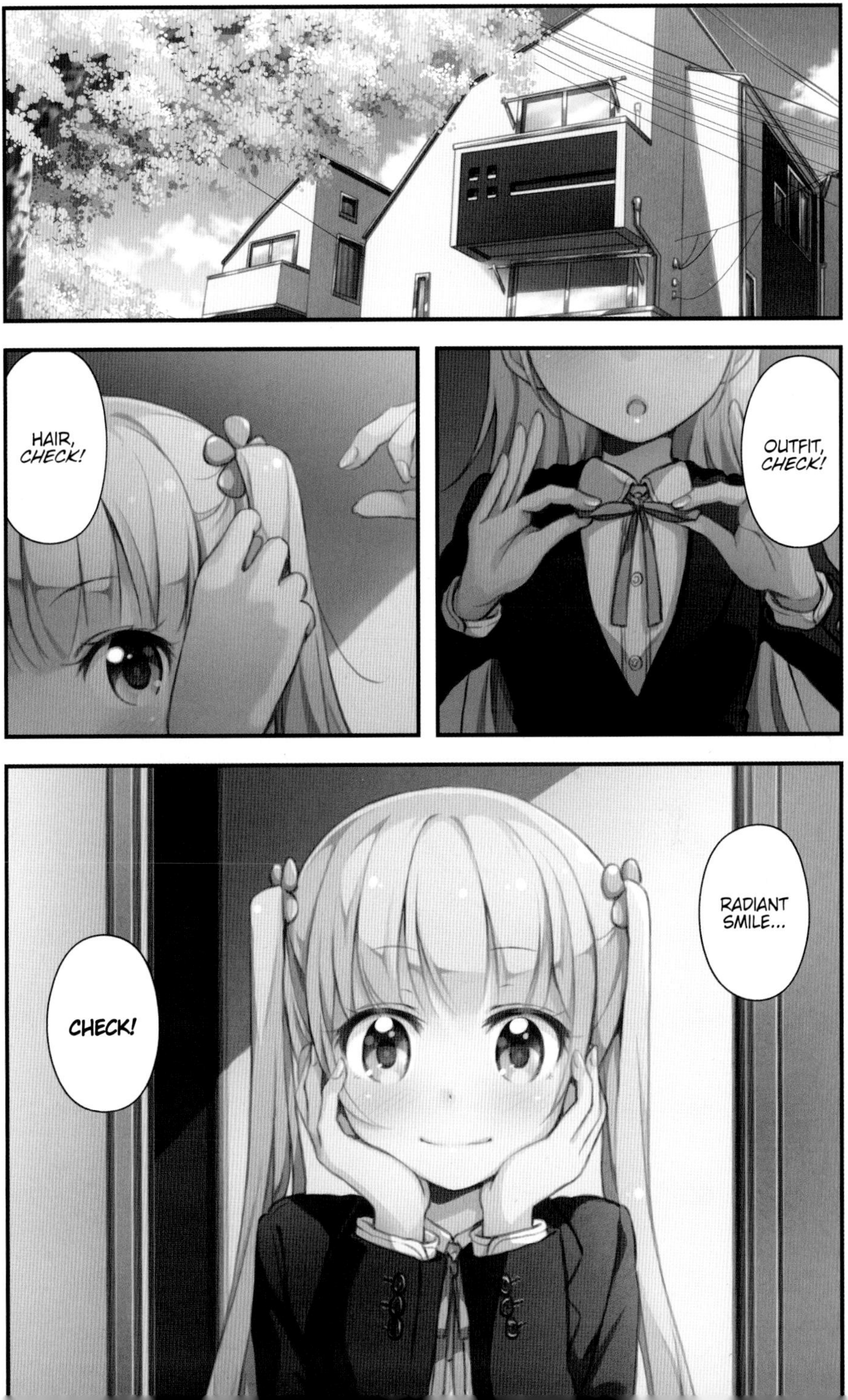
OUTFIT, CHECK!
HAIR, CHECK!
RADIANT SMILE...
CHECK!

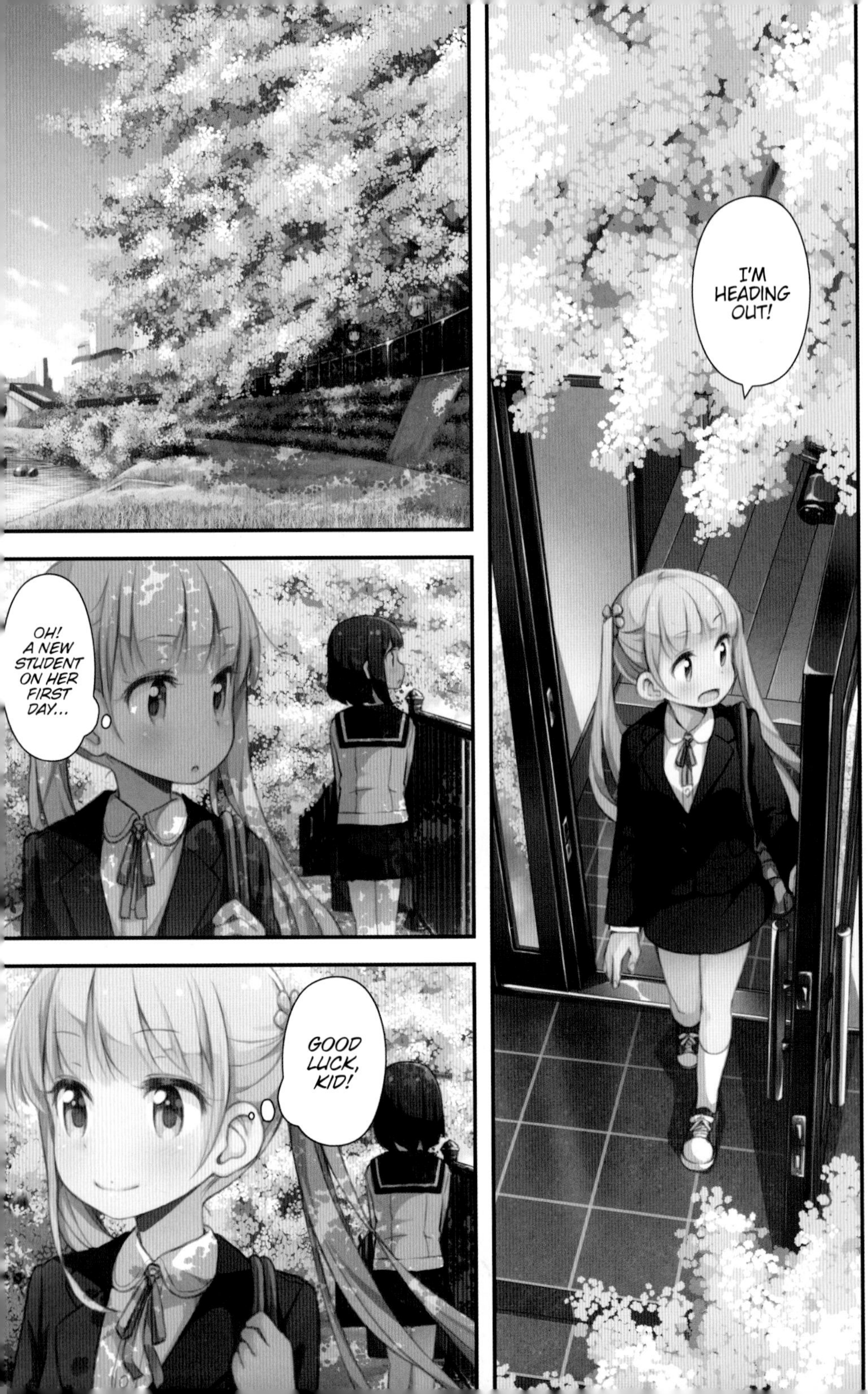
I'M HEADING OUT!
OH! A NEW STUDENT ON HER FIRST DAY...
GOOD LUCK, KID!

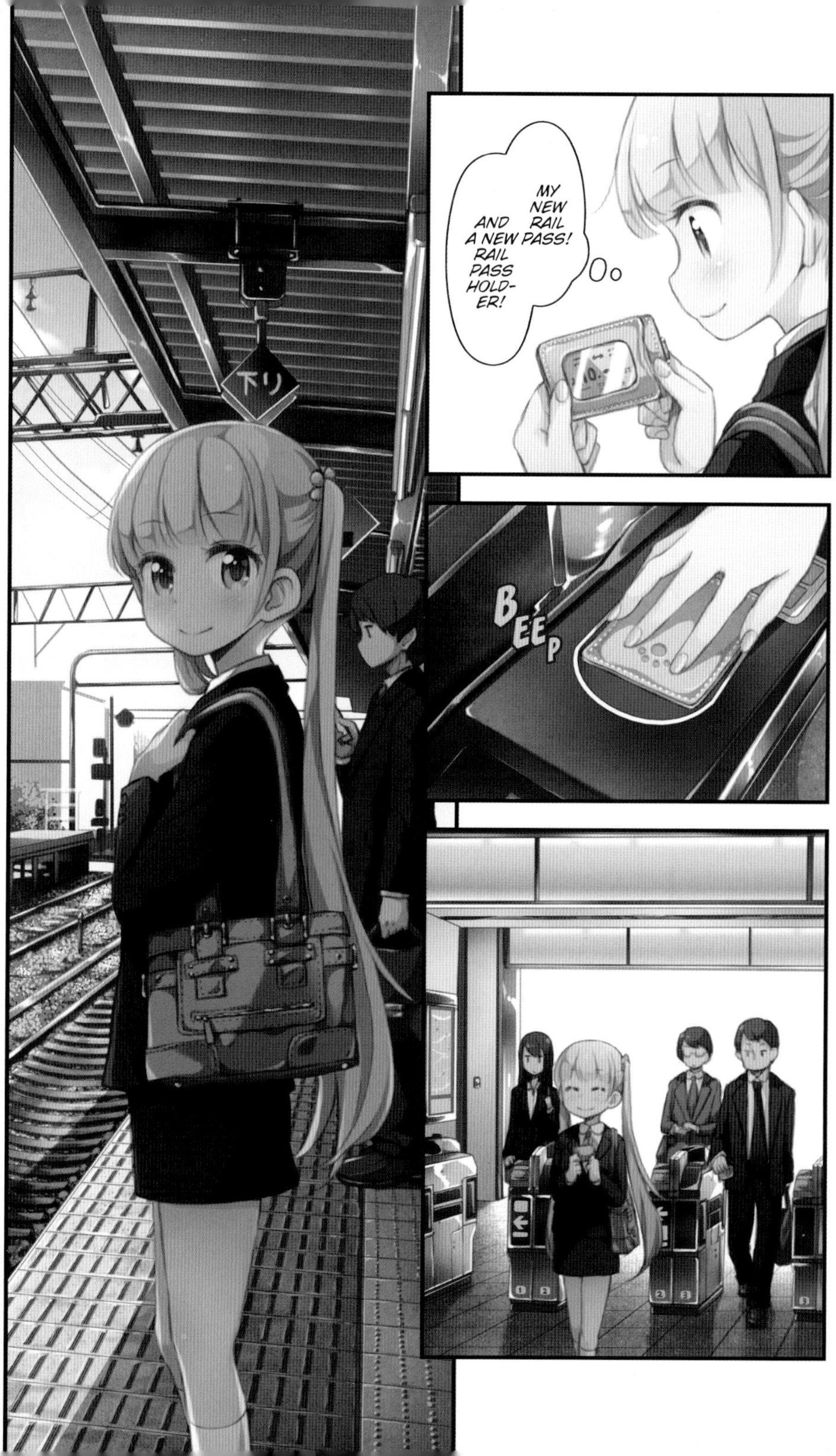
MY NEW RAIL PASS!
AND A NEW RAIL PASS HOLDER!
Oo
BEEP
下り

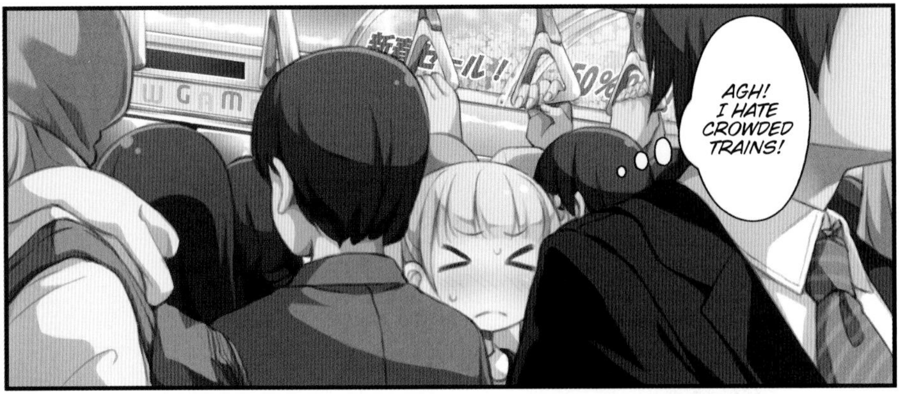
AGH! I HATE CROWDED TRAINS!

*Sign: New Clothing Sale! 50% Off

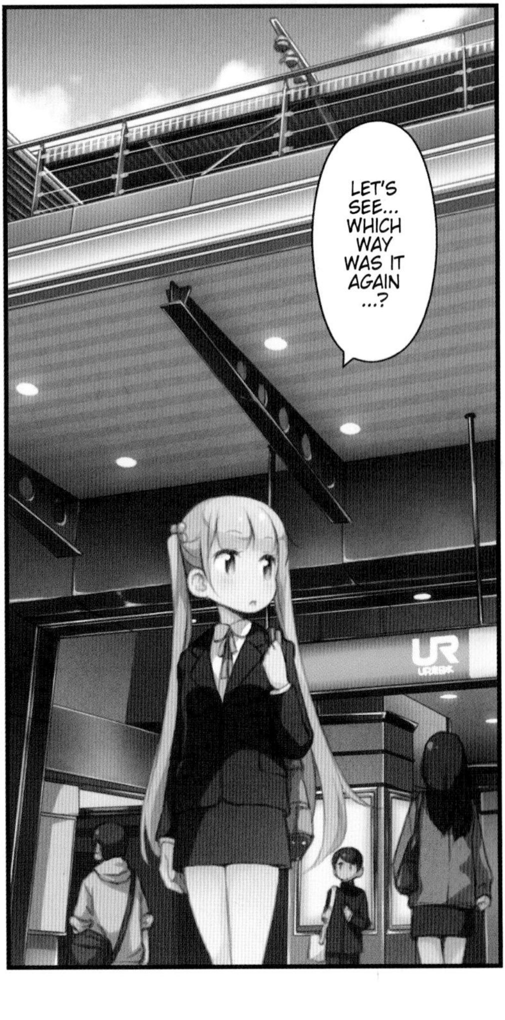
LET'S SEE... WHICH WAY WAS IT AGAIN ...?
UR

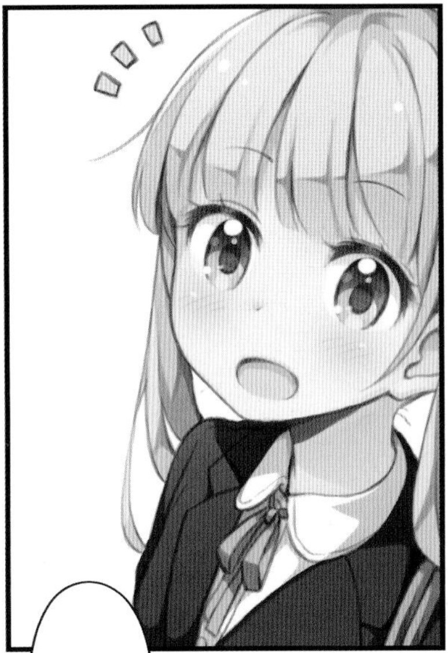

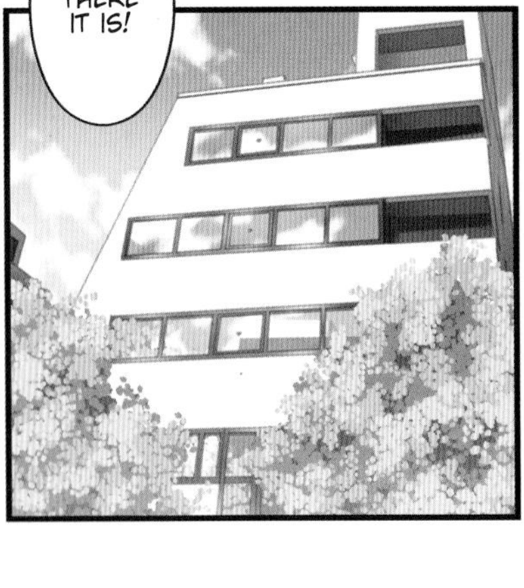
THERE IT IS!

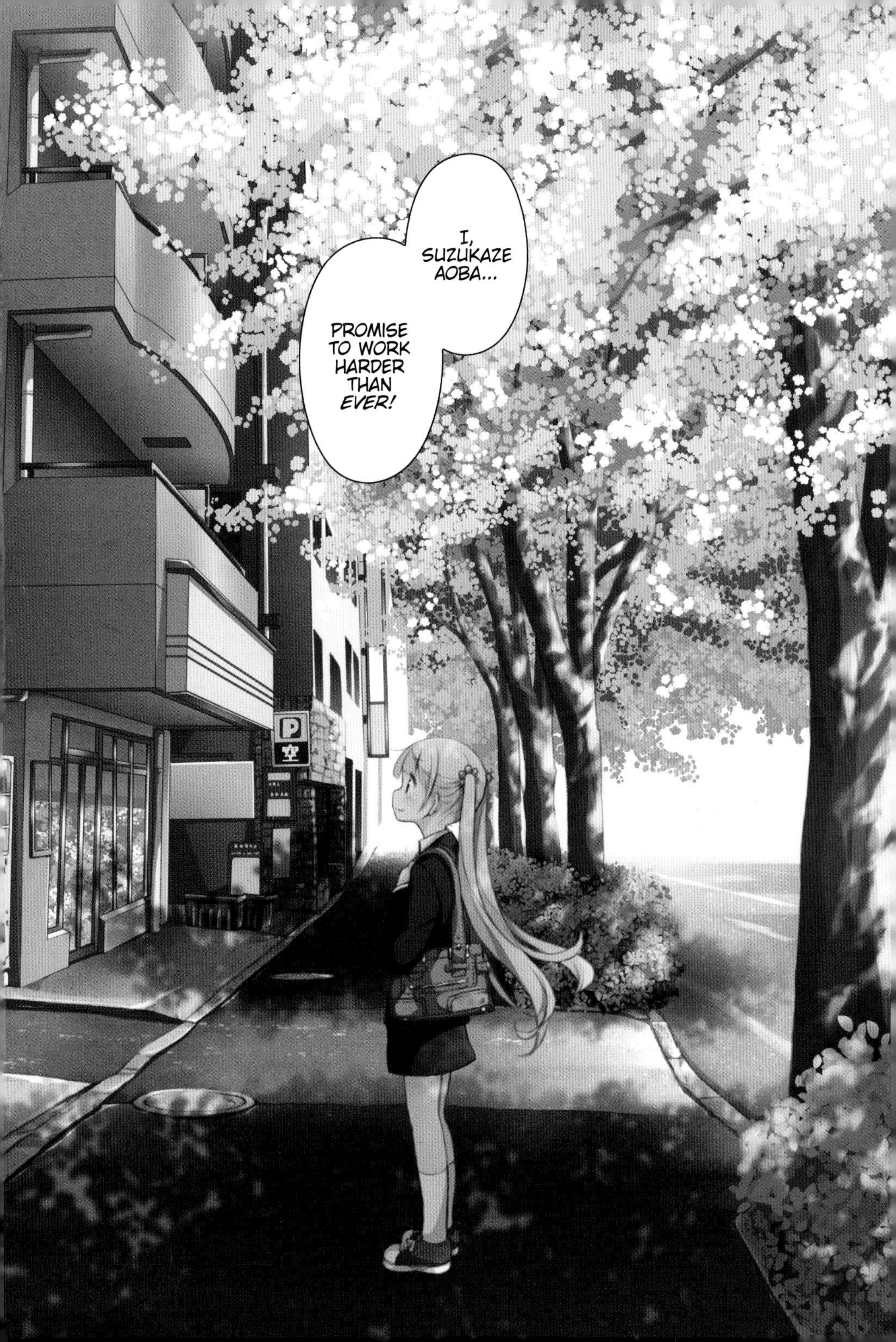
I, SUZUKAZE AOBA...
PROMISE TO WORK HARDER THAN *EVER!*
P
空

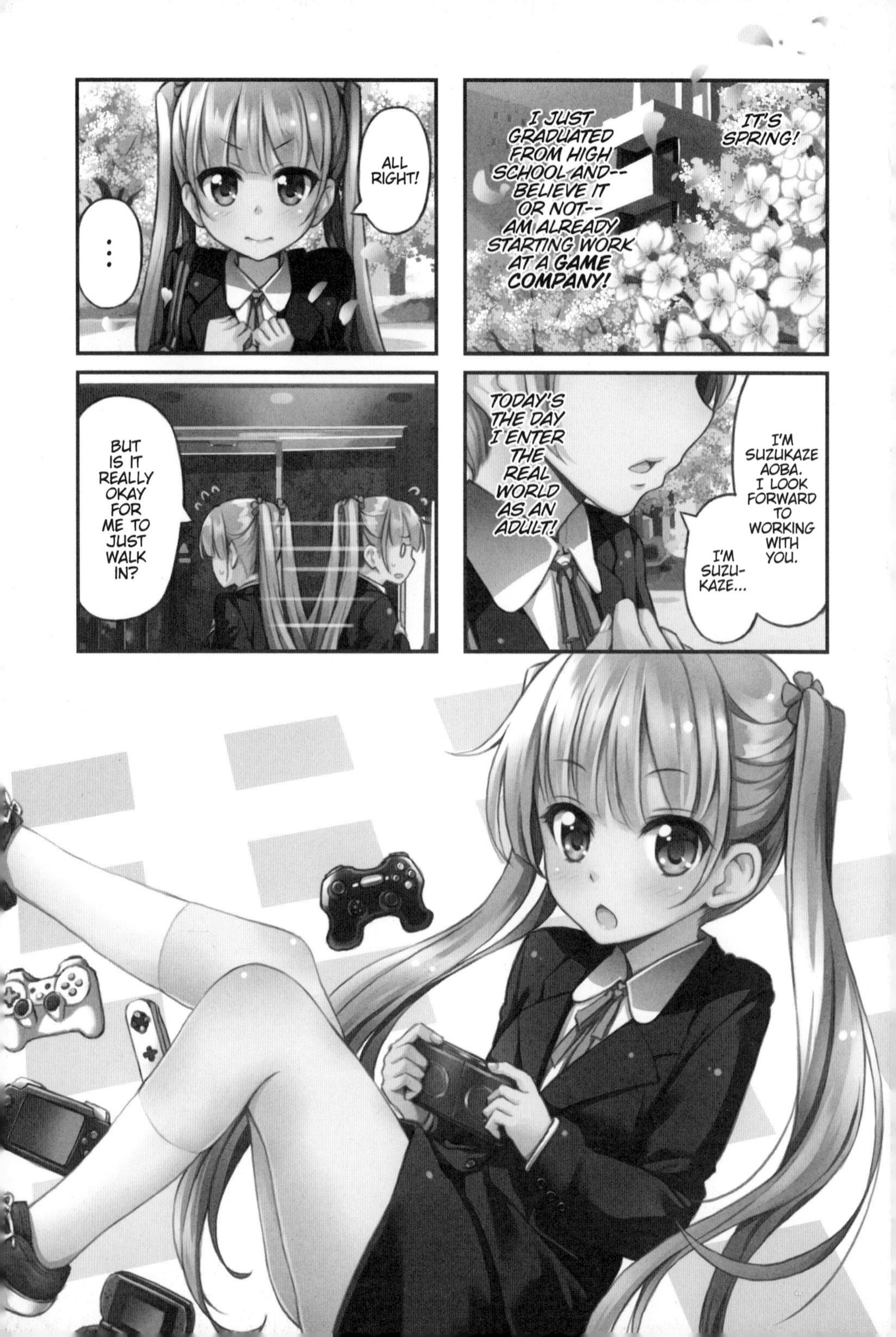
IT'S SPRING!
I JUST GRADUATED FROM HIGH SCHOOL AND-- BELIEVE IT OR NOT-- AM ALREADY STARTING WORK AT A **GAME COMPANY!**
ALL RIGHT!
...
I'M SUZUKAZE AOBA. I LOOK FORWARD TO WORKING WITH YOU.
I'M SUZUKAZE...
TODAY'S THE DAY I ENTER THE REAL WORLD AS AN ADULT!
BUT IS IT REALLY OKAY FOR ME TO JUST WALK IN?

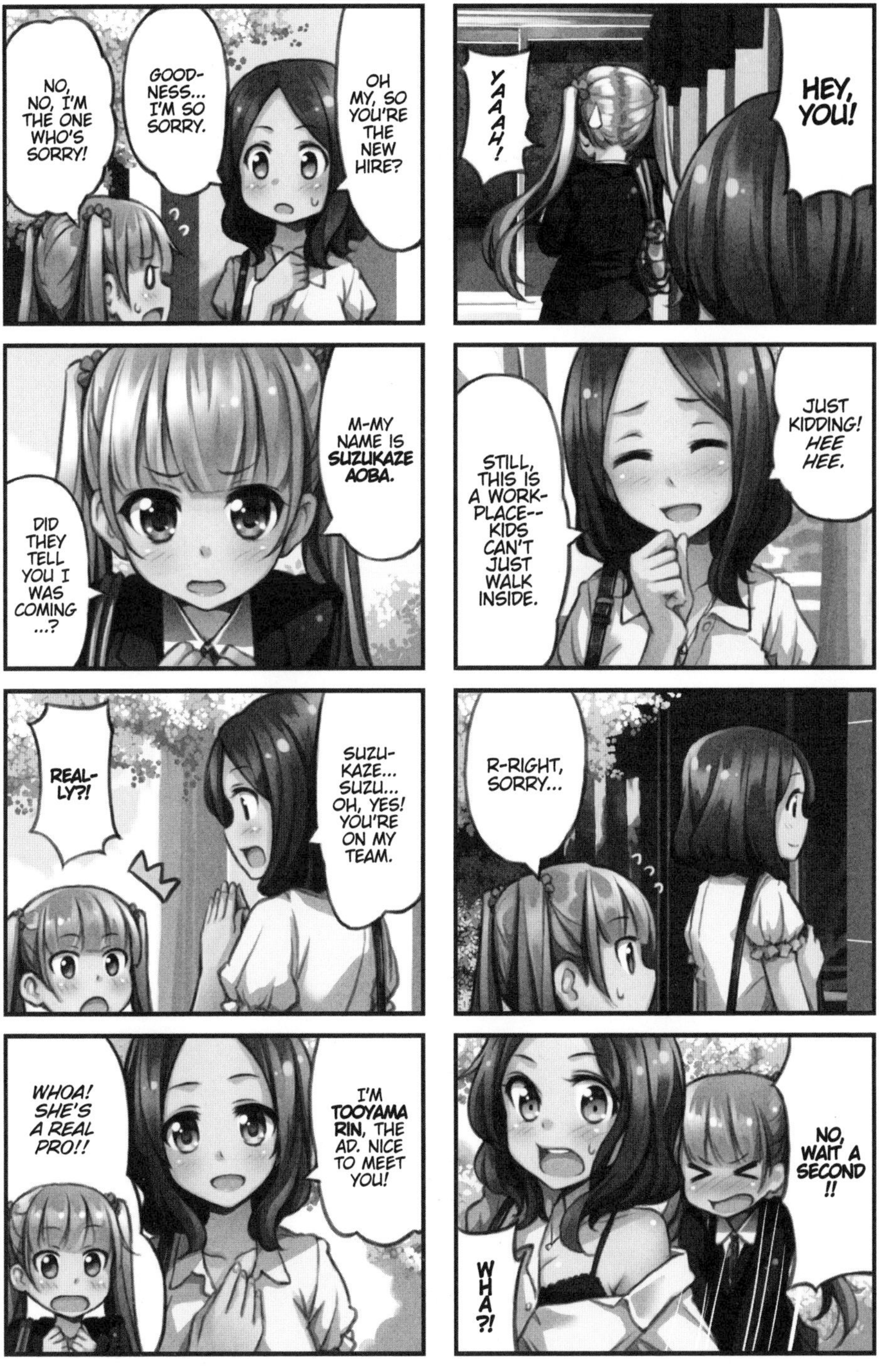
HEY, YOU!
YAAAH!
OH MY, SO YOU'RE THE NEW HIRE?
GOODNESS... I'M SO SORRY.
NO, NO, I'M THE ONE WHO'S SORRY!
JUST KIDDING! HEE HEE.
STILL, THIS IS A WORKPLACE--KIDS CAN'T JUST WALK INSIDE.
M-MY NAME IS SUZUKAZE AOBA.
DID THEY TELL YOU I WAS COMING...?
R-RIGHT, SORRY...
SUZUKAZE... SUZU... OH, YES! YOU'RE ON MY TEAM.
REALLY?!
NO, WAIT A SECOND!!
WHA?!
I'M TOOYAMA RIN, THE AD. NICE TO MEET YOU!
WHOA! SHE'S A REAL PRO!!

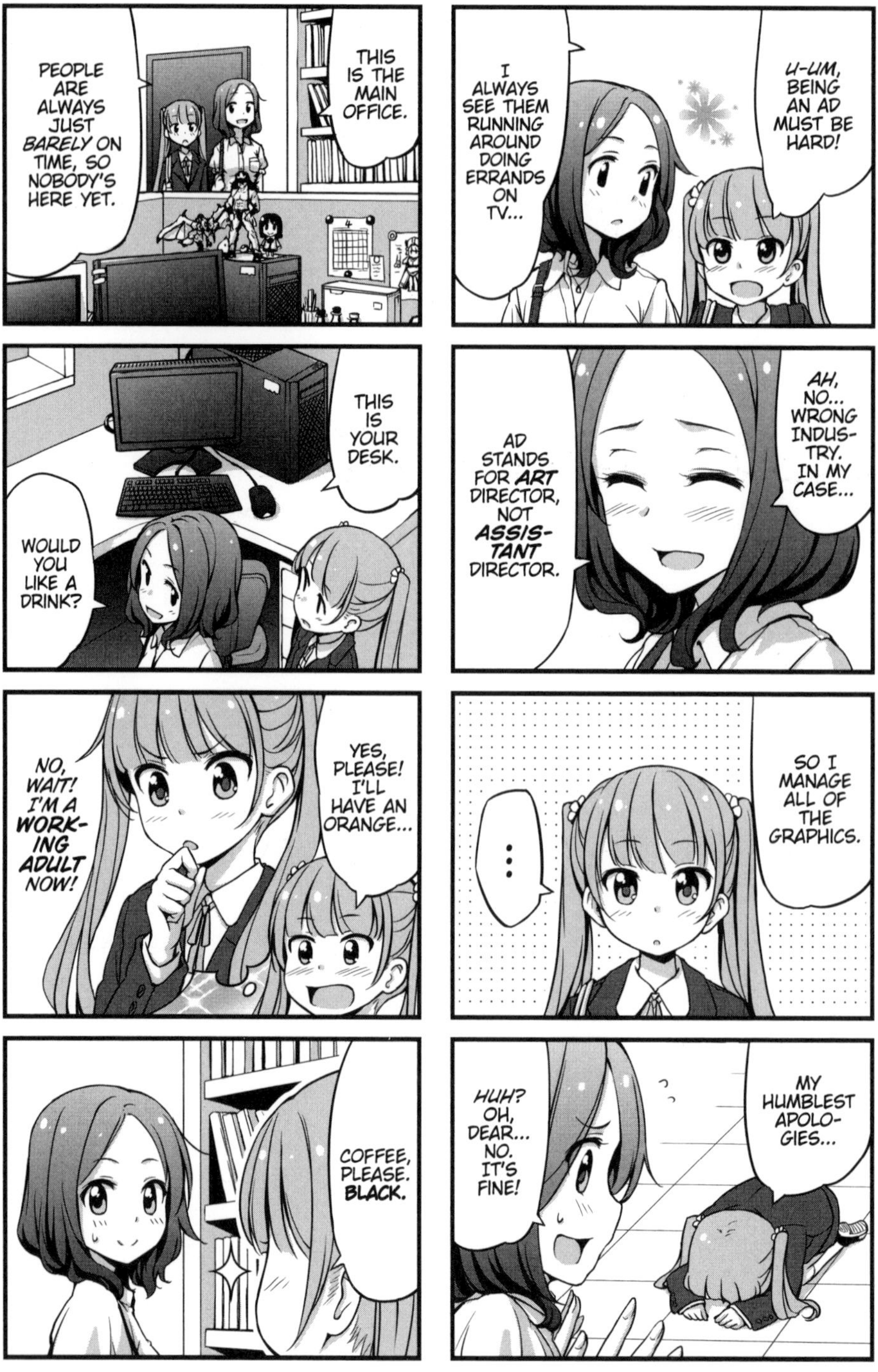
U-UM, BEING AN AD MUST BE HARD!
I ALWAYS SEE THEM RUNNING AROUND DOING ERRANDS ON TV...
AH, NO... WRONG INDUSTRY. IN MY CASE...
AD STANDS FOR ART DIRECTOR, NOT ASSISTANT DIRECTOR.
SO I MANAGE ALL OF THE GRAPHICS.
...
MY HUMBLEST APOLOGIES...
HUH? OH, DEAR... NO. IT'S FINE!
THIS IS THE MAIN OFFICE.
PEOPLE ARE ALWAYS JUST BARELY ON TIME, SO NOBODY'S HERE YET.
THIS IS YOUR DESK.
WOULD YOU LIKE A DRINK?
YES, PLEASE! I'LL HAVE AN ORANGE...
NO, WAIT! I'M A WORKING ADULT NOW!
COFFEE, PLEASE. BLACK.

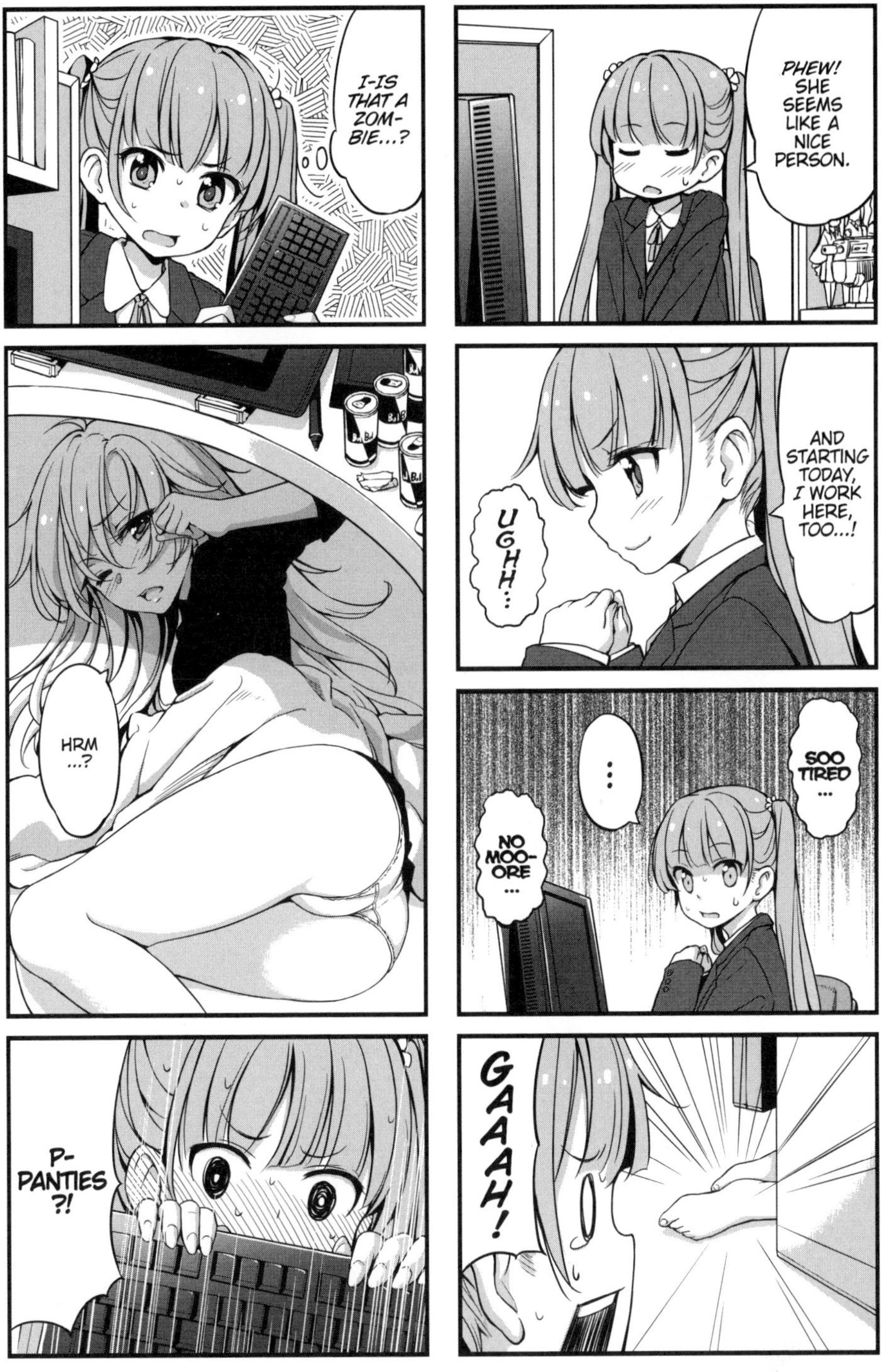
PHEW! SHE SEEMS LIKE A NICE PERSON.
I-IS THAT A ZOM-BIE...?
AND STARTING TODAY, I WORK HERE, TOO...!
UGHH...
SOO TIRED ...
...
NO MOOORE ...
HRM ...?
GAAAH!
P-PANTIES ?!

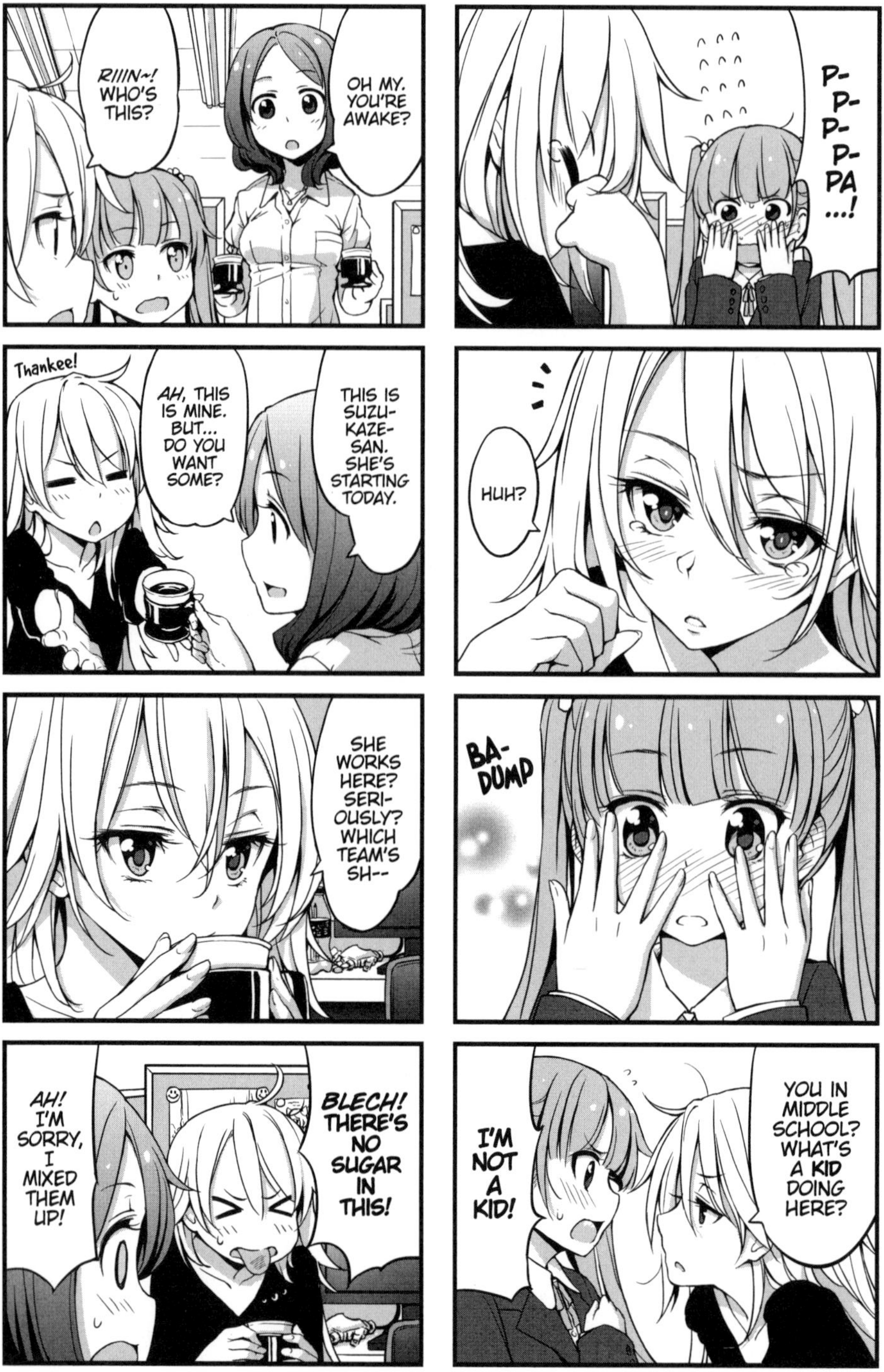
P-P-P-P-PA...!
HUH?
BA-DUMP
YOU IN MIDDLE SCHOOL? WHAT'S A KID DOING HERE?
I'M NOT A KID!
OH MY. YOU'RE AWAKE?
RIIIN~! WHO'S THIS?
THIS IS SUZUKAZE-SAN. SHE'S STARTING TODAY.
AH, THIS IS MINE. BUT... DO YOU WANT SOME?
Thankee!
SHE WORKS HERE? SERIOUSLY? WHICH TEAM'S SH--
BLECH! THERE'S NO SUGAR IN THIS!
AH! I'M SORRY, I MIXED THEM UP!

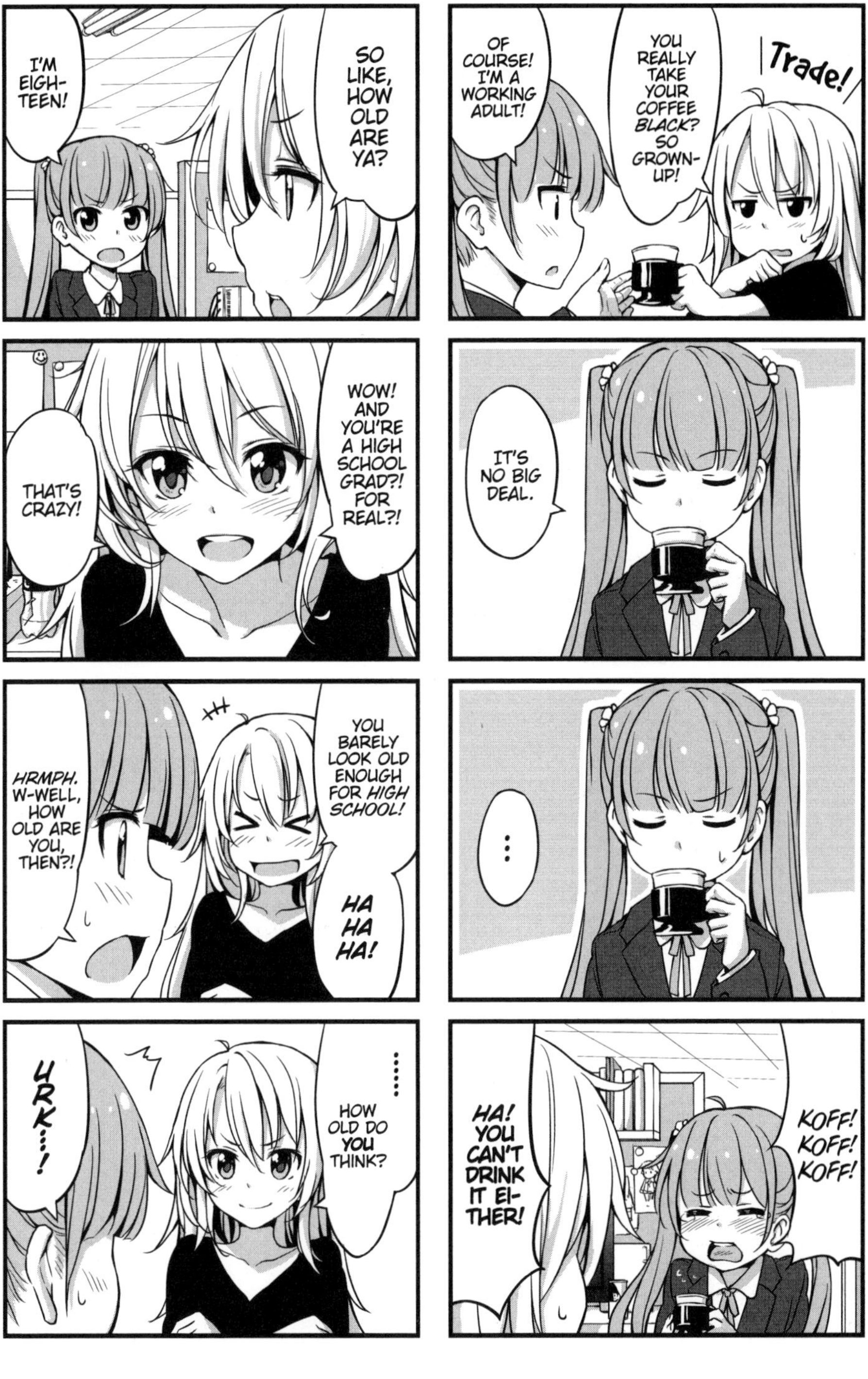
Trade!
YOU REALLY TAKE YOUR COFFEE *BLACK*? SO GROWN-UP!
OF COURSE! I'M A WORKING ADULT!
IT'S NO BIG DEAL.
...
KOFF! KOFF! KOFF!
HA! YOU CAN'T DRINK IT EI-THER!
SO LIKE, HOW OLD ARE YA?
I'M EIGH-TEEN!
WOW! AND YOU'RE A HIGH SCHOOL GRAD?! FOR REAL?!
THAT'S CRAZY!
YOU BARELY LOOK OLD ENOUGH FOR *HIGH SCHOOL*!
HA HA HA!
HRMPH. W-WELL, HOW OLD ARE YOU, THEN?!
......
HOW OLD DO **YOU** THINK?
URK...!

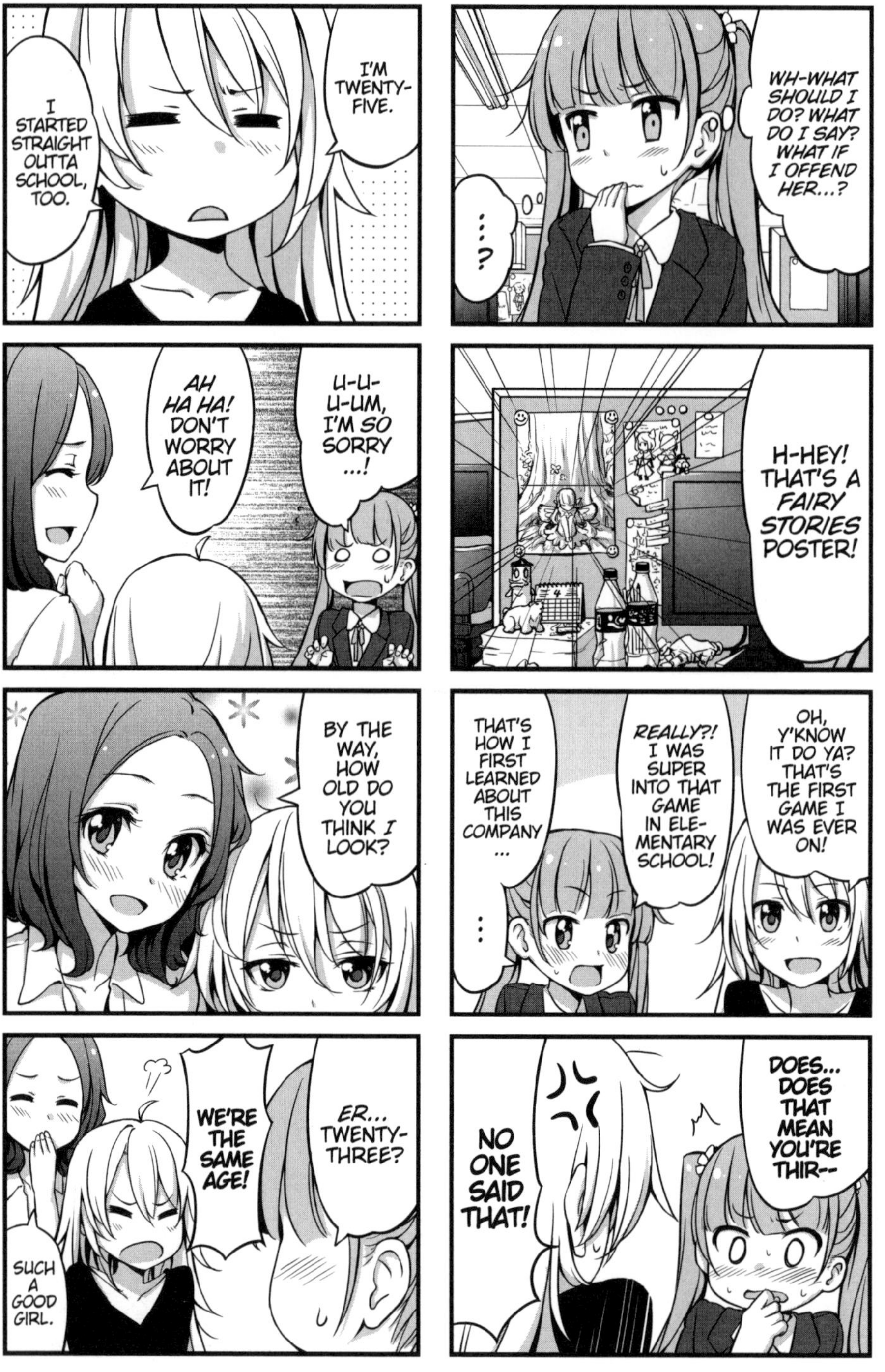
WH-WHAT SHOULD I DO? WHAT DO I SAY? WHAT IF I OFFEND HER...?
...?
I'M TWENTY-FIVE.
I STARTED STRAIGHT OUTTA SCHOOL, TOO.
H-HEY! THAT'S A FAIRY STORIES POSTER!
U-U-U-UM, I'M SO SORRY ...!
AH HA HA! DON'T WORRY ABOUT IT!
OH, Y'KNOW IT DO YA? THAT'S THE FIRST GAME I WAS EVER ON!
REALLY?! I WAS SUPER INTO THAT GAME IN ELEMENTARY SCHOOL!
THAT'S HOW I FIRST LEARNED ABOUT THIS COMPANY...
...
BY THE WAY, HOW OLD DO YOU THINK I LOOK?
DOES... DOES THAT MEAN YOU'RE THIR--
NO ONE SAID THAT!
ER... TWENTY-THREE?
WE'RE THE SAME AGE!
SUCH A GOOD GIRL.

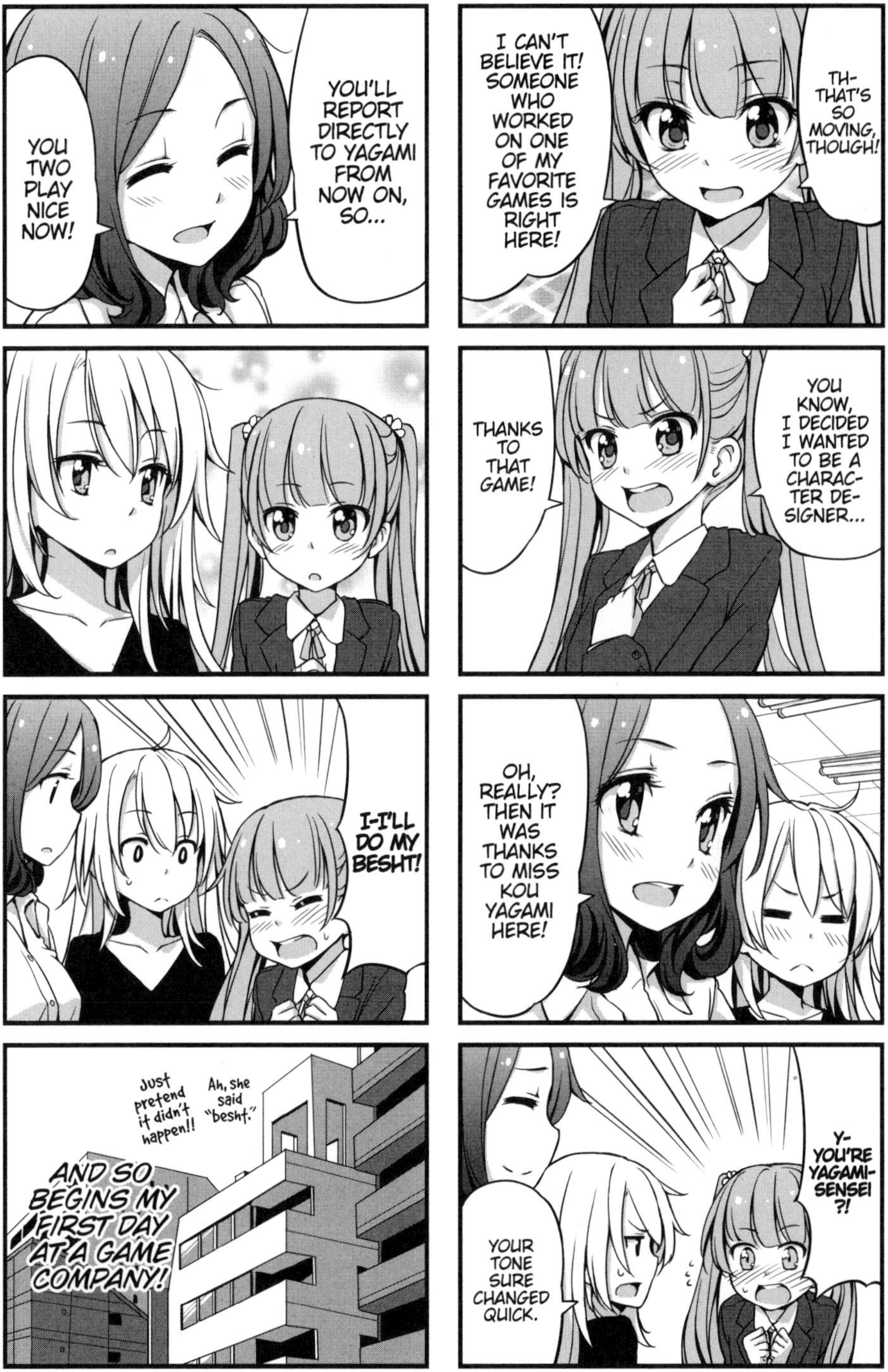
I CAN'T BELIEVE IT! SOMEONE WHO WORKED ON ONE OF MY FAVORITE GAMES IS RIGHT HERE!
TH-THAT'S SO MOVING, THOUGH!
YOU'LL REPORT DIRECTLY TO YAGAMI FROM NOW ON, SO...
YOU TWO PLAY NICE NOW!
YOU KNOW, I DECIDED I WANTED TO BE A CHARACTER DESIGNER...
THANKS TO THAT GAME!
OH, REALLY? THEN IT WAS THANKS TO MISS KOU YAGAMI HERE!
I-I'LL DO MY BESHT!
Y-YOU'RE YAGAMI-SENSEI?!
YOUR TONE SURE CHANGED QUICK.
Ah, she said "besht."
Just pretend it didn't happen!!
AND SO, BEGINS MY FIRST DAY AT A GAME COMPANY!

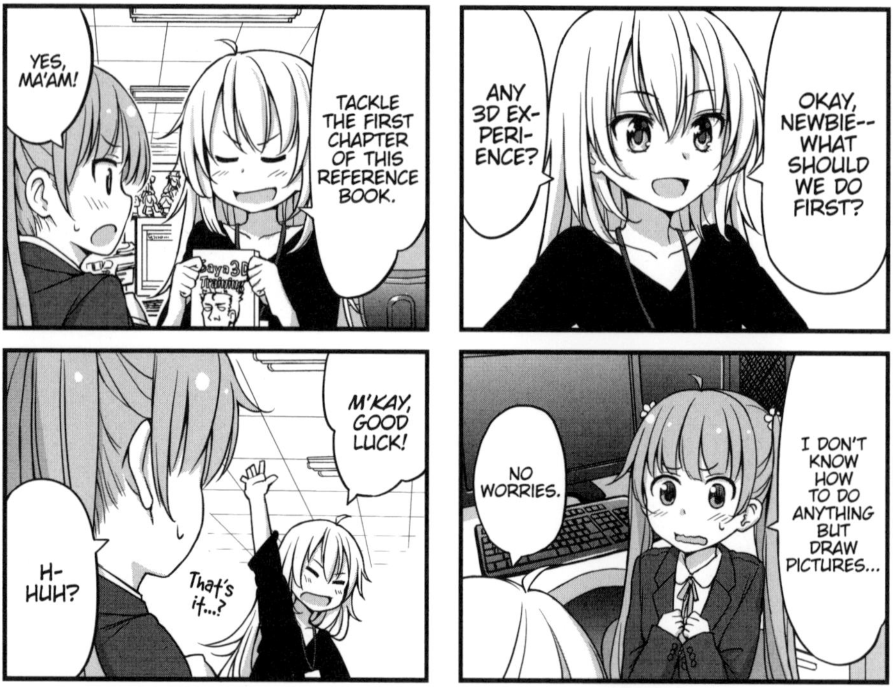
OKAY, NEWBIE-- WHAT SHOULD WE DO FIRST?
ANY 3D EXPERIENCE?
TACKLE THE FIRST CHAPTER OF THIS REFERENCE BOOK.
YES, MA'AM!
Saya 3D Training
I DON'T KNOW HOW TO DO ANYTHING BUT DRAW PICTURES...
NO WORRIES.
M'KAY, GOOD LUCK!
That's it...?
H-HUH?
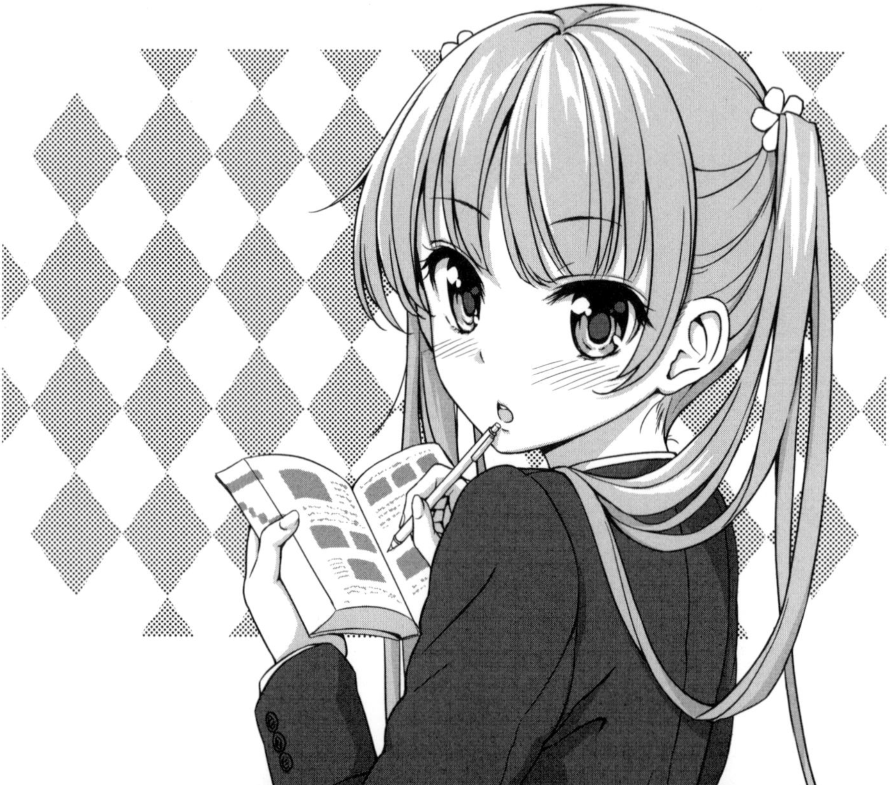

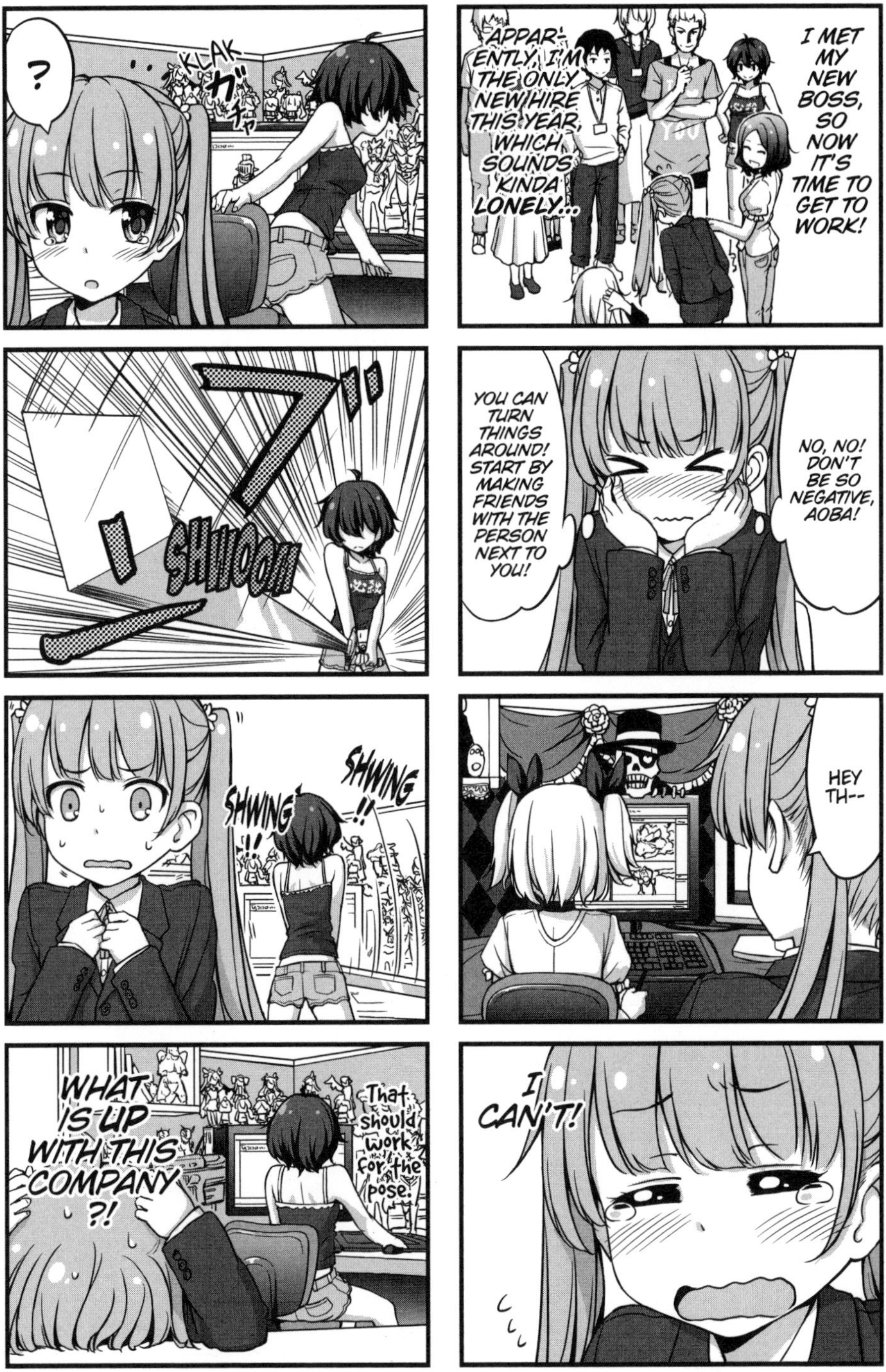
I MET MY NEW BOSS, SO NOW IT'S TIME TO GET TO WORK!
APPARENTLY, I'M THE ONLY NEW HIRE THIS YEAR, WHICH SOUNDS KINDA LONELY...
NO, NO! DON'T BE SO NEGATIVE, AOBA!
YOU CAN TURN THINGS AROUND! START BY MAKING FRIENDS WITH THE PERSON NEXT TO YOU!
HEY TH--
I CAN'T!
?
KLAK
ガチャ
SHWOOM
SHWING!!
SHWING!!
That should work for the pose.
WHAT IS UP WITH THIS COMPANY?!

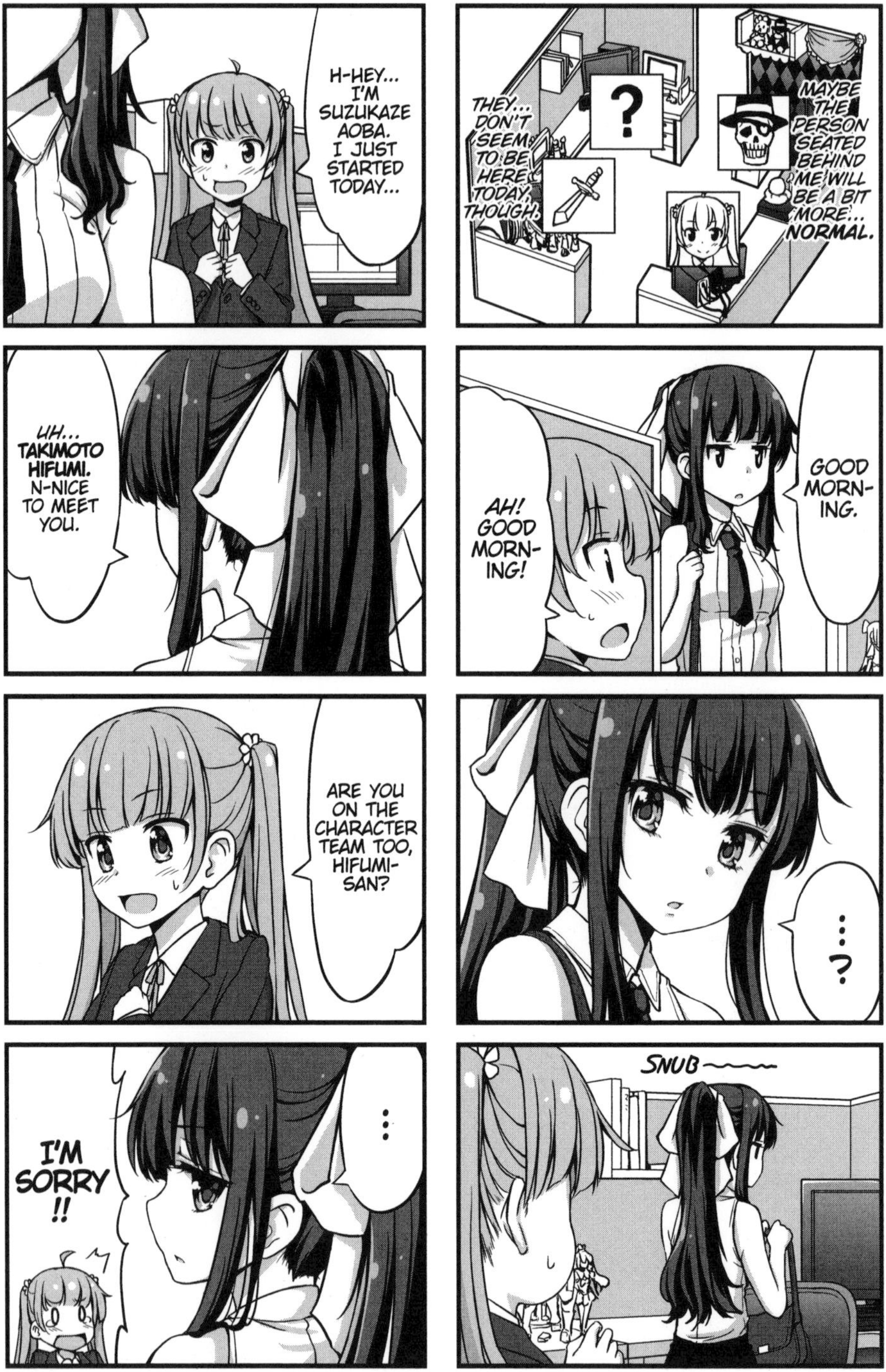
MAYBE THE PERSON SEATED BEHIND ME WILL BE A BIT MORE... NORMAL.
THEY... DON'T SEEM TO BE HERE TODAY, THOUGH.
H-HEY... I'M SUZUKAZE AOBA. I JUST STARTED TODAY...
GOOD MORN-ING.
AH! GOOD MORN-ING!
UH... TAKIMOTO HIFUMI. N-NICE TO MEET YOU.
...?
ARE YOU ON THE CHARACTER TEAM TOO, HIFUMI-SAN?
SNUB~~~
...
I'M SORRY!!

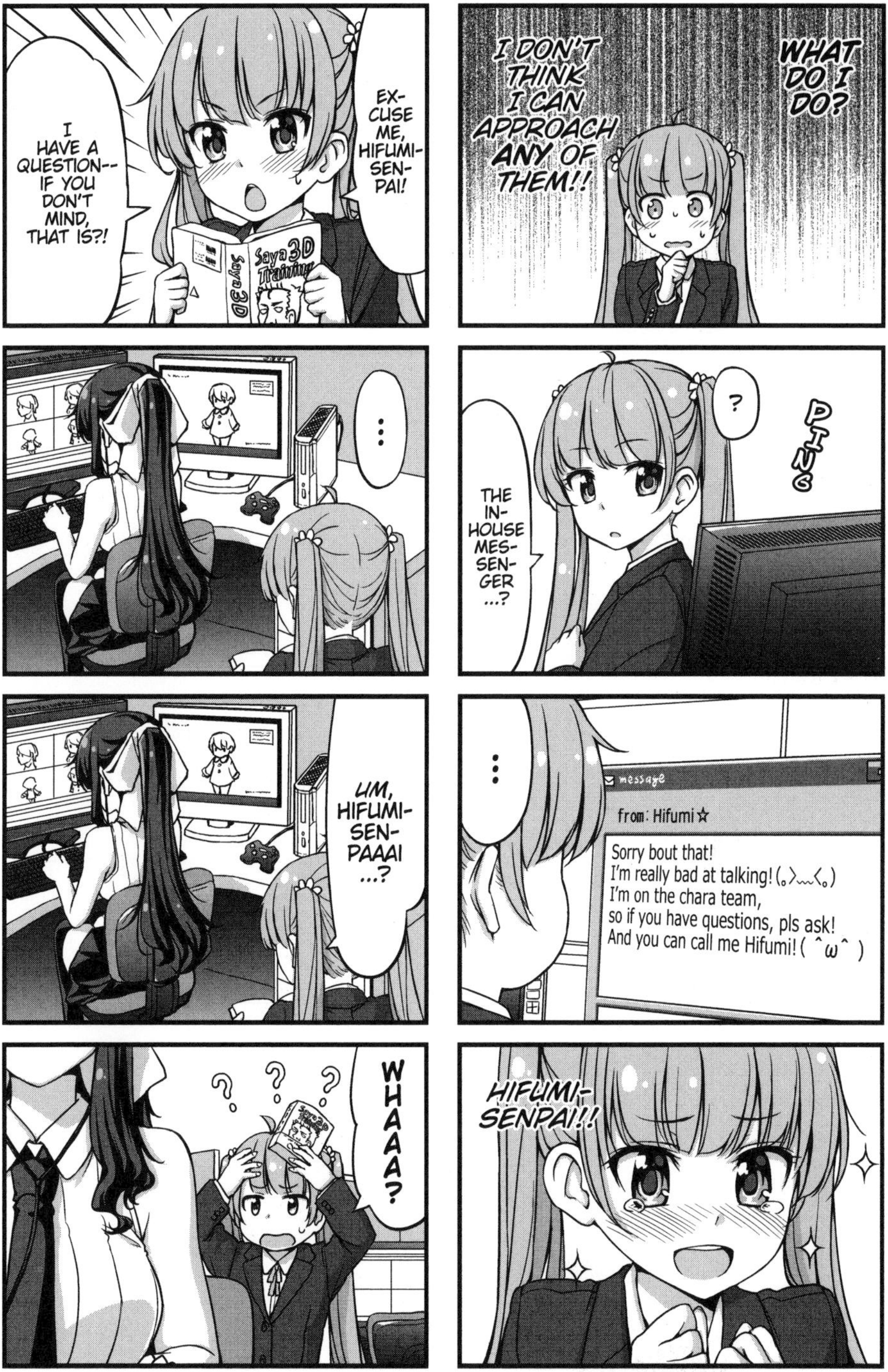
WHAT DO I DO?
I DON'T THINK I CAN APPROACH ANY OF THEM!!
EXCUSE ME, HIFUMI-SENPAI!
I HAVE A QUESTION--IF YOU DON'T MIND, THAT IS?!
Saya 3D Training
Saya 3D
PING
?
THE IN-HOUSE MESSENGER ...?
...
...
message
from: Hifumi☆
Sorry bout that!
I'm really bad at talking! (｡>﹏<｡)
I'm on the chara team,
so if you have questions, pls ask!
And you can call me Hifumi! (ˆωˆ)
UM, HIFUMI-SENPAAAI ...?
HIFUMI-SENPAI!!
WHAAAA?
? ? ?

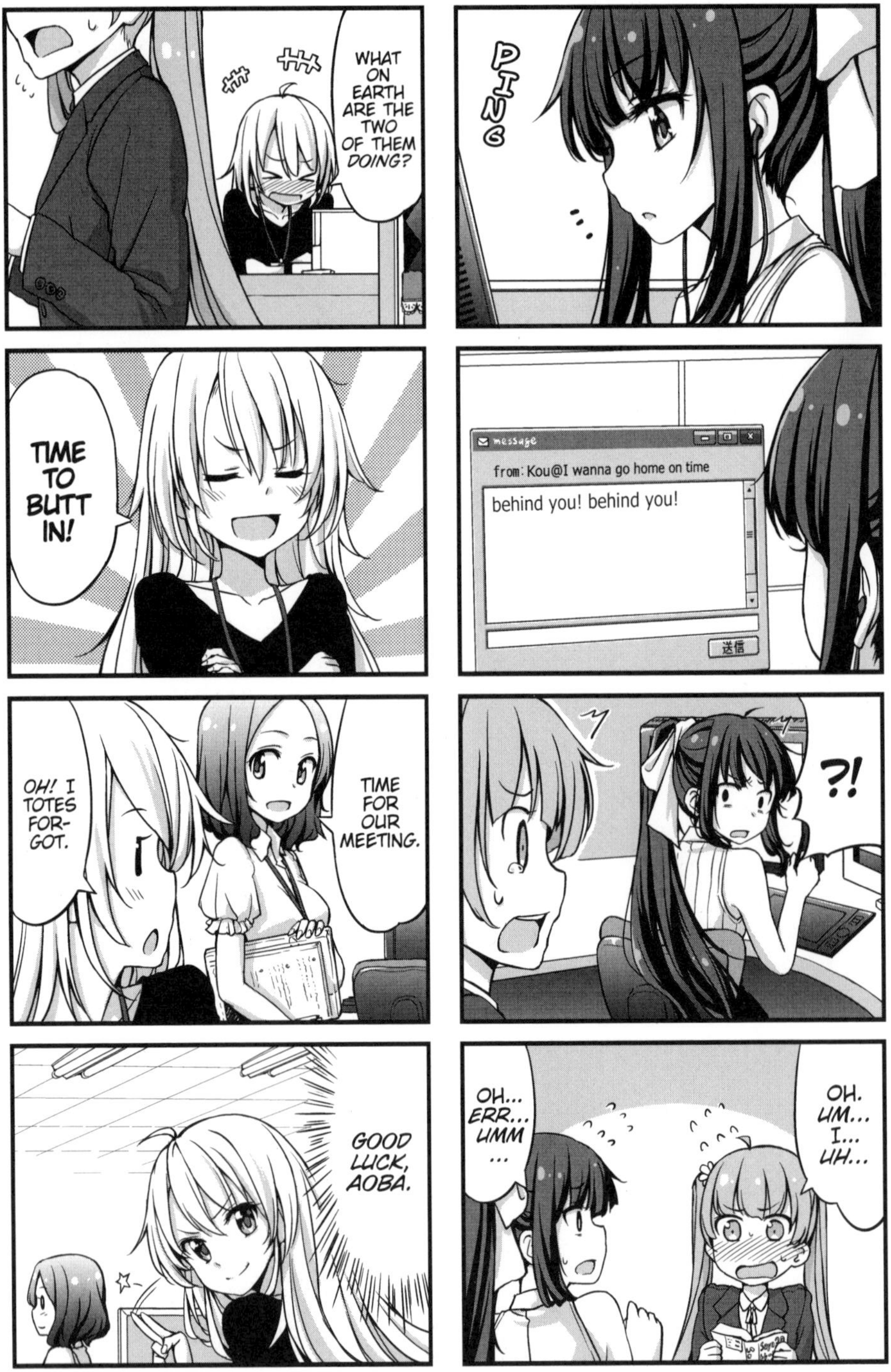
PING
...
WHAT ON EARTH ARE THE TWO OF THEM DOING?
message
from: Kou@I wanna go home on time
behind you! behind you!
送信
TIME TO BUTT IN!
?!
TIME FOR OUR MEETING.
OH! I TOTES FOR-GOT.
OH. UM... I... UH...
OH... ERR... UMM ...
GOOD LUCK, AOBA.

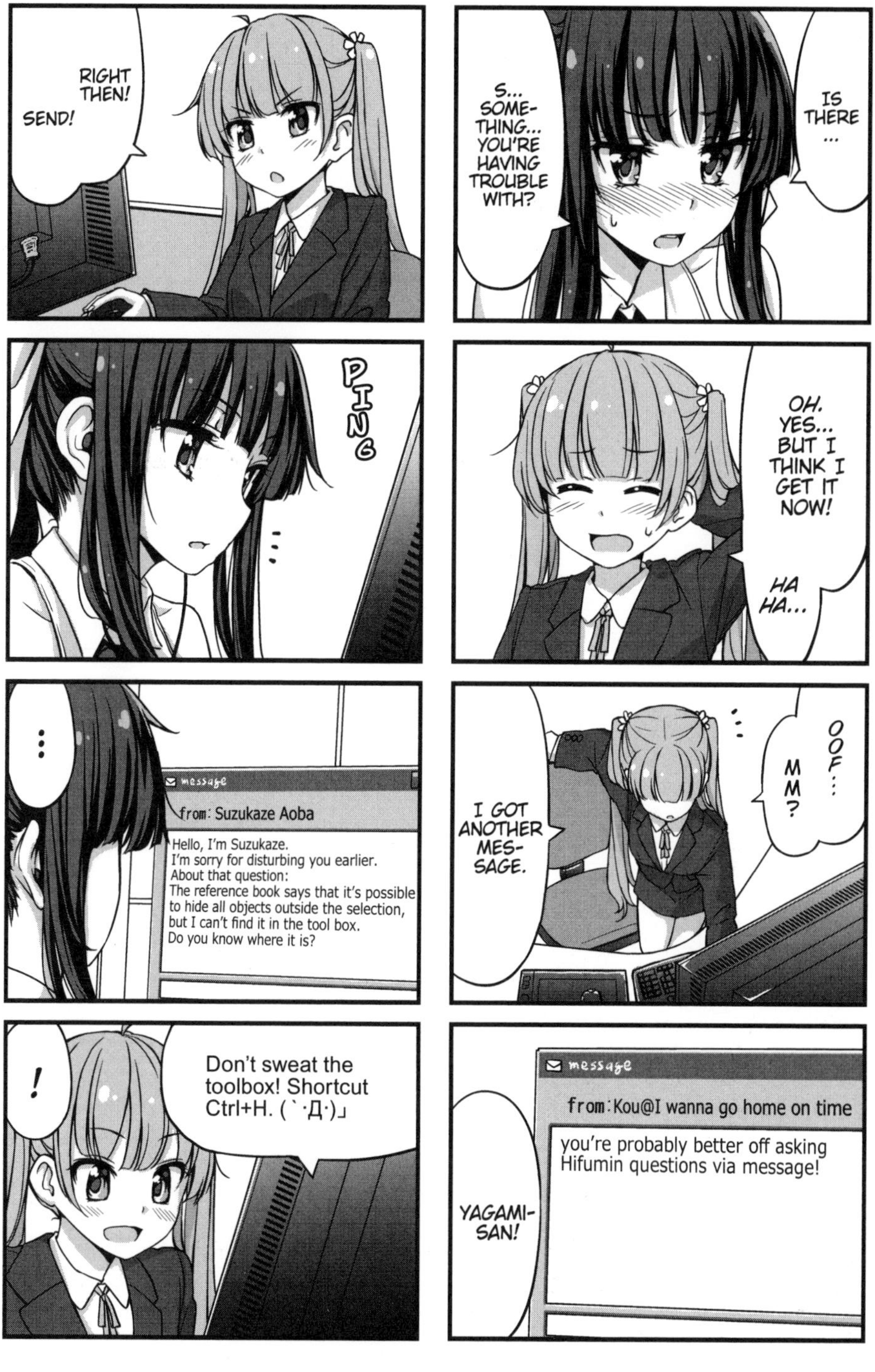
IS THERE ...
S... SOME-THING... YOU'RE HAVING TROUBLE WITH?
RIGHT THEN!
SEND!
OH. YES... BUT I THINK I GET IT NOW!
HA HA...
PING
...
OOF... MM?
...
I GOT ANOTHER MES-SAGE.
...
message
from: Suzukaze Aoba
Hello, I'm Suzukaze.
I'm sorry for disturbing you earlier.
About that question:
The reference book says that it's possible to hide all objects outside the selection, but I can't find it in the tool box.
Do you know where it is?
message
from: Kou@I wanna go home on time
you're probably better off asking Hifumin questions via message!
YAGAMI-SAN!
Don't sweat the toolbox! Shortcut Ctrl+H. (`·Д·)」
!

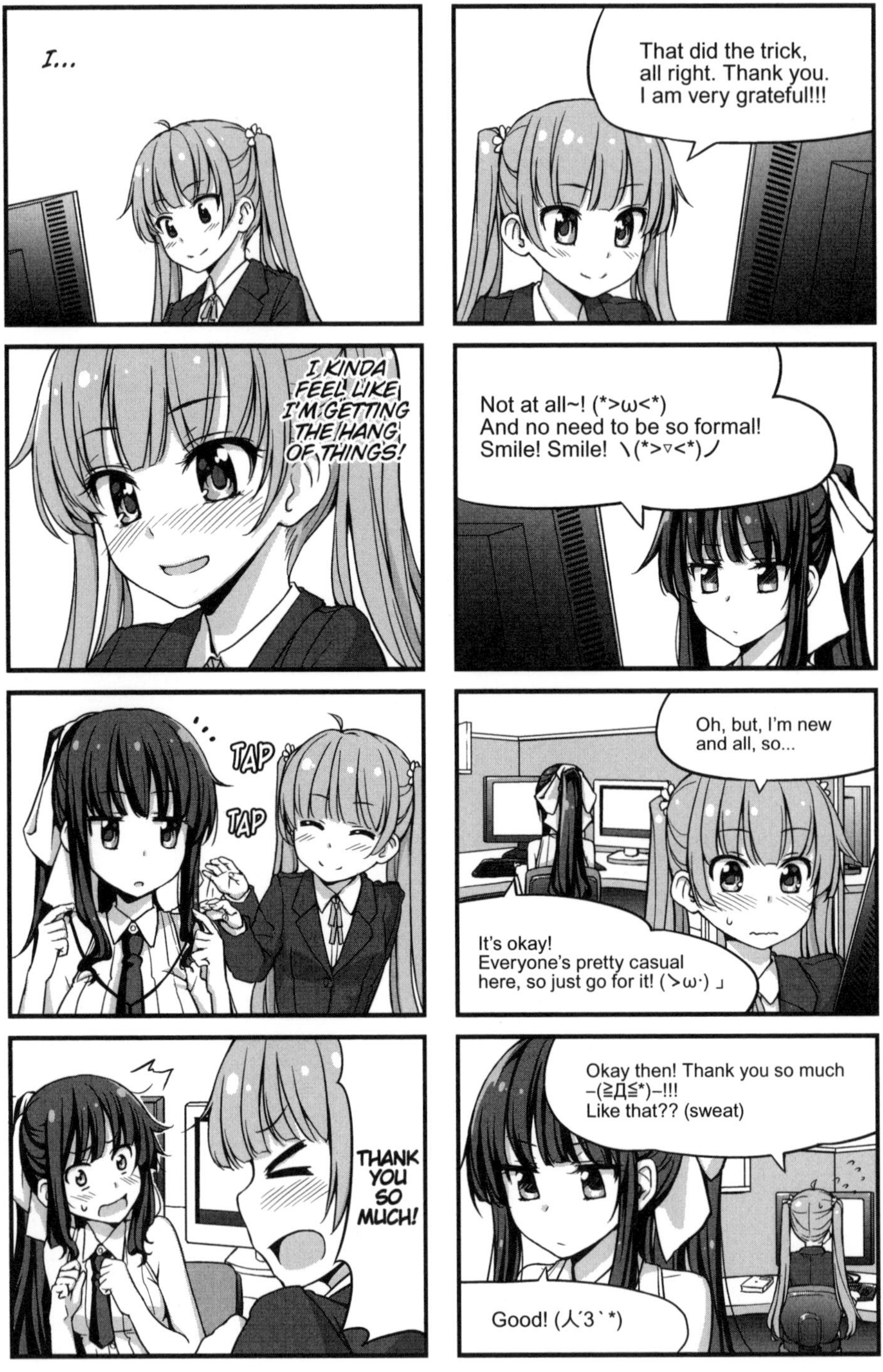
That did the trick, all right. Thank you. I am very grateful!!!
I...
Not at all~! (*>ω<*) And no need to be so formal! Smile! Smile! \(*>▿<*)ノ
I KINDA FEEL LIKE I'M GETTING THE HANG OF THINGS!
Oh, but, I'm new and all, so...
It's okay! Everyone's pretty casual here, so just go for it! (ゝω·) 」
...
TAP
TAP
Okay then! Thank you so much –(≧Д≦*)–!!! Like that?? (sweat)
Good! (人´3`*)
THANK YOU SO MUCH!

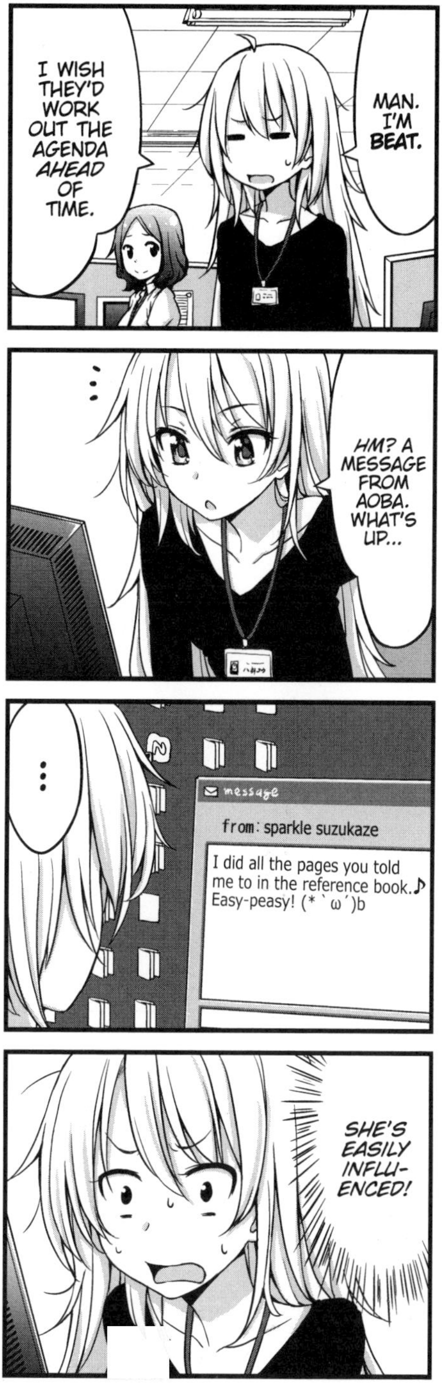
MAN. I'M BEAT.
I WISH THEY'D WORK OUT THE AGENDA AHEAD OF TIME.
...
HM? A MESSAGE FROM AOBA. WHAT'S UP...
...
message
from: sparkle suzukaze
I did all the pages you told me to in the reference book.♪ Easy-peasy! (*｀ω´)b
SHE'S EASILY INFLU-ENCED!

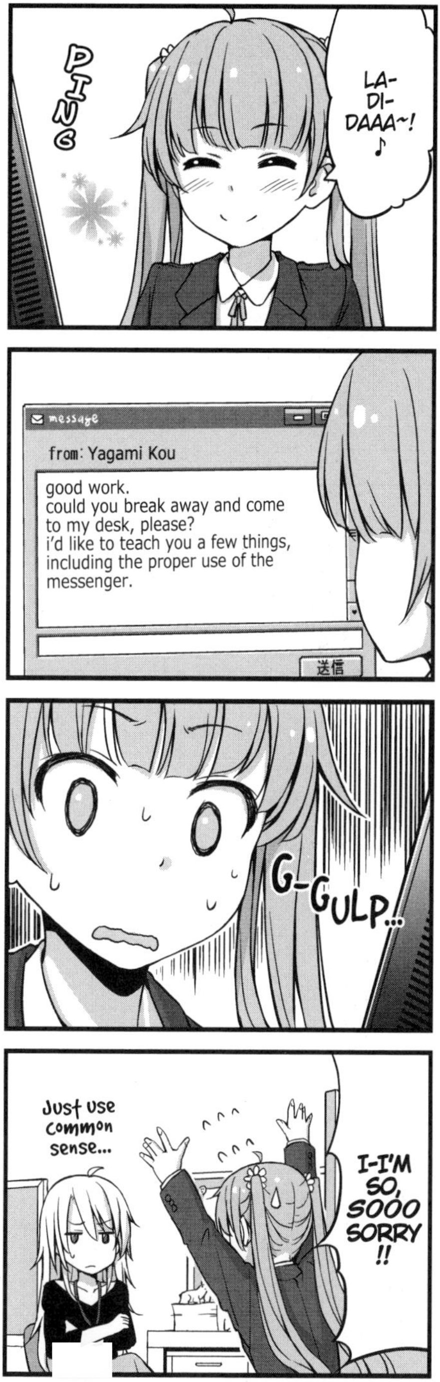
LA-DI-DAAA~! ♪
PING
message
from: Yagami Kou
good work. could you break away and come to my desk, please? i'd like to teach you a few things, including the proper use of the messenger.
送信
G-GULP...
I-I'M SO, SOOO SORRY !!
Just use common sense...

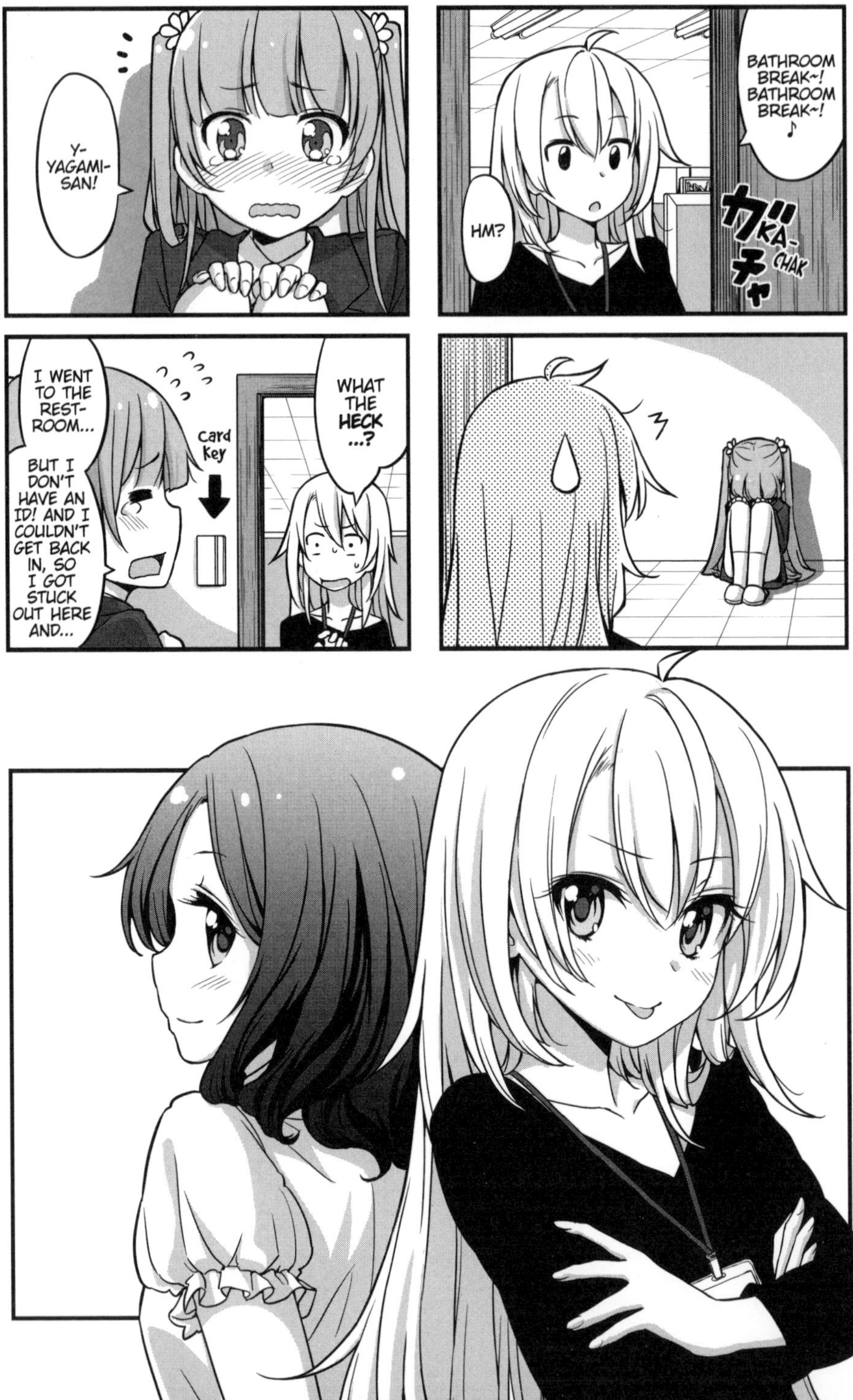
BATHROOM BREAK~! BATHROOM BREAK~! ♪
カチャ KA-CHAK
HM?
Y-YAGAMI-SAN!
WHAT THE HECK ...?
card Key
I WENT TO THE REST-ROOM...
BUT I DON'T HAVE AN ID! AND I COULDN'T GET BACK IN, SO I GOT STUCK OUT HERE AND...

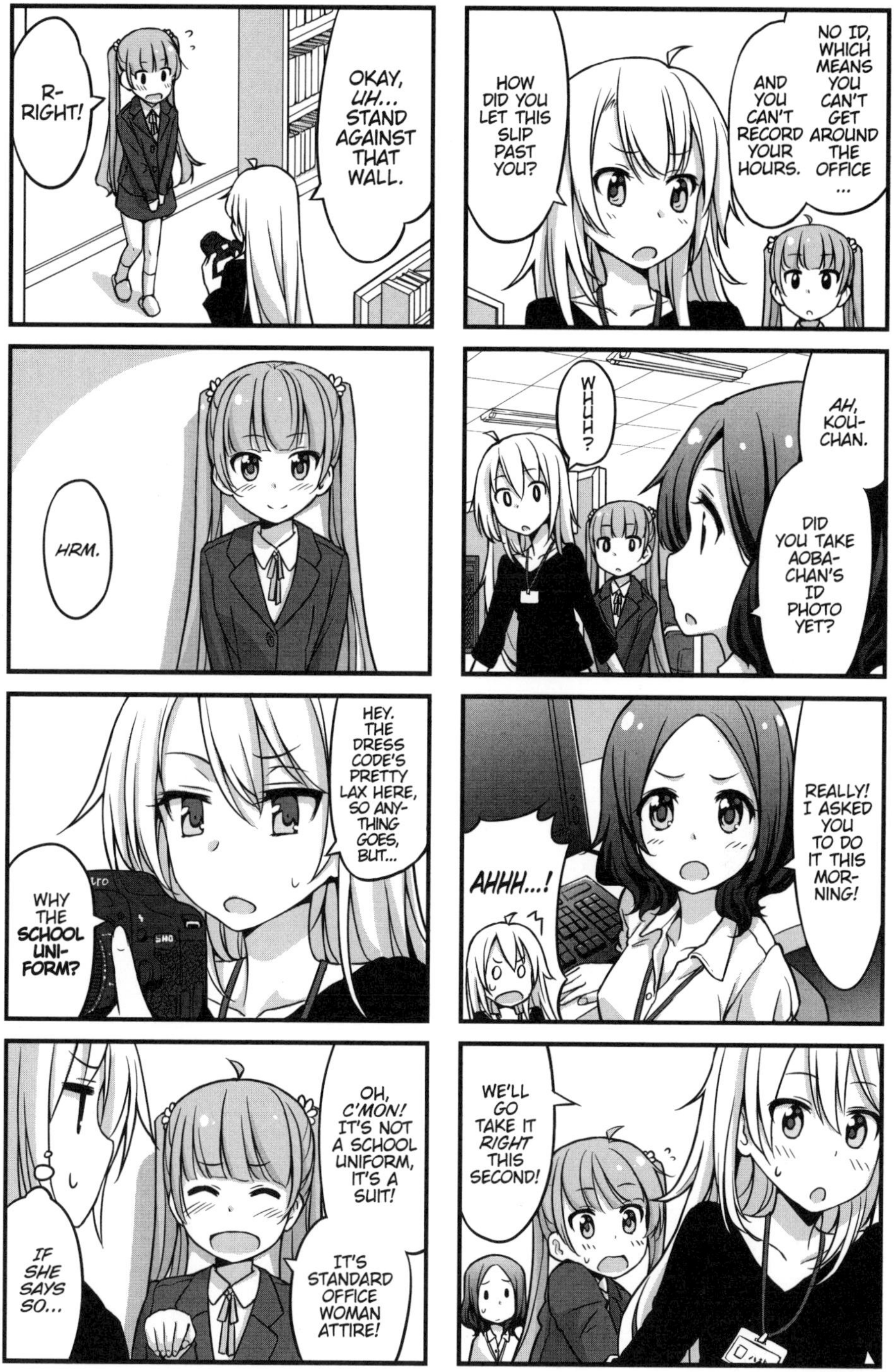
NO ID, WHICH MEANS YOU CAN'T GET AROUND THE OFFICE ...
AND YOU CAN'T RECORD YOUR HOURS.
HOW DID YOU LET THIS SLIP PAST YOU?
AH, KOU-CHAN.
DID YOU TAKE AOBA-CHAN'S ID PHOTO YET?
WHUH?
REALLY! I ASKED YOU TO DO IT THIS MORNING!
AHHH...!
WE'LL GO TAKE IT RIGHT THIS SECOND!
OKAY, UH... STAND AGAINST THAT WALL.
R-RIGHT!
HRM.
HEY. THE DRESS CODE'S PRETTY LAX HERE, SO ANYTHING GOES, BUT...
WHY THE SCHOOL UNIFORM?
OH, C'MON! IT'S NOT A SCHOOL UNIFORM, IT'S A SUIT!
IT'S STANDARD OFFICE WOMAN ATTIRE!
IF SHE SAYS SO...

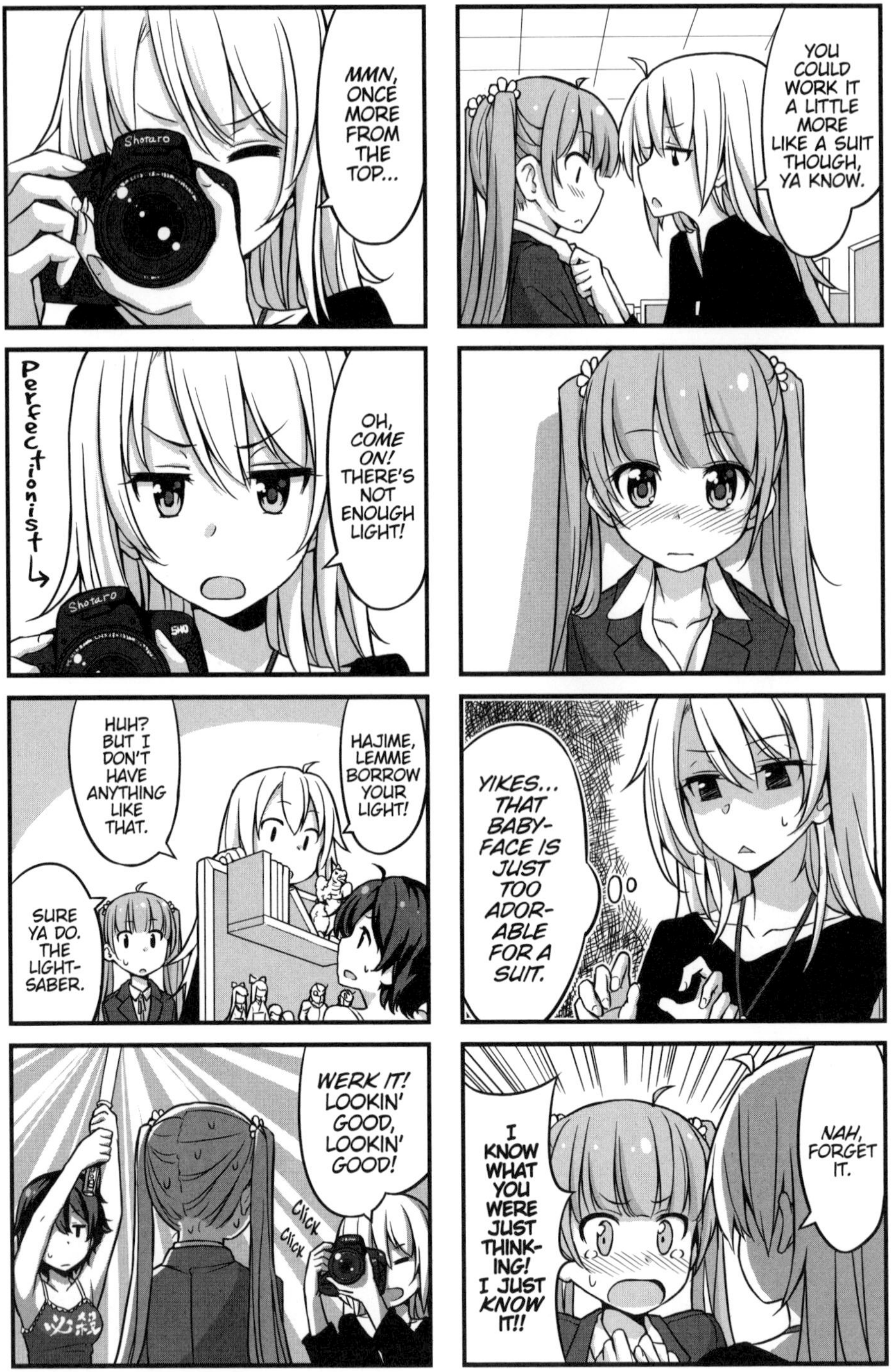
YOU COULD WORK IT A LITTLE MORE LIKE A SUIT THOUGH, YA KNOW.
YIKES... THAT BABY-FACE IS JUST TOO ADORABLE FOR A SUIT.
NAH, FORGET IT.
I KNOW WHAT YOU WERE JUST THINKING! I JUST KNOW IT!!
MMN, ONCE MORE FROM THE TOP...
Shotaro
OH, COME ON! THERE'S NOT ENOUGH LIGHT!
Perfectionist
Shotaro
HAJIME, LEMME BORROW YOUR LIGHT!
HUH? BUT I DON'T HAVE ANYTHING LIKE THAT.
SURE YA DO. THE LIGHT-SABER.
WERK IT! LOOKIN' GOOD, LOOKIN' GOOD!
Click
Click

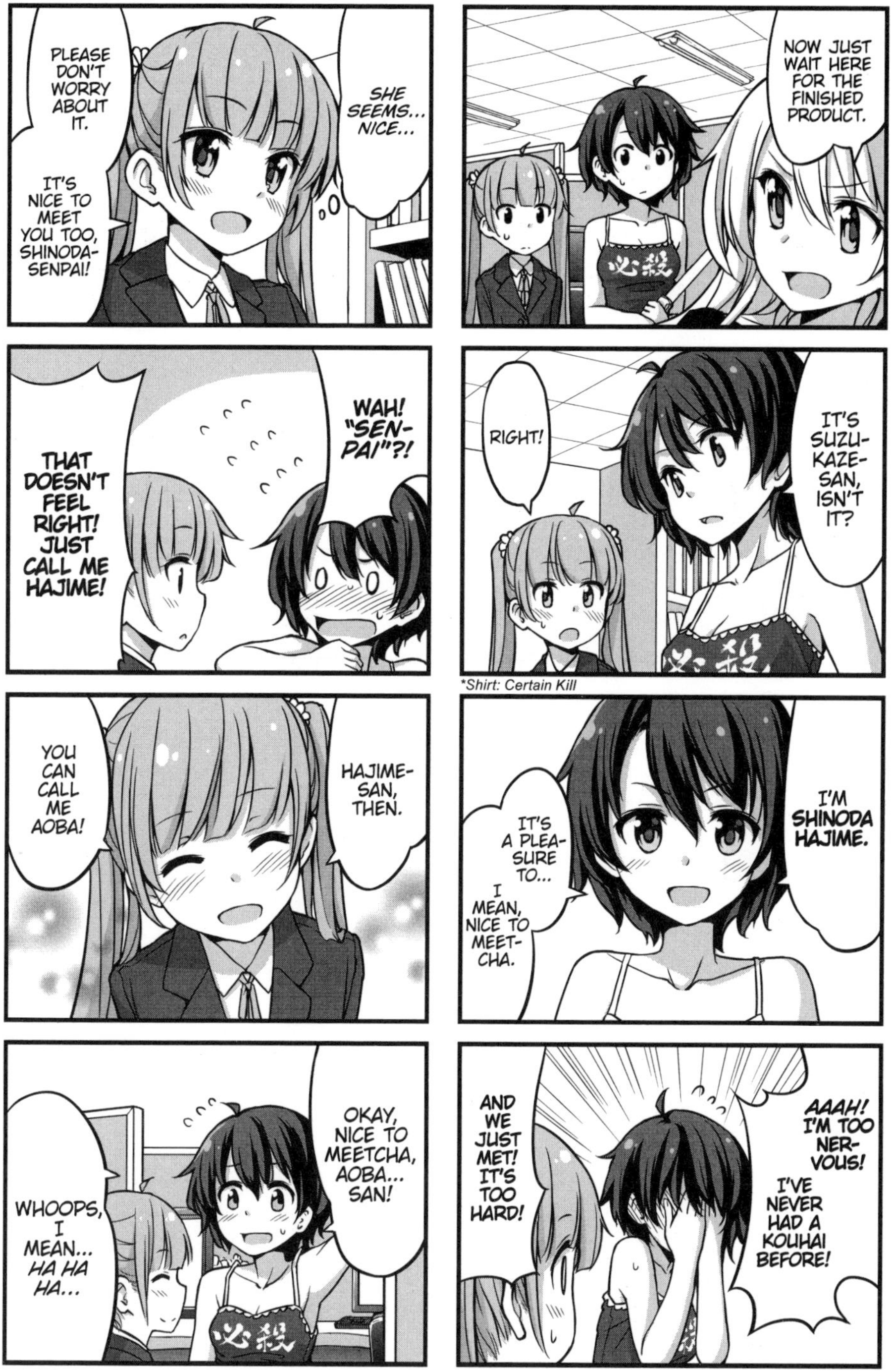
NOW JUST WAIT HERE FOR THE FINISHED PRODUCT.
SHE SEEMS... NICE...
PLEASE DON'T WORRY ABOUT IT.
IT'S NICE TO MEET YOU TOO, SHINODA-SENPAI!
IT'S SUZUKAZE-SAN, ISN'T IT?
RIGHT!
WAH! "SEN-PAI"?!
THAT DOESN'T FEEL RIGHT! JUST CALL ME HAJIME!
I'M SHINODA HAJIME.
IT'S A PLEA-SURE TO... I MEAN, NICE TO MEET-CHA.
HAJIME-SAN, THEN.
YOU CAN CALL ME AOBA!
AAAH! I'M TOO NER-VOUS!
I'VE NEVER HAD A KOUHAI BEFORE!
AND WE JUST MET! IT'S TOO HARD!
OKAY, NICE TO MEETCHA, AOBA... SAN!
WHOOPS, I MEAN... HA HA HA...

*Shirt: Certain Kill

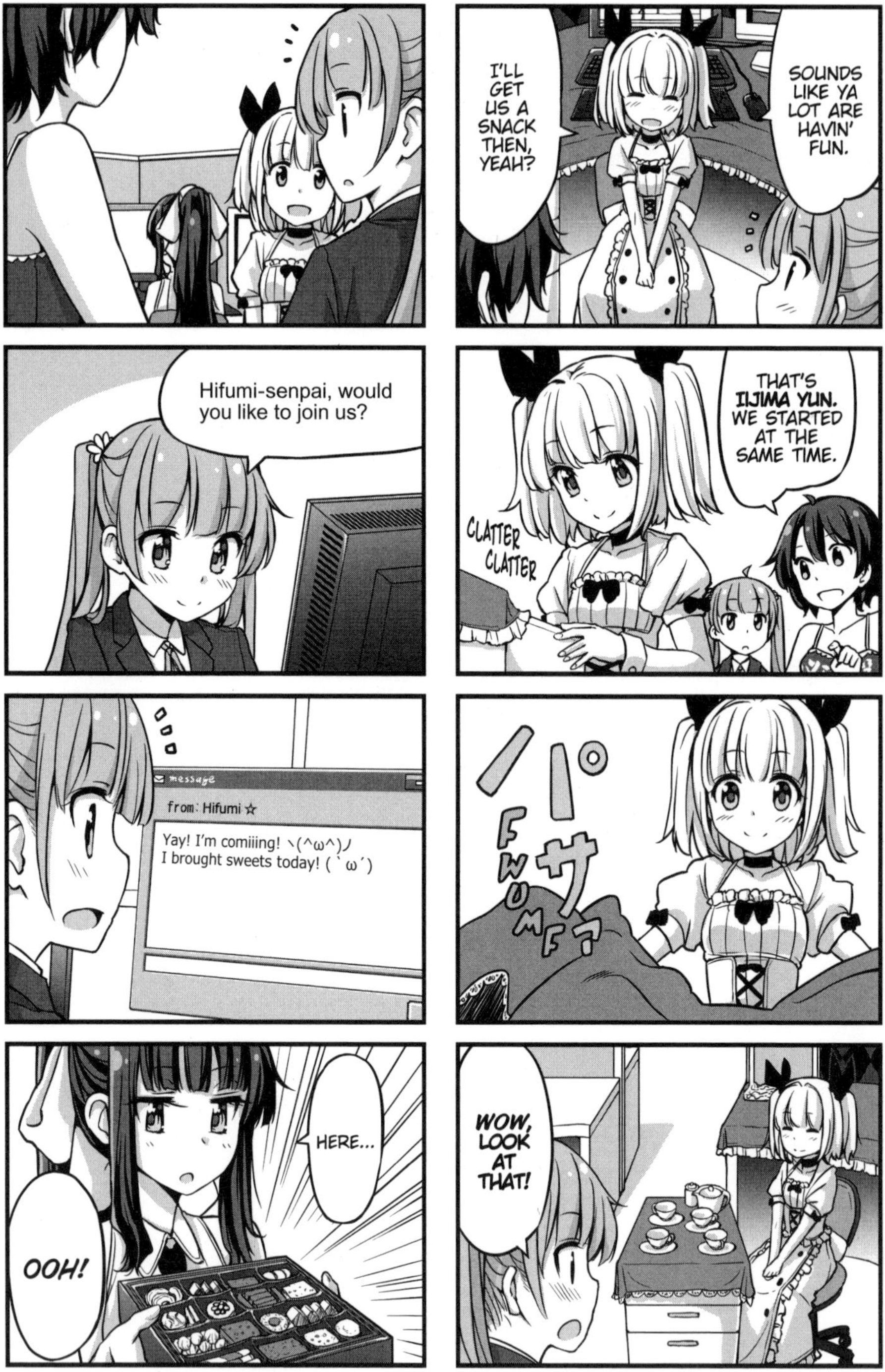
SOUNDS LIKE YA LOT ARE HAVIN' FUN.
I'LL GET US A SNACK THEN, YEAH?
THAT'S IIJIMA YUN. WE STARTED AT THE SAME TIME.
CLATTER CLATTER
Hifumi-senpai, would you like to join us?
パサァ
FWUMF
message
from: Hifumi ☆
Yay! I'm comiiing! ヽ(^ω^)ノ
I brought sweets today! (｀ω´)
WOW, LOOK AT THAT!
HERE...
OOH!

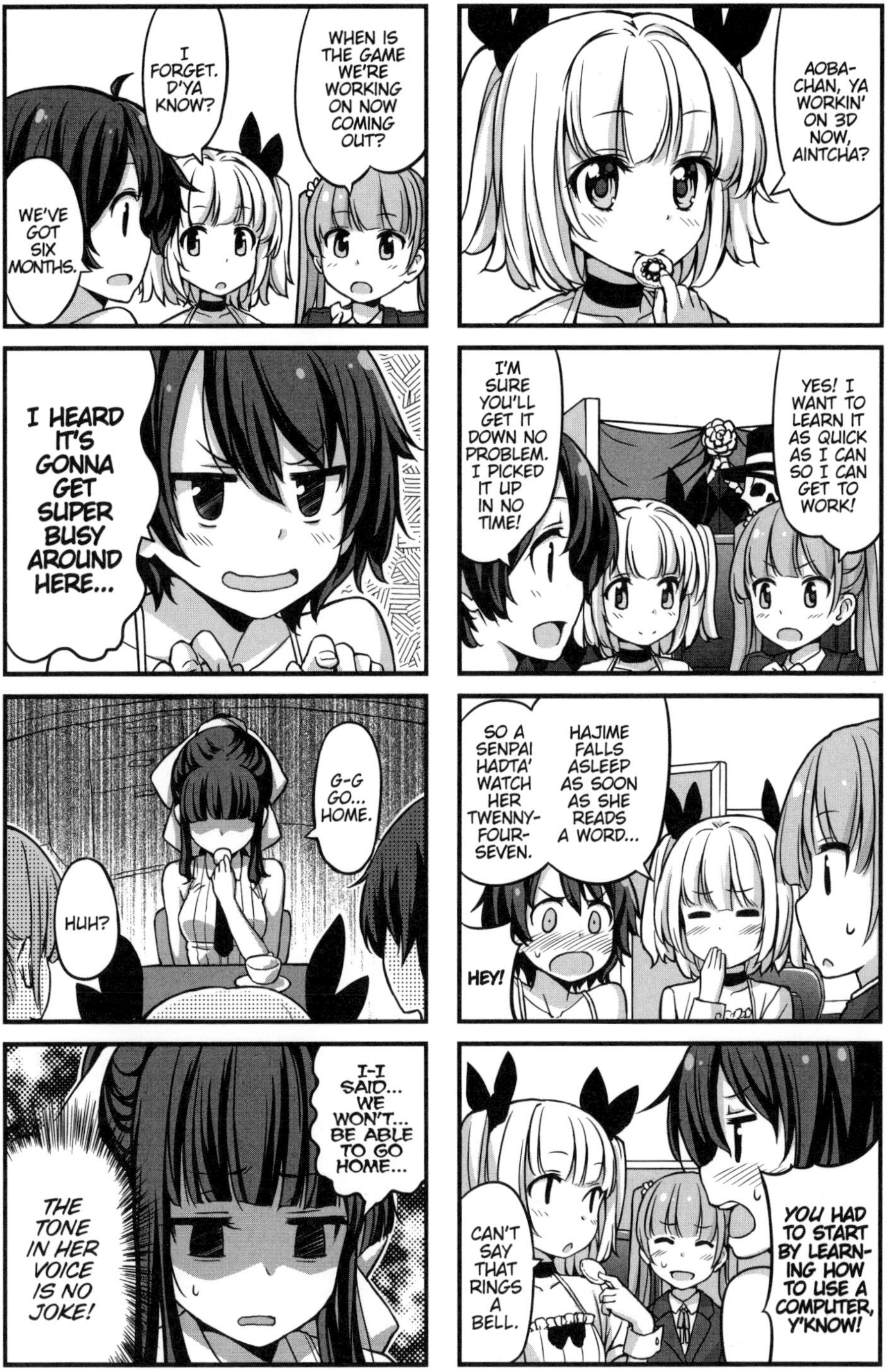
AOBA-CHAN, YA WORKIN' ON 3D NOW, AINTCHA?
YES! I WANT TO LEARN IT AS QUICK AS I CAN SO I CAN GET TO WORK!
I'M SURE YOU'LL GET IT DOWN NO PROBLEM. I PICKED IT UP IN NO TIME!
HAJIME FALLS ASLEEP AS SOON AS SHE READS A WORD...
SO A SENPAI HADTA' WATCH HER TWENNY-FOUR-SEVEN.
HEY!
YOU HAD TO START BY LEARNING HOW TO USE A COMPUTER, Y'KNOW!
CAN'T SAY THAT RINGS A BELL.
WHEN IS THE GAME WE'RE WORKING ON NOW COMING OUT?
I FORGET. D'YA KNOW?
WE'VE GOT SIX MONTHS.
I HEARD IT'S GONNA GET SUPER BUSY AROUND HERE...
G-G GO... HOME.
HUH?
I-I SAID... WE WON'T... BE ABLE TO GO HOME...
THE TONE IN HER VOICE IS NO JOKE!

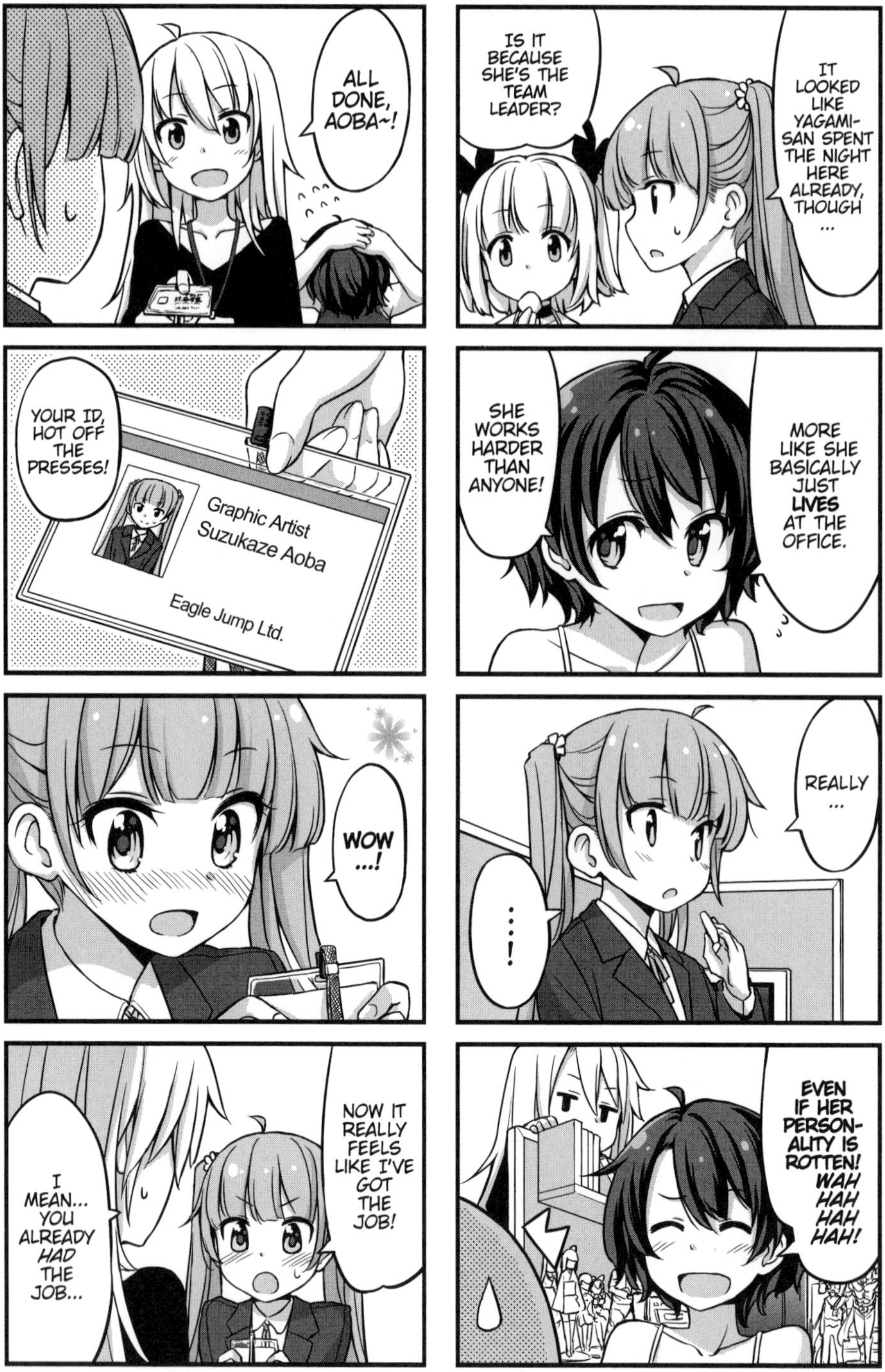
IT LOOKED LIKE YAGAMI-SAN SPENT THE NIGHT HERE ALREADY, THOUGH...
IS IT BECAUSE SHE'S THE TEAM LEADER?
ALL DONE, AOBA~!
MORE LIKE SHE BASICALLY JUST **LIVES** AT THE OFFICE.
SHE WORKS HARDER THAN ANYONE!
YOUR ID, HOT OFF THE PRESSES!
Graphic Artist
Suzukaze Aoba
Eagle Jump Ltd.
REALLY...
...!
WOW...!
EVEN IF HER PERSONALITY IS ROTTEN! *WAH HAH HAH HAH!*
NOW IT REALLY FEELS LIKE I'VE GOT THE JOB!
I MEAN... YOU ALREADY *HAD* THE JOB...

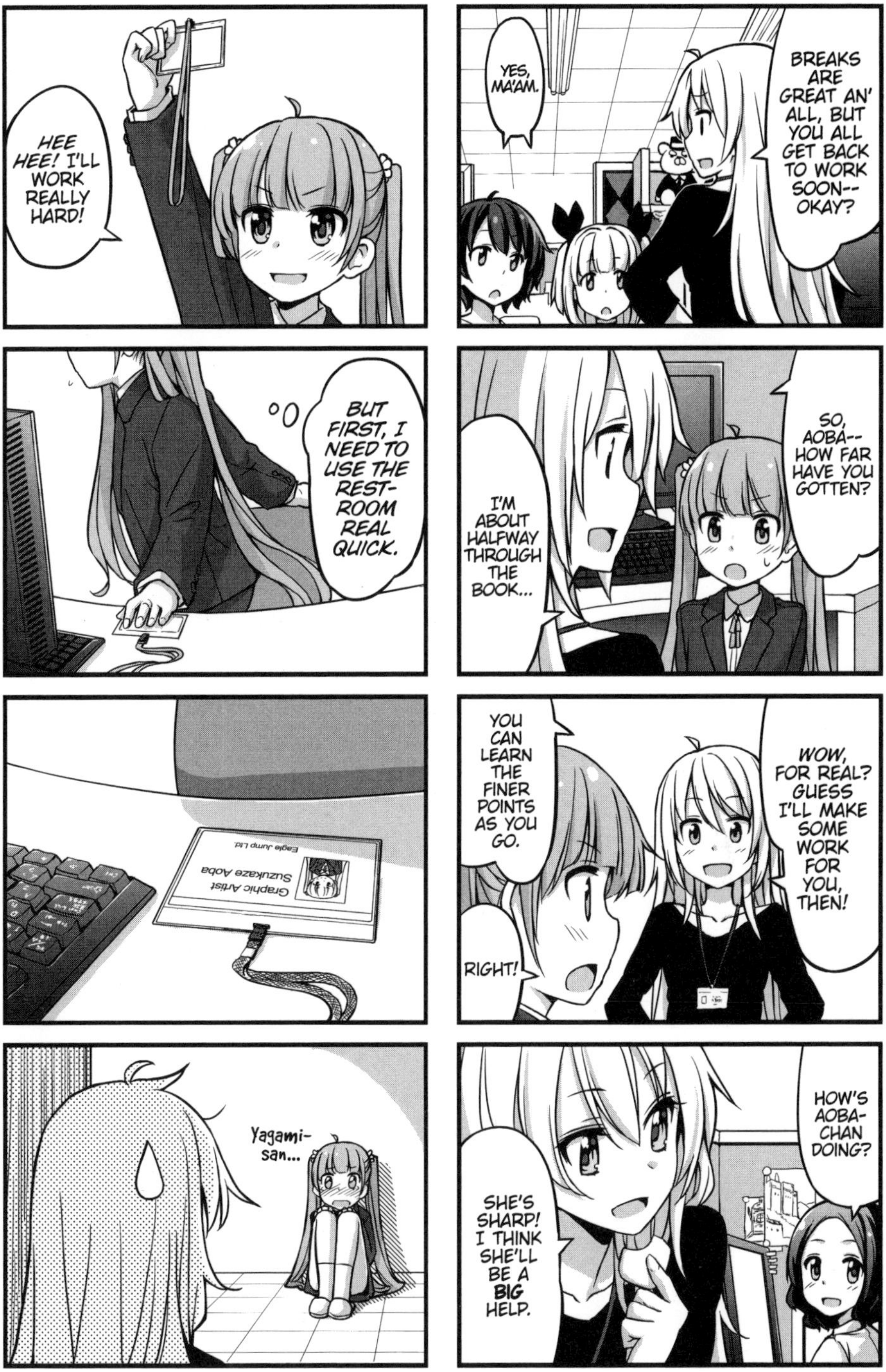
BREAKS ARE GREAT AN' ALL, BUT YOU ALL GET BACK TO WORK SOON--OKAY?
YES, MA'AM.
SO, AOBA--HOW FAR HAVE YOU GOTTEN?
I'M ABOUT HALFWAY THROUGH THE BOOK...
WOW, FOR REAL? GUESS I'LL MAKE SOME WORK FOR YOU, THEN!
YOU CAN LEARN THE FINER POINTS AS YOU GO.
RIGHT!
HOW'S AOBA-CHAN DOING?
SHE'S SHARP! I THINK SHE'LL BE A BIG HELP.
HEE HEE! I'LL WORK REALLY HARD!
BUT FIRST, I NEED TO USE THE REST-ROOM REAL QUICK.
Graphic Artist
Suzukaze Aoba
Eagle Jump Ltd.
Yagami-san...

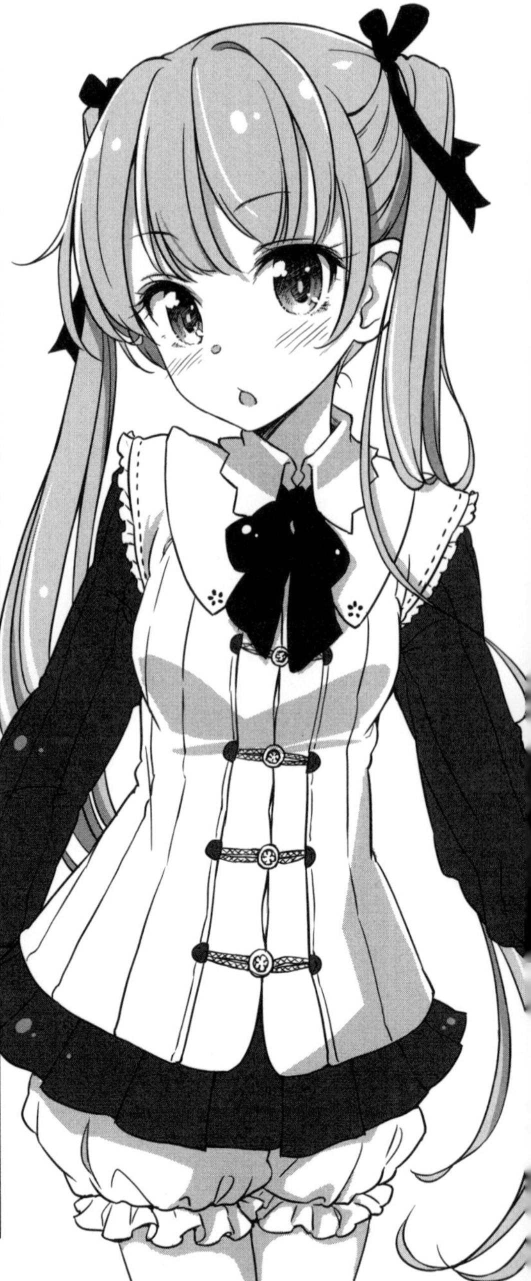

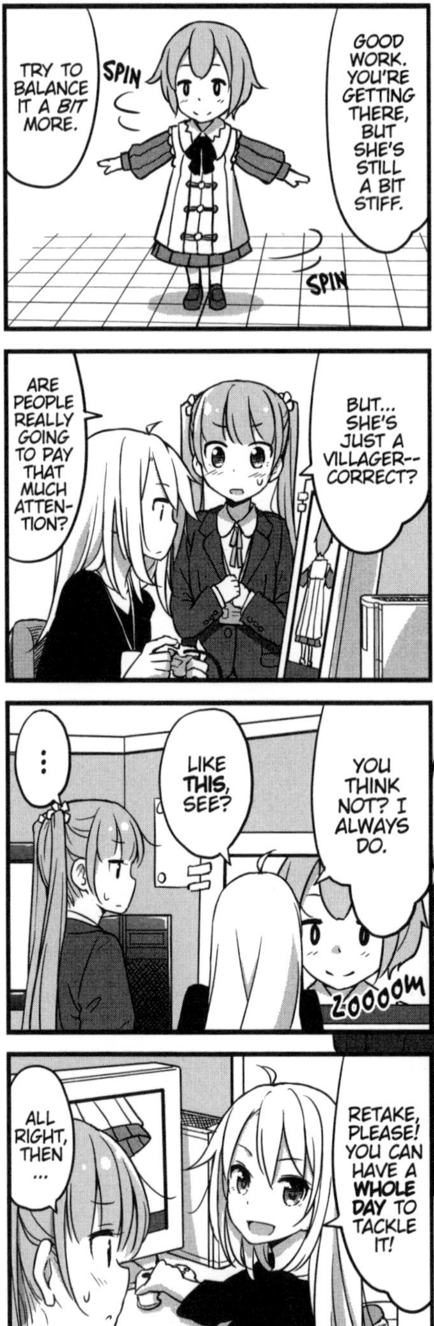
GOOD WORK. YOU'RE GETTING THERE, BUT SHE'S STILL A BIT STIFF.
SPIN
TRY TO BALANCE IT A *BIT* MORE.
SPIN
BUT... SHE'S JUST A VILLAGER--CORRECT?
ARE PEOPLE REALLY GOING TO PAY THAT MUCH ATTENTION?
YOU THINK NOT? I ALWAYS DO.
LIKE **THIS,** SEE?
...
ZOOOOOM
RETAKE, PLEASE! YOU CAN HAVE A **WHOLE DAY** TO TACKLE IT!
ALL RIGHT, THEN...

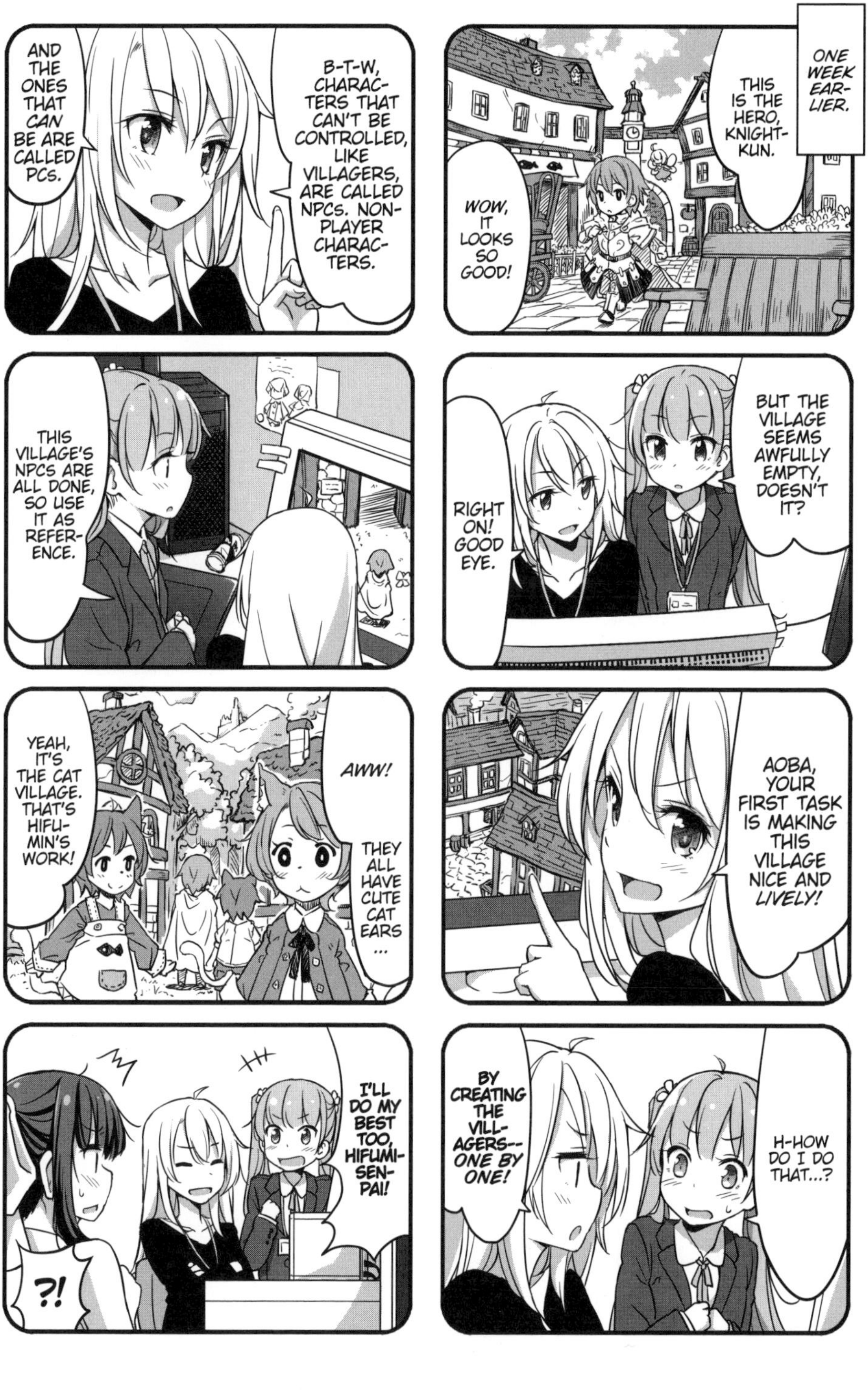
ONE WEEK EARLIER.
THIS IS THE HERO, KNIGHT-KUN.
WOW, IT LOOKS SO GOOD!
B-T-W, CHARACTERS THAT CAN'T BE CONTROLLED, LIKE VILLAGERS, ARE CALLED NPCs. NON-PLAYER CHARACTERS.
AND THE ONES THAT CAN BE ARE CALLED PCs.
BUT THE VILLAGE SEEMS AWFULLY EMPTY, DOESN'T IT?
RIGHT ON! GOOD EYE.
THIS VILLAGE'S NPCS ARE ALL DONE, SO USE IT AS REFERENCE.
AOBA, YOUR FIRST TASK IS MAKING THIS VILLAGE NICE AND LIVELY!
AWW!
THEY ALL HAVE CUTE CAT EARS...
YEAH, IT'S THE CAT VILLAGE. THAT'S HIFUMIN'S WORK!
H-HOW DO I DO THAT...?
BY CREATING THE VILLAGERS-- ONE BY ONE!
I'LL DO MY BEST TOO, HIFUMI-SENPAI!
?!

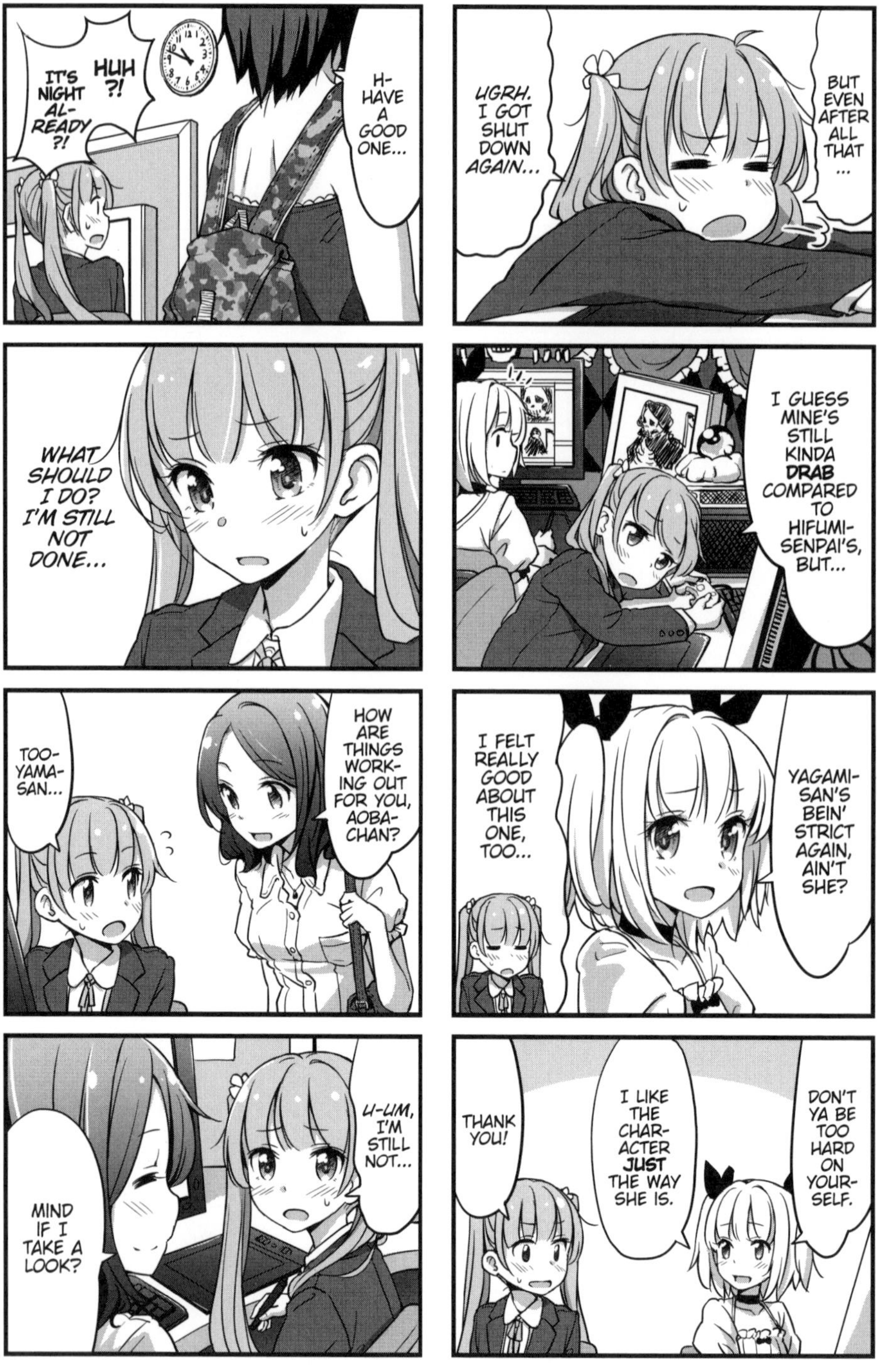
BUT EVEN AFTER ALL THAT...
UGRH. I GOT SHUT DOWN AGAIN...
I GUESS MINE'S STILL KINDA **DRAB** COMPARED TO HIFUMI-SENPAI'S, BUT...
YAGAMI-SAN'S BEIN' STRICT AGAIN, AIN'T SHE?
I FELT REALLY GOOD ABOUT THIS ONE, TOO...
DON'T YA BE TOO HARD ON YOURSELF.
I LIKE THE CHARACTER **JUST** THE WAY SHE IS.
THANK YOU!
H-HAVE A GOOD ONE...
HUH?!
IT'S NIGHT ALREADY?!
WHAT SHOULD I DO? I'M STILL NOT DONE...
HOW ARE THINGS WORKING OUT FOR YOU, AOBA-CHAN?
TOOYAMA-SAN...
U-UM, I'M STILL NOT...
MIND IF I TAKE A LOOK?

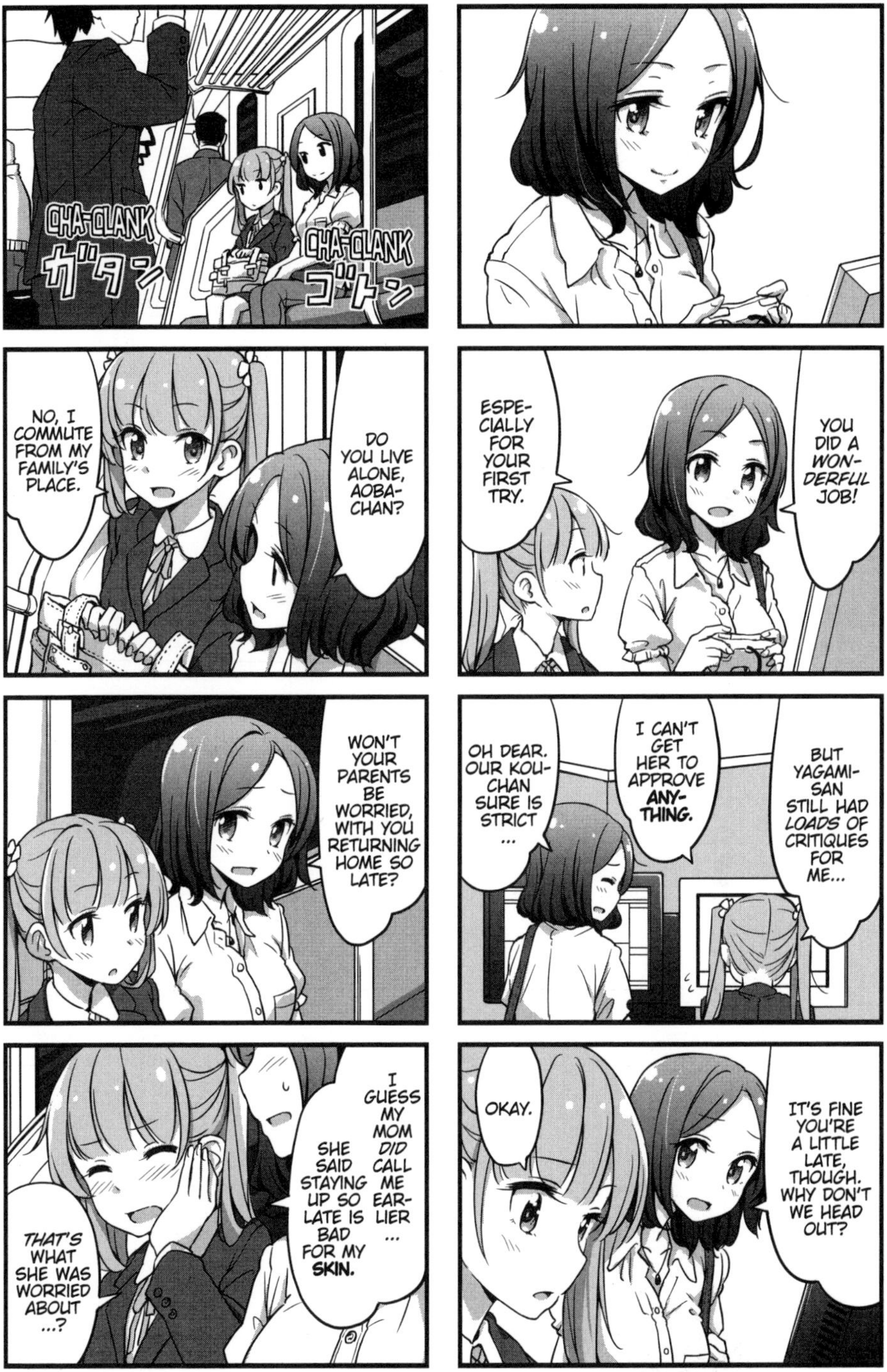
YOU DID A *WONDERFUL* JOB!
ESPECIALLY FOR YOUR FIRST TRY.
BUT YAGAMI-SAN STILL HAD *LOADS* OF CRITIQUES FOR ME...
I CAN'T GET HER TO APPROVE **ANYTHING.**
OH DEAR. OUR KOU-CHAN SURE IS STRICT...
IT'S FINE YOU'RE A LITTLE LATE, THOUGH. WHY DON'T WE HEAD OUT?
OKAY.
CHA-CLANK
ゴトン
CHA-CLANK
ガタン
DO YOU LIVE ALONE, AOBA-CHAN?
NO, I COMMUTE FROM MY FAMILY'S PLACE.
WON'T YOUR PARENTS BE WORRIED, WITH YOU RETURNING HOME SO LATE?
I GUESS MY MOM *DID* CALL ME EARLIER...
SHE SAID STAYING UP SO LATE IS BAD FOR MY **SKIN.**
THAT'S WHAT SHE WAS WORRIED ABOUT...?

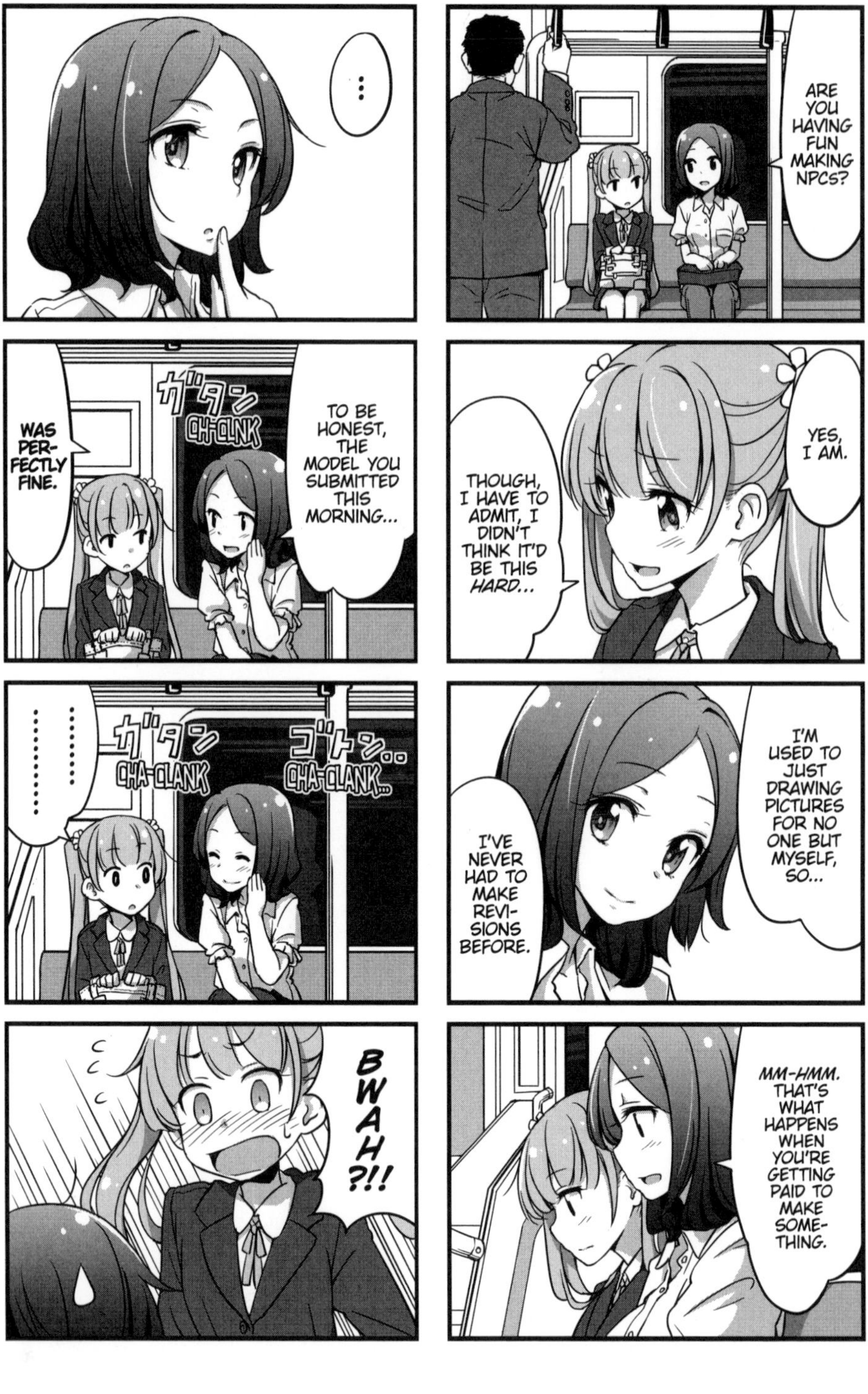
ARE YOU HAVING FUN MAKING NPCS?
...
YES, I AM.
THOUGH, I HAVE TO ADMIT, I DIDN'T THINK IT'D BE THIS *HARD*...
TO BE HONEST, THE MODEL YOU SUBMITTED THIS MORNING...
ガタン
CHA-CLNK
WAS PERFECTLY FINE.
I'M USED TO JUST DRAWING PICTURES FOR NO ONE BUT MYSELF, SO...
I'VE NEVER HAD TO MAKE REVISIONS BEFORE.
ゴトン..
CHA-CLANK...
ガタン
CHA-CLANK
....
MM-HMM. THAT'S WHAT HAPPENS WHEN YOU'RE GETTING PAID TO MAKE SOMETHING.
BWAH?!!

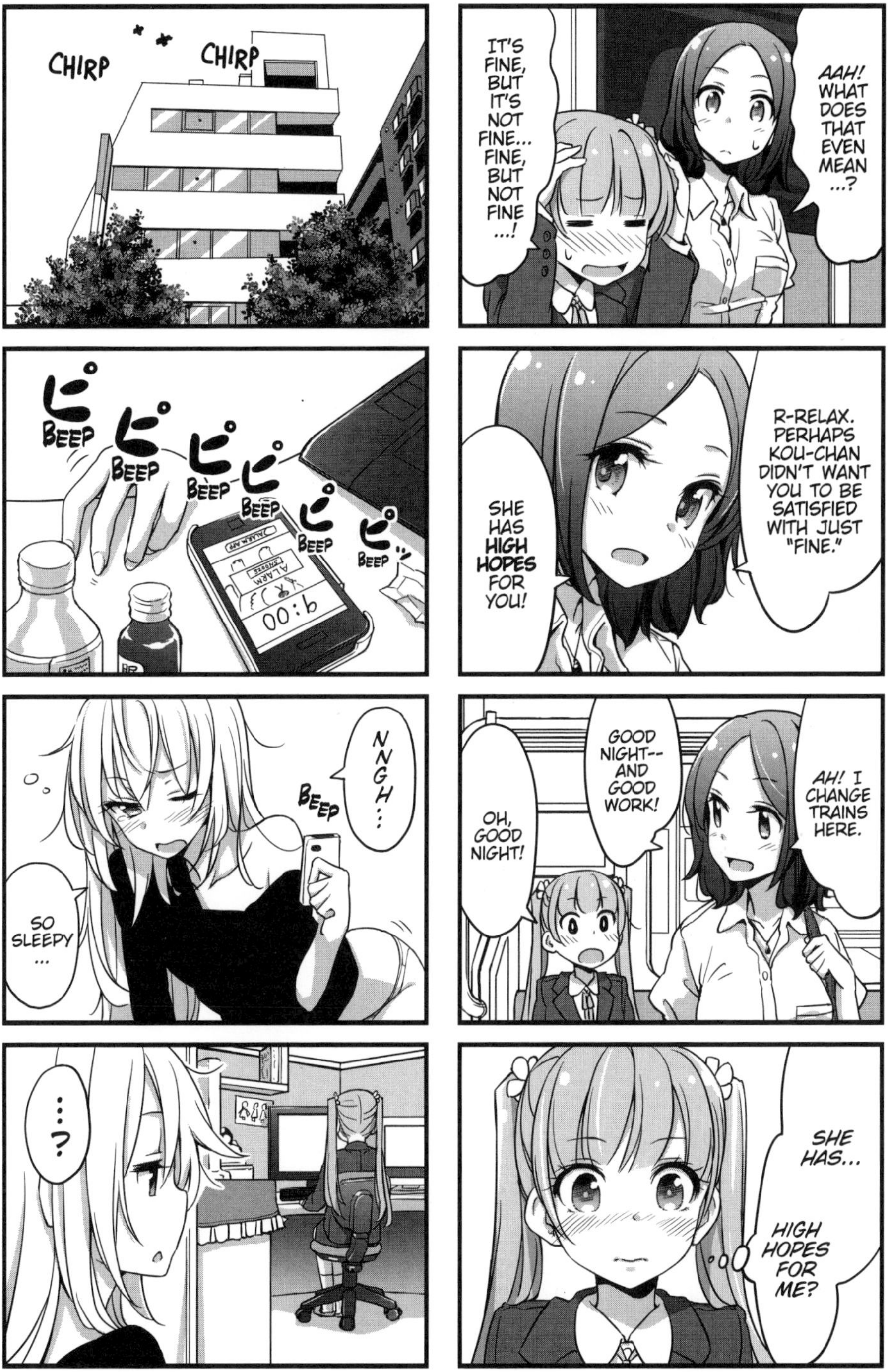
AAH! WHAT DOES THAT EVEN MEAN...?
IT'S FINE, BUT IT'S NOT FINE... FINE, BUT NOT FINE...!
R-RELAX. PERHAPS KOU-CHAN DIDN'T WANT YOU TO BE SATISFIED WITH JUST "FINE."
SHE HAS **HIGH HOPES** FOR YOU!
AH! I CHANGE TRAINS HERE.
GOOD NIGHT-- AND GOOD WORK!
OH, GOOD NIGHT!
SHE HAS...
HIGH HOPES FOR ME?
CHIRP
CHIRP
ピ BEEP
ピ BEEP
ピ BEEP
ピ BEEP
ピ BEEP
ピ BEEP
9:00
NNGH...
BEEP
SO SLEEPY...
...?

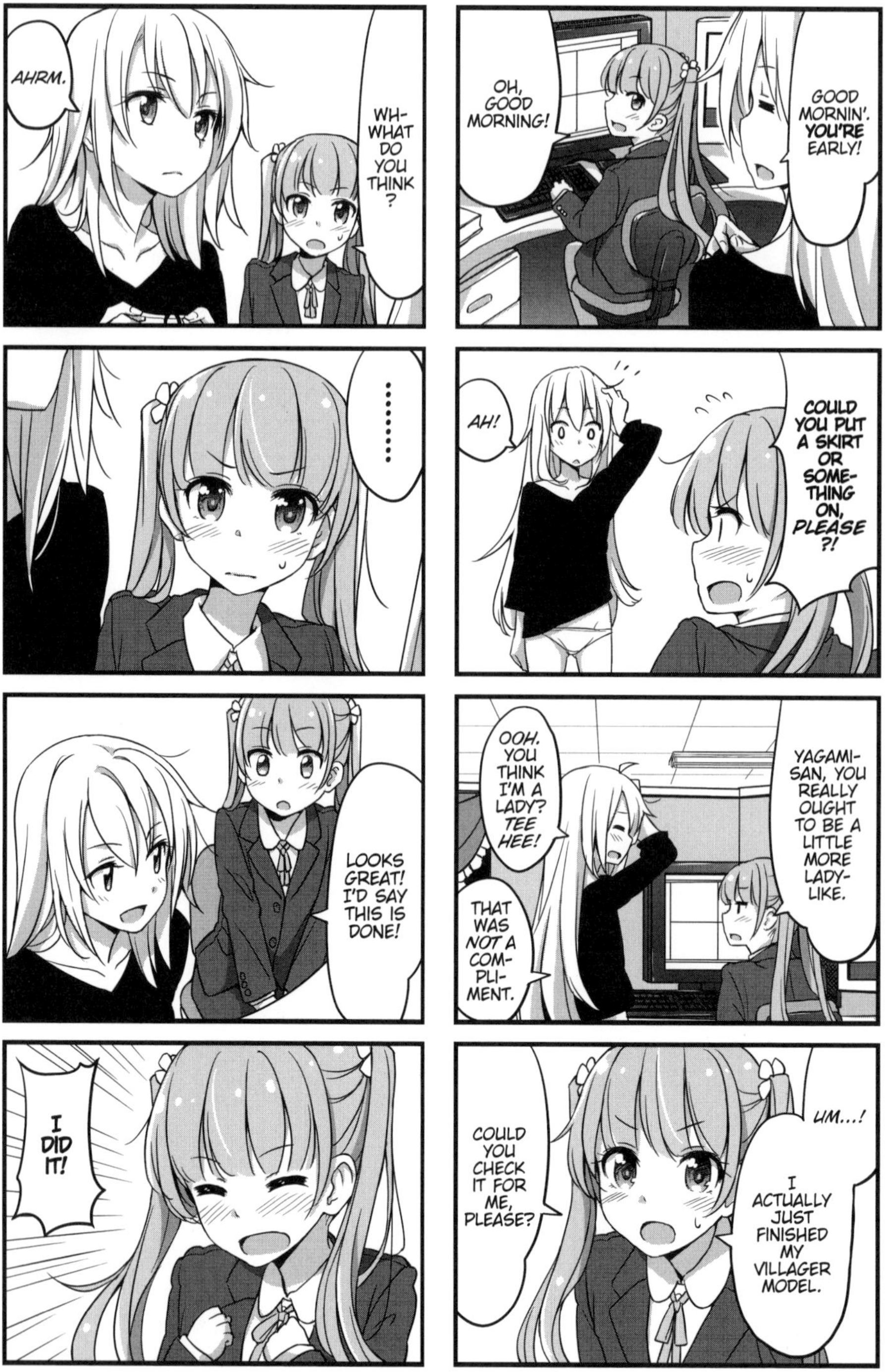
GOOD MORNIN'. YOU'RE EARLY!
OH, GOOD MORNING!
COULD YOU PUT A SKIRT OR SOMETHING ON, PLEASE?!
AH!
YAGAMI-SAN, YOU REALLY OUGHT TO BE A LITTLE MORE LADY-LIKE.
OOH. YOU THINK I'M A LADY? TEE HEE!
THAT WAS NOT A COMPLIMENT.
UM...!
I ACTUALLY JUST FINISHED MY VILLAGER MODEL.
COULD YOU CHECK IT FOR ME, PLEASE?
WH-WHAT DO YOU THINK?
AHRM.
....
LOOKS GREAT! I'D SAY THIS IS DONE!
I DID IT!

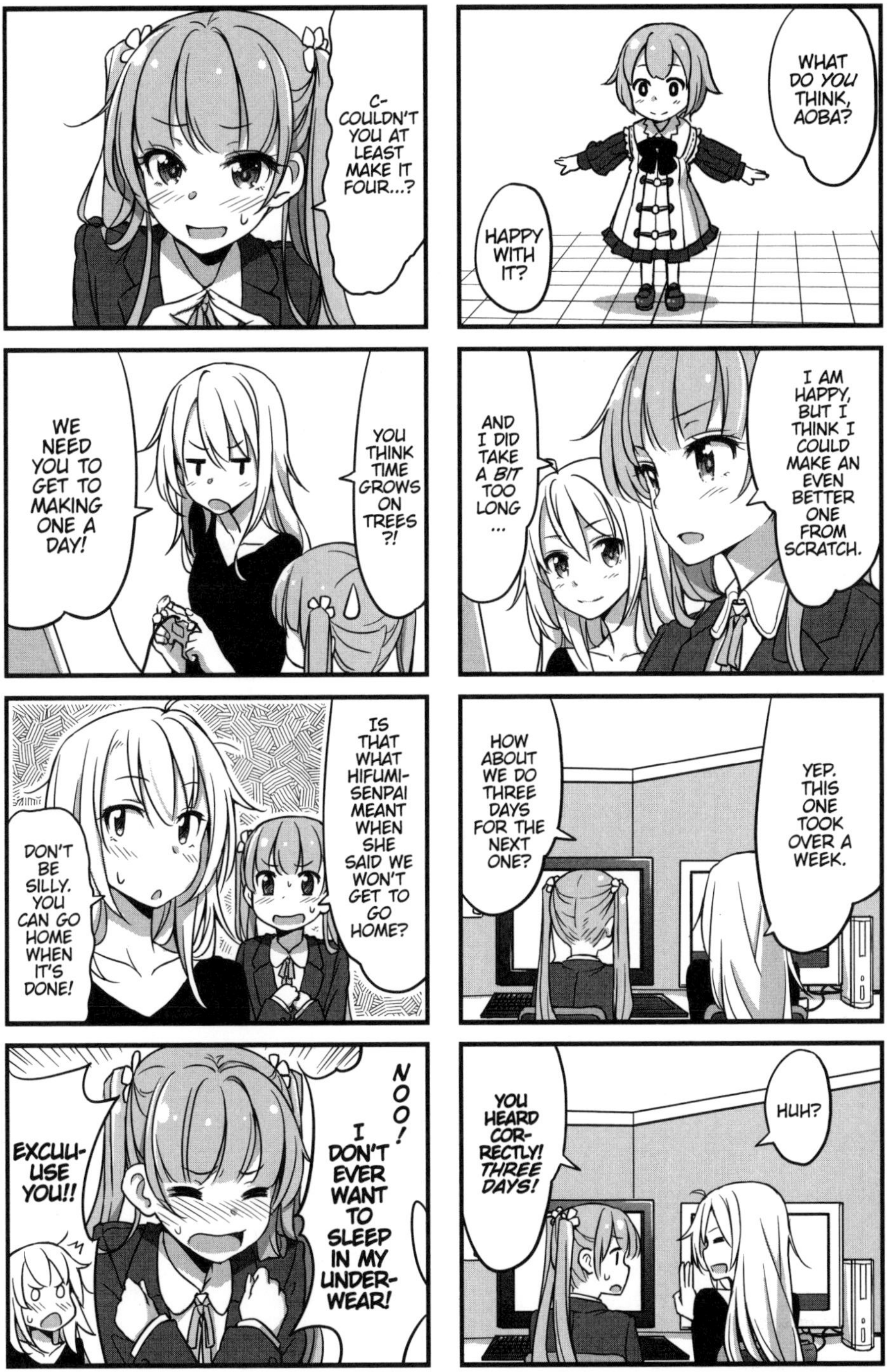
WHAT DO *YOU* THINK, AOBA?
HAPPY WITH IT?
I AM HAPPY, BUT I THINK I COULD MAKE AN EVEN BETTER ONE FROM SCRATCH.
AND I DID TAKE A *BIT* TOO LONG...
YEP. THIS ONE TOOK OVER A WEEK.
HOW ABOUT WE DO THREE DAYS FOR THE NEXT ONE?
HUH?
YOU HEARD COR-RECTLY! *THREE DAYS!*
C-COULDN'T YOU AT LEAST MAKE IT FOUR...?
YOU THINK TIME GROWS ON TREES?!
WE NEED YOU TO GET TO MAKING ONE A DAY!
IS THAT WHAT HIFUMI-SENPAI MEANT WHEN SHE SAID WE WON'T GET TO GO HOME?
DON'T BE SILLY. YOU CAN GO HOME WHEN IT'S DONE!
NOO! I DON'T EVER WANT TO SLEEP IN MY UNDER-WEAR!
EXCUU-USE YOU!!

NEW GAME!

NEW GAME!

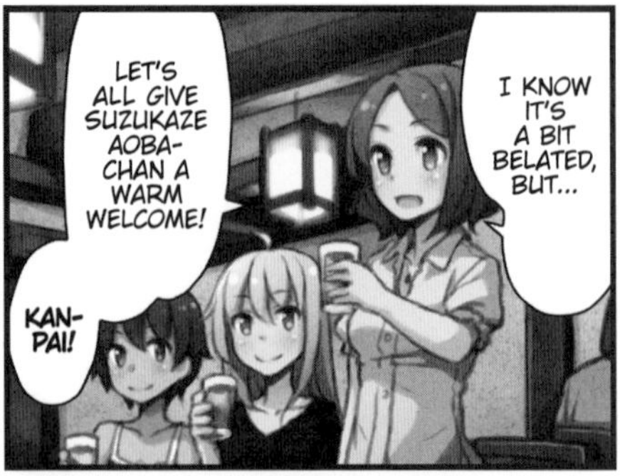
I KNOW IT'S A BIT BELATED, BUT...
LET'S ALL GIVE SUZUKAZE AOBA-CHAN A WARM WELCOME!
KAN-PAI!
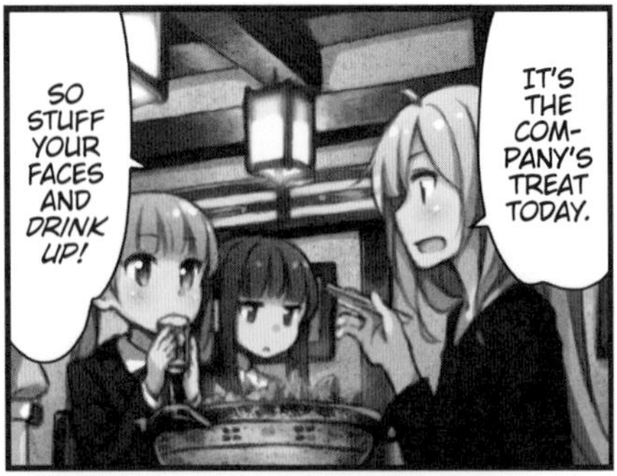
IT'S THE COMPANY'S TREAT TODAY.
SO STUFF YOUR FACES AND DRINK UP!
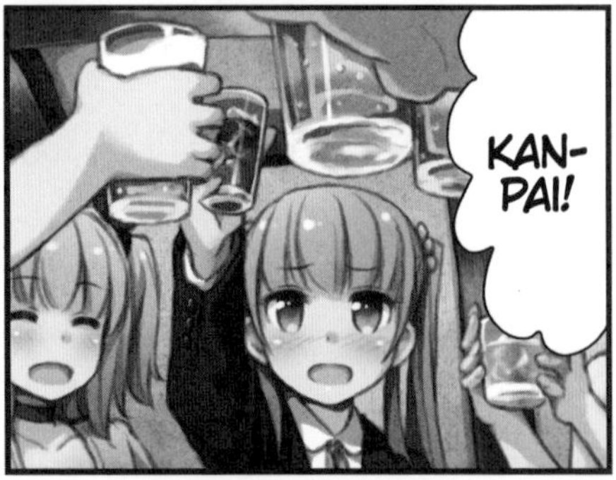
KAN-PAI!
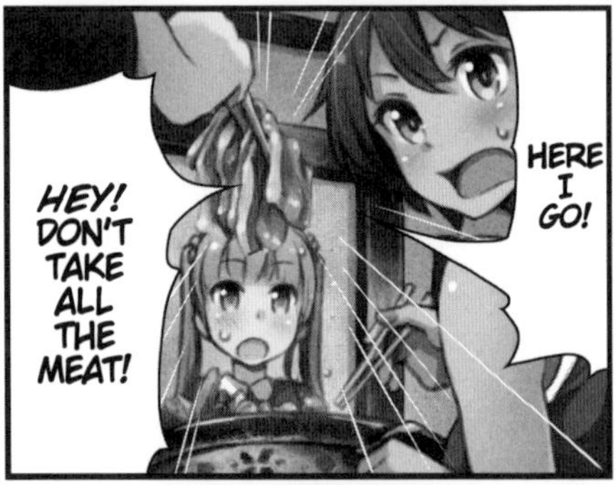
HERE I GO!
HEY! DON'T TAKE ALL THE MEAT!
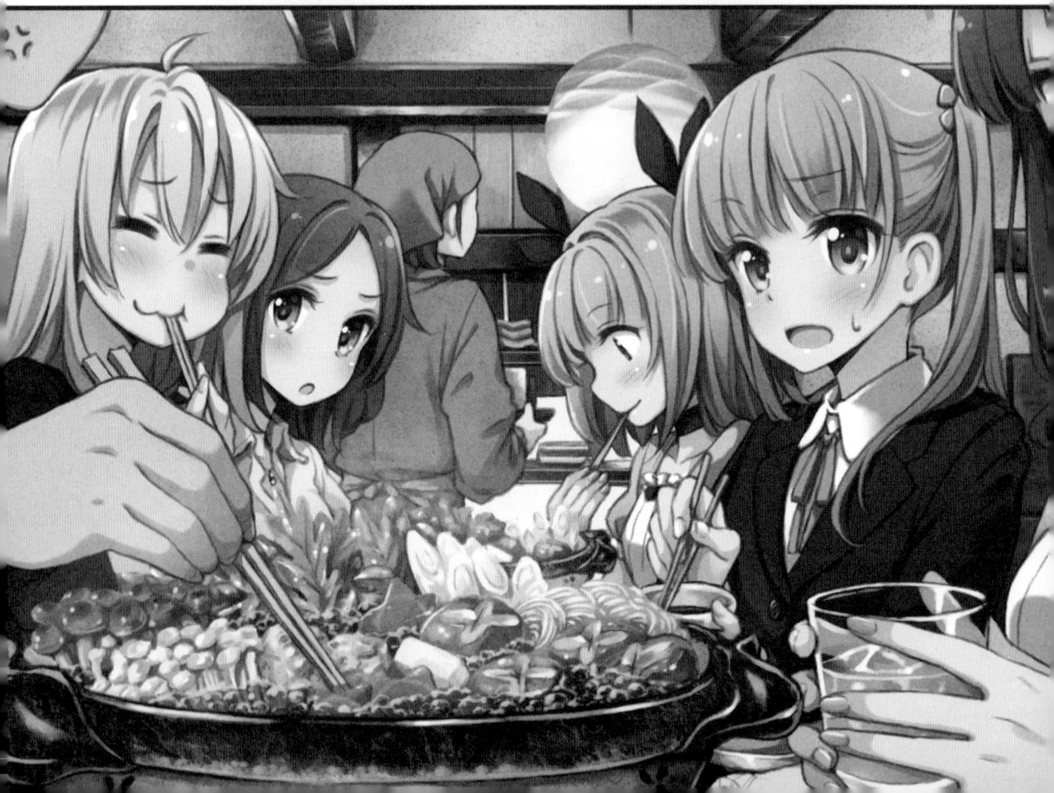

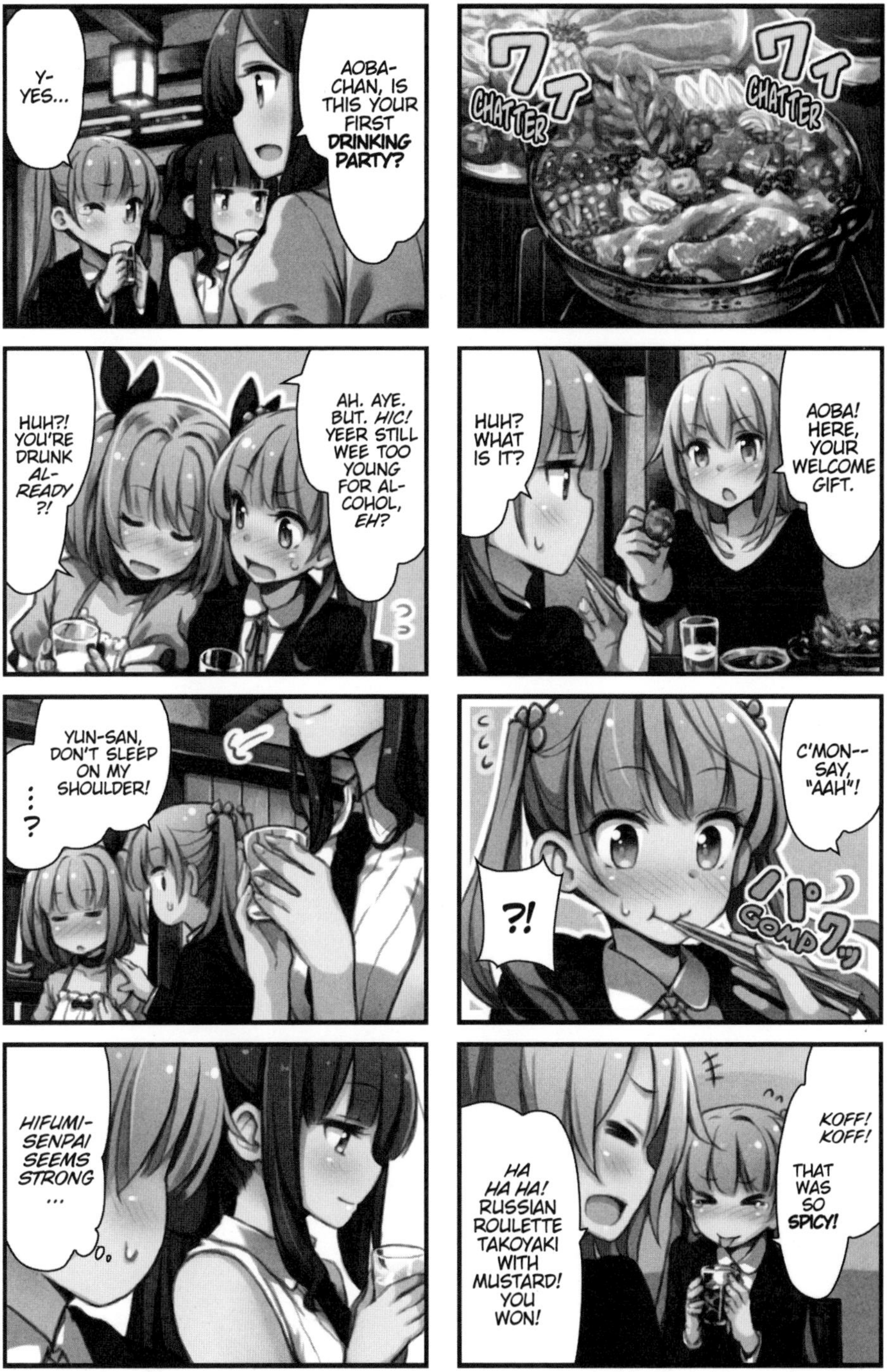
ワイ CHATTER
ワイ CHATTER
AOBA! HERE, YOUR WELCOME GIFT.
HUH? WHAT IS IT?
C'MON-- SAY, "AAH"!
?!
パクッ GOMP
KOFF! KOFF!
THAT WAS SO SPICY!
HA HA HA! RUSSIAN ROULETTE TAKOYAKI WITH MUSTARD! YOU WON!
AOBA-CHAN, IS THIS YOUR FIRST DRINKING PARTY?
Y-YES...
AH. AYE. BUT. HIC! YEER STILL WEE TOO YOUNG FOR AL-COHOL, EH?
HUH?! YOU'RE DRUNK AL-READY?!
YUN-SAN, DON'T SLEEP ON MY SHOULDER!
...?
HIFUMI-SENPAI SEEMS STRONG...

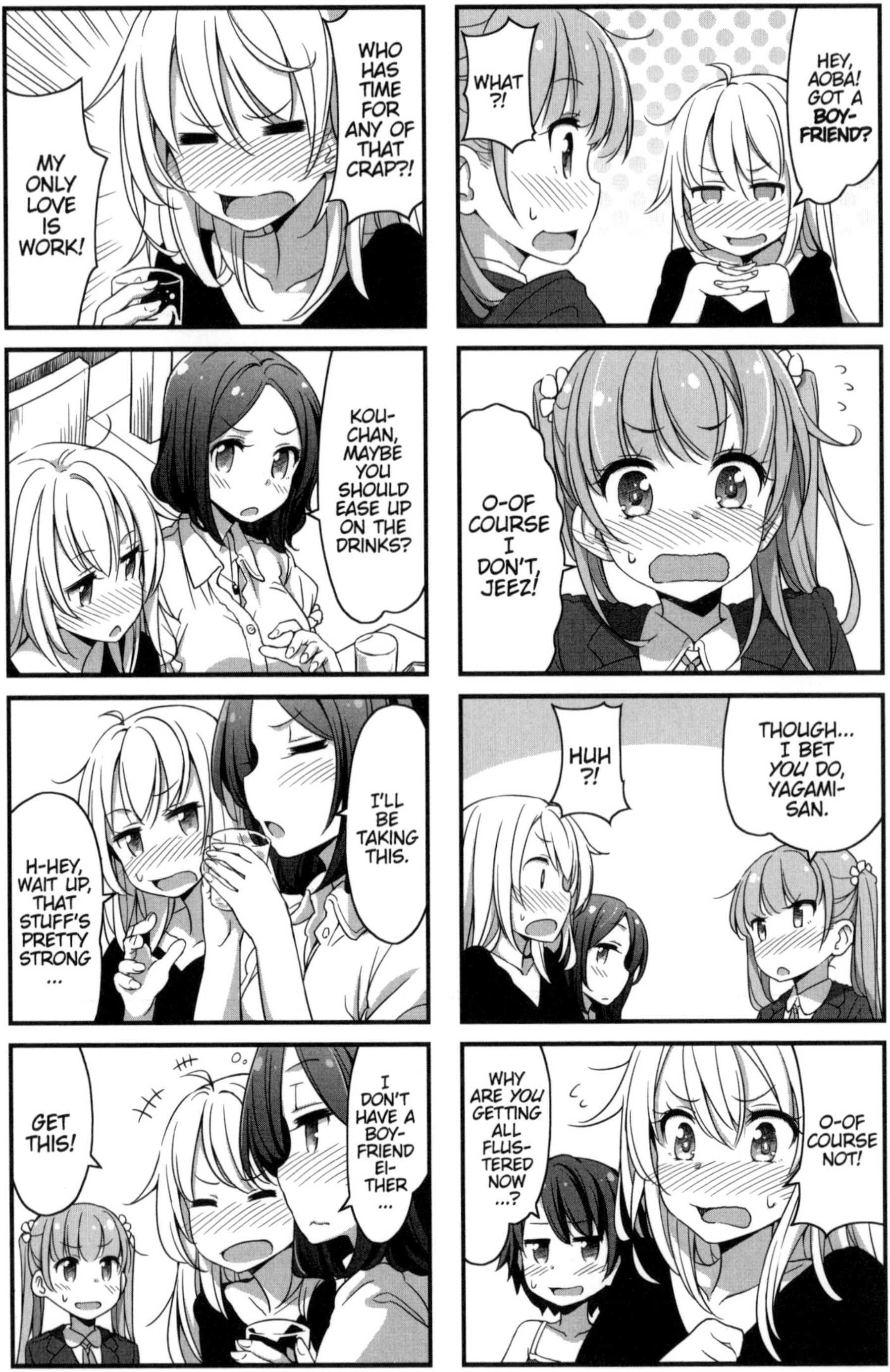
HEY, AOBA! GOT A BOY-FRIEND?
WHAT ?!
O-OF COURSE I DON'T, JEEZ!
THOUGH... I BET YOU DO, YAGAMI-SAN.
HUH ?!
O-OF COURSE NOT!
WHY ARE YOU GETTING ALL FLUS-TERED NOW ...?
WHO HAS TIME FOR ANY OF THAT CRAP?!
MY ONLY LOVE IS WORK!
KOU-CHAN, MAYBE YOU SHOULD EASE UP ON THE DRINKS?
I'LL BE TAKING THIS.
H-HEY, WAIT UP, THAT STUFF'S PRETTY STRONG ...
I DON'T HAVE A BOY-FRIEND EI-THER ...
GET THIS!

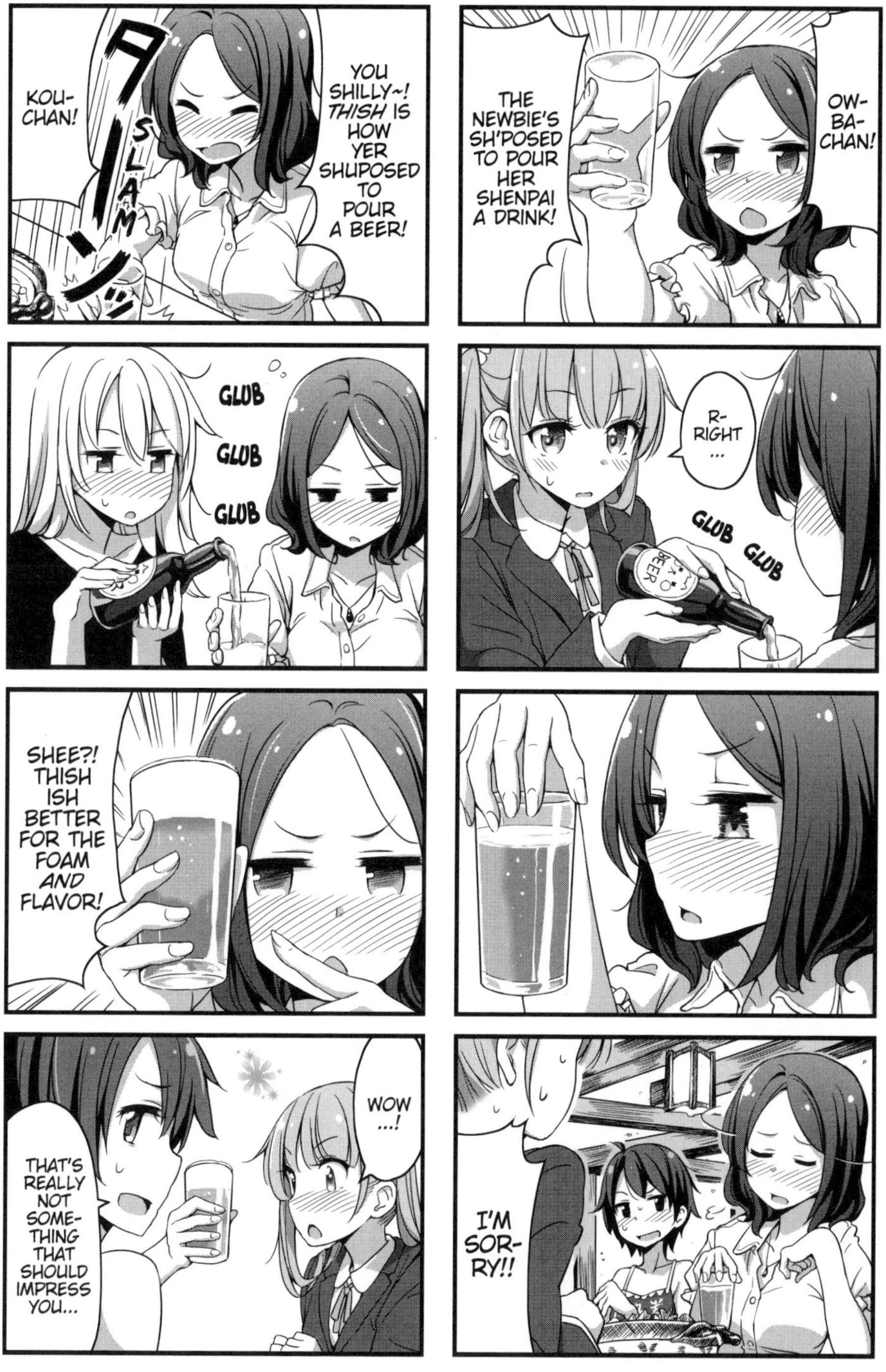
OW-BA-CHAN!
THE NEWBIE'S SH'POSED TO POUR HER SHENPAI A DRINK!
YOU SHILLY~! THISH IS HOW YER SHUPOSED TO POUR A BEER!
KOU-CHAN!
SLAM
R-RIGHT ...
GLUB GLUB
BEER
GLUB
GLUB
GLUB
SHEE?! THISH ISH BETTER FOR THE FOAM AND FLAVOR!
I'M SOR-RY!!
WOW ...!
THAT'S REALLY NOT SOME-THING THAT SHOULD IMPRESS YOU...

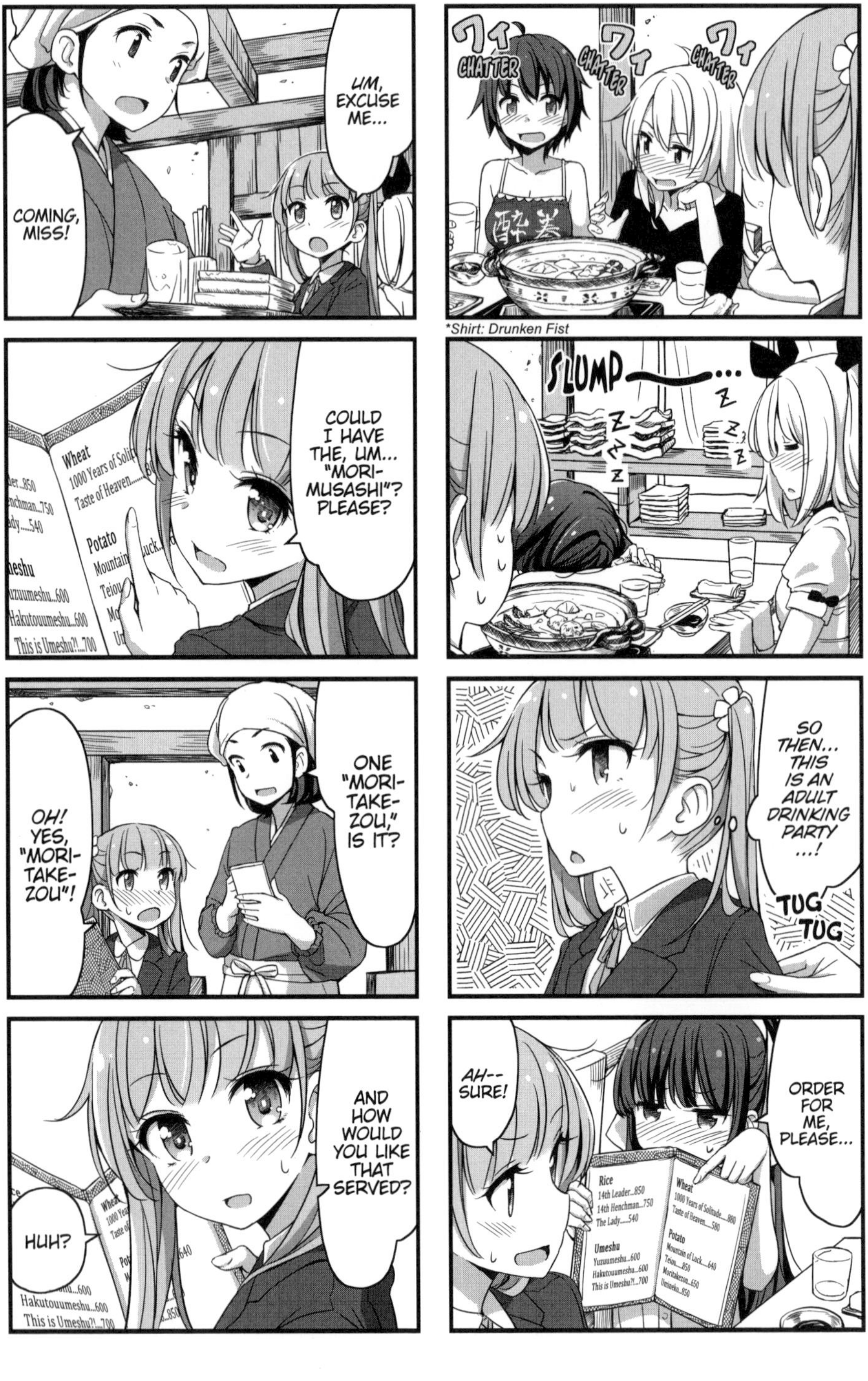

ワイ
CHATTER
ワイ
CHATTER
ワイ
CHATTER
UM, EXCUSE ME...
COMING, MISS!
SLUMP———...
Z Z Z Z Z Z
COULD I HAVE THE, UM... "MORI-MUSASHI"? PLEASE?
SO THEN... THIS IS AN ADULT DRINKING PARTY...!
TUG TUG
ONE "MORI-TAKE-ZOU," IS IT?
OH! YES, "MORI-TAKE-ZOU"!
ORDER FOR ME, PLEASE...
AH-- SURE!
Rice
14th Leader...850
14th Henchman...750
The Lady.....540
Umeshu
Yuzuumeshu...600
Hakutouumeshu...600
This is Umeshu?!...700
Wheat
1000 Years of Solitude.....880
Taste of Heaven.....500
Potato
Mountain of Luck....640
Teiou.....850
Moritakezou....650
Umineko...850
AND HOW WOULD YOU LIKE THAT SERVED?
HUH?

*Shirt: Drunken Fist

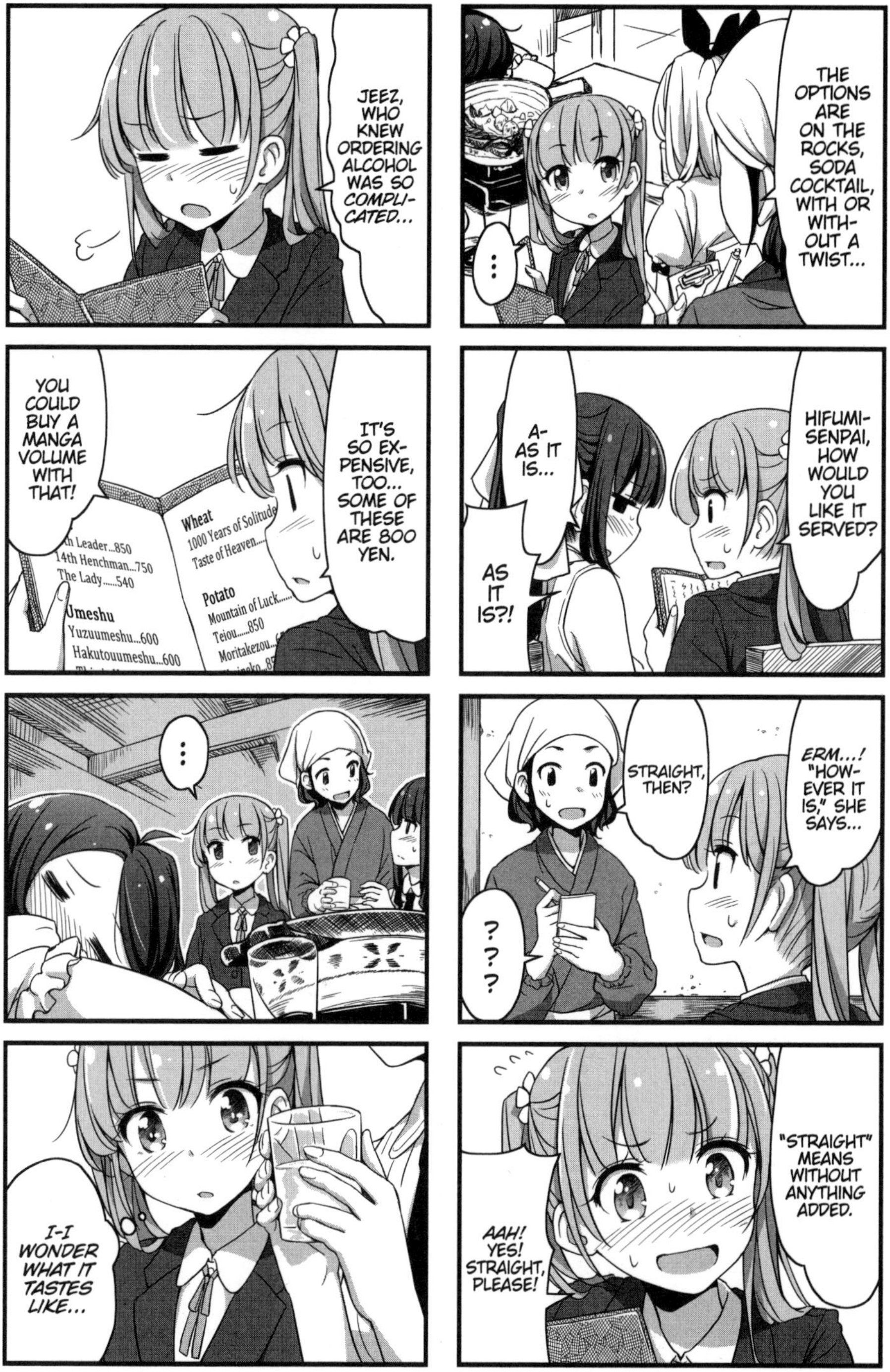
THE OPTIONS ARE ON THE ROCKS, SODA COCKTAIL, WITH OR WITHOUT A TWIST...
...
HIFUMI-SENPAI, HOW WOULD YOU LIKE IT SERVED?
A-AS IT IS...
AS IT IS?!
ERM...! "HOWEVER IT IS," SHE SAYS...
STRAIGHT, THEN?
???
"STRAIGHT" MEANS WITHOUT ANYTHING ADDED.
AAH! YES! STRAIGHT, PLEASE!
JEEZ, WHO KNEW ORDERING ALCOHOL WAS SO COMPLICATED...
IT'S SO EXPENSIVE, TOO... SOME OF THESE ARE 800 YEN.
YOU COULD BUY A MANGA VOLUME WITH THAT!
14th Henchman...750
The Lady......540
Umeshu
Yuzuumeshu...600
Hakutouumeshu...600
Wheat
1000 Years of Solitude
Taste of Heaven
Potato
Mountain of Luck
Teiou...850
...
I-I WONDER WHAT IT TASTES LIKE...

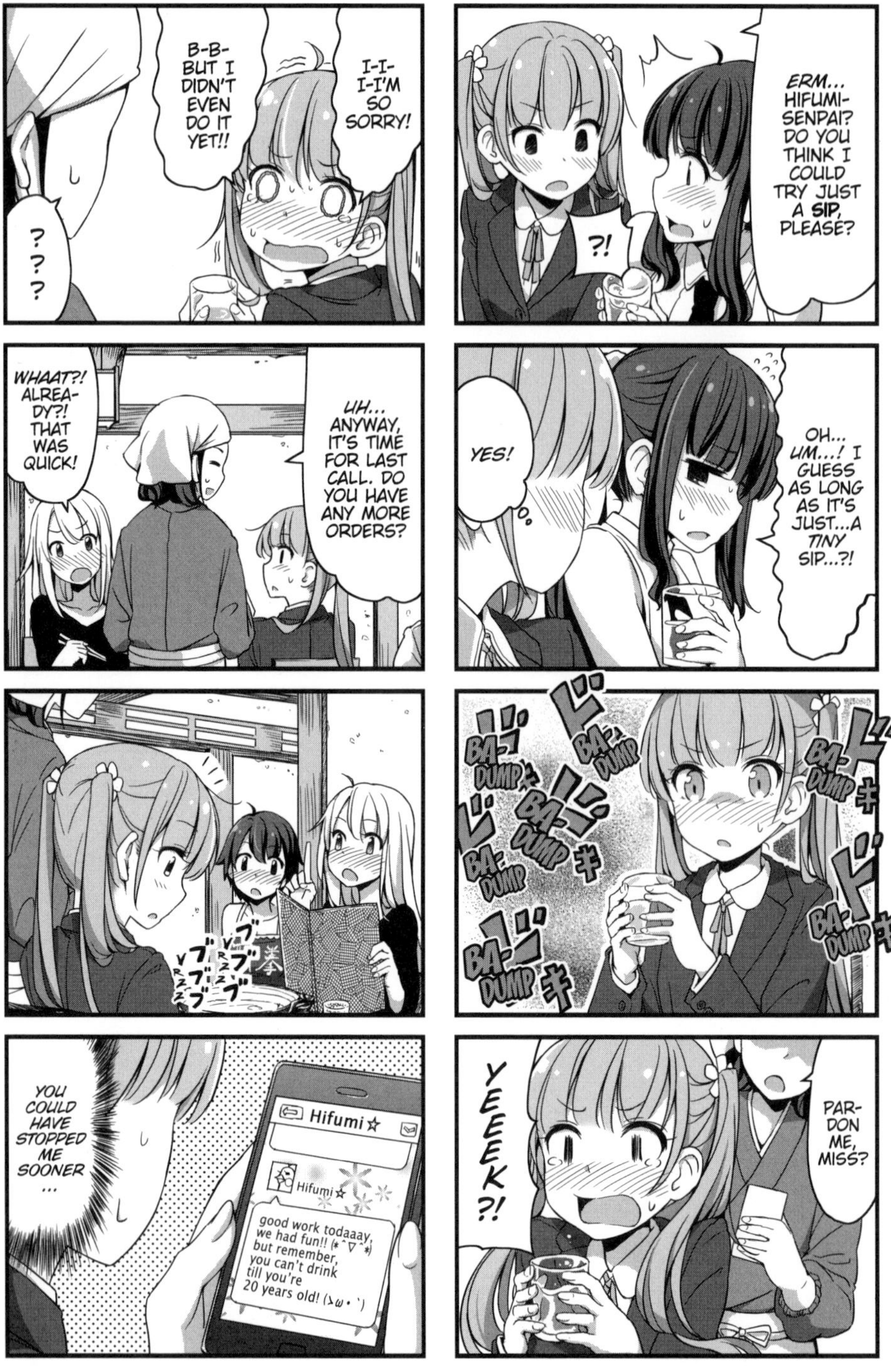
ERM... HIFUMI-SENPAI? DO YOU THINK I COULD TRY JUST A **SIP**, PLEASE?
?!
OH... UM...! I GUESS AS LONG AS IT'S JUST...A *TINY* SIP...?!
YES!
BA-DUMP
BA-DUMP
BA-DUMP
BA-DUMP
BA-DUMP
BA-DUMP
BA-DUMP
PAR-DON ME, MISS?
YEEEK?!
I-I-I-I'M SO SORRY!
B-B-BUT I DIDN'T EVEN DO IT YET!!
???
UH... ANYWAY, IT'S TIME FOR LAST CALL. DO YOU HAVE ANY MORE ORDERS?
WHAAT?! ALREA-DY?! THAT WAS QUICK!
ZZZ
Hifumi☆
Hifumi☆
good work todaaay, we had fun!! (*^▽^*) but remember, you can't drink till you're 20 years old! (ゝω・`)
YOU COULD HAVE STOPPED ME SOONER...

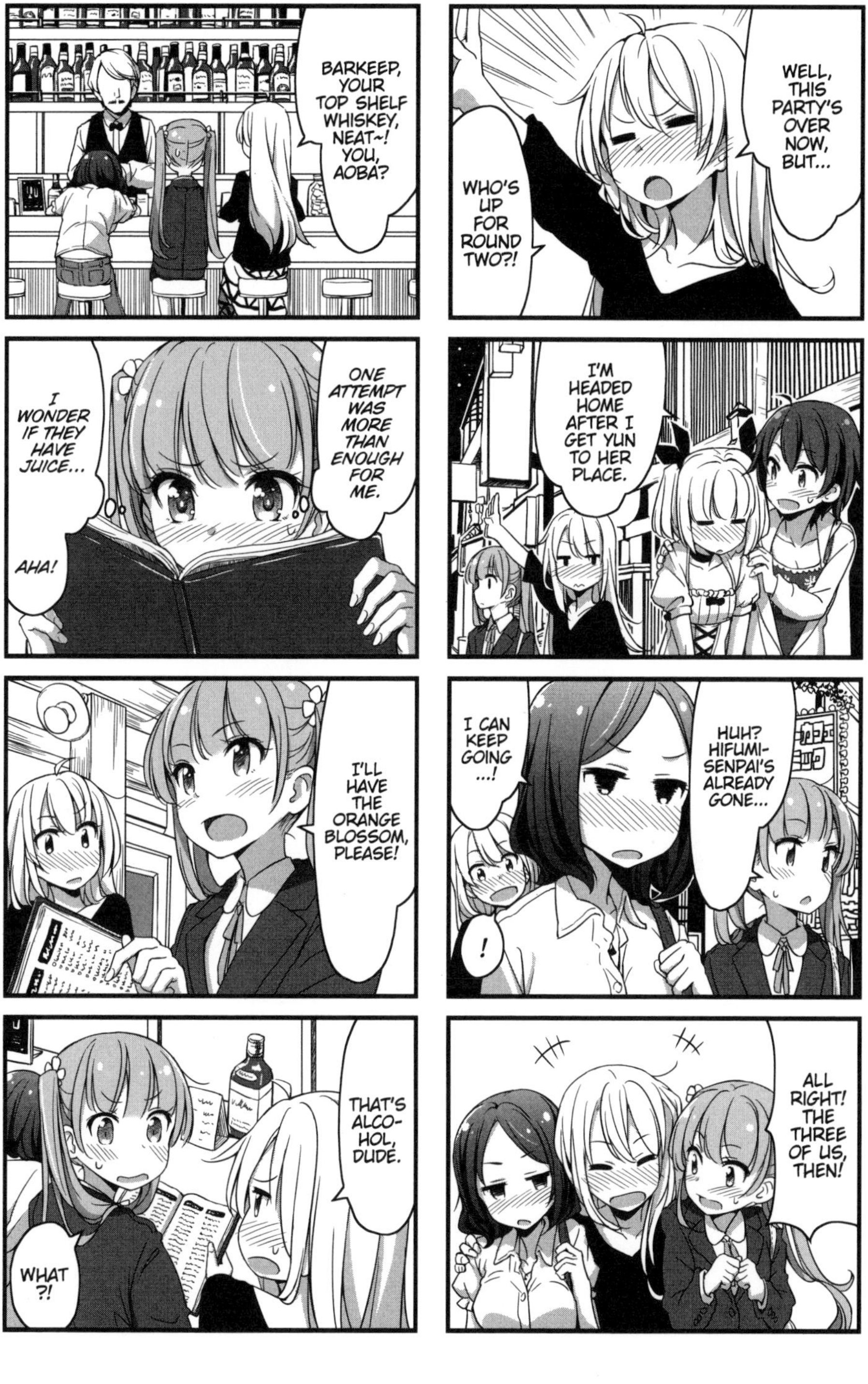
WELL, THIS PARTY'S OVER NOW, BUT...
WHO'S UP FOR ROUND TWO?!
I'M HEADED HOME AFTER I GET YUN TO HER PLACE.
HUH? HIFUMI-SENPAI'S ALREADY GONE...
I CAN KEEP GOING...!
!
ALL RIGHT! THE THREE OF US, THEN!
BARKEEP, YOUR TOP SHELF WHISKEY, NEAT~! YOU, AOBA?
ONE ATTEMPT WAS MORE THAN ENOUGH FOR ME.
I WONDER IF THEY HAVE JUICE...
AHA!
I'LL HAVE THE ORANGE BLOSSOM, PLEASE!
THAT'S ALCOHOL, DUDE.
WHAT?!

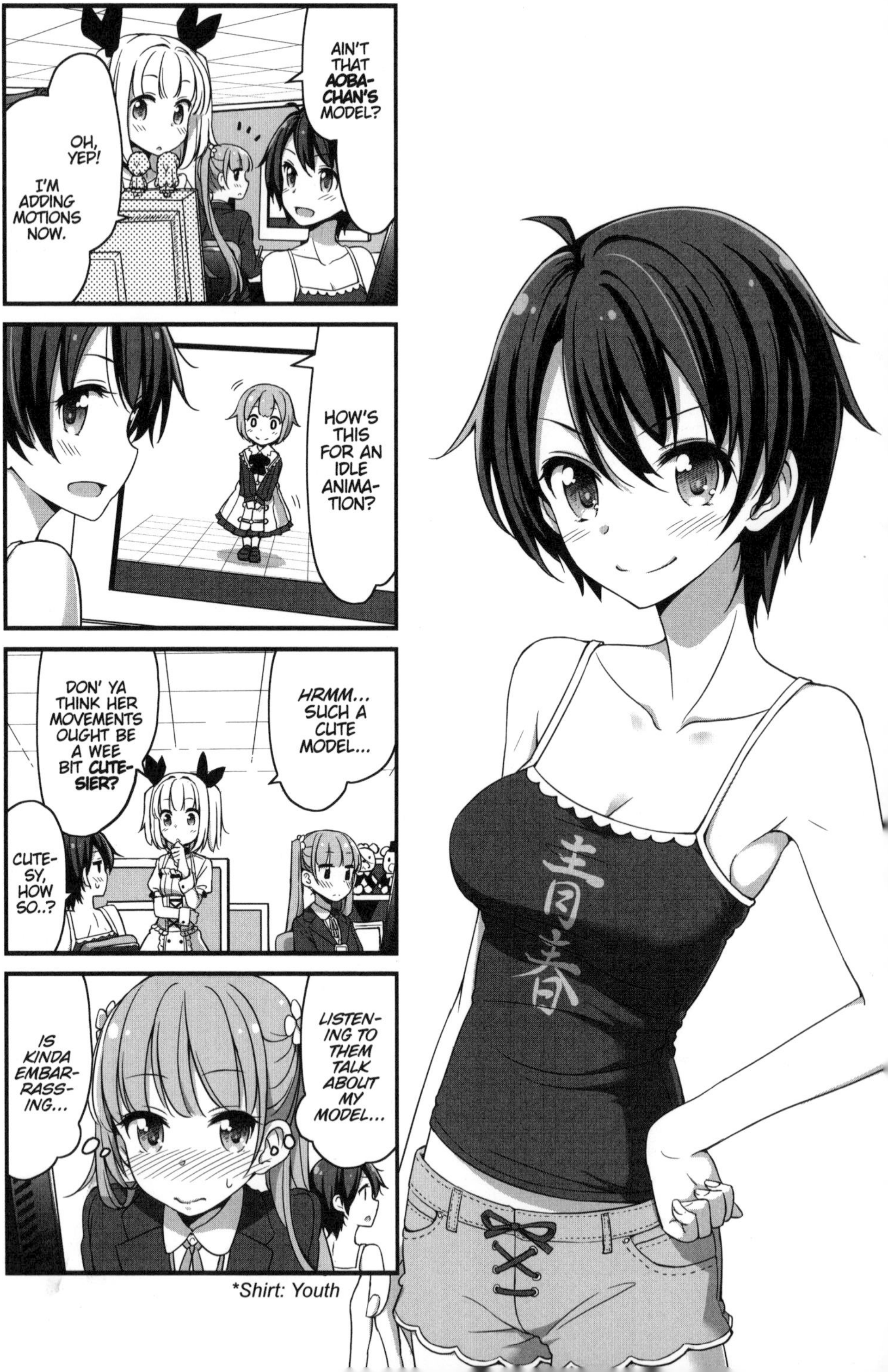
青春
AIN'T THAT AOBA-CHAN'S MODEL?
OH, YEP! I'M ADDING MOTIONS NOW.
HOW'S THIS FOR AN IDLE ANIMATION?
HRMM... SUCH A CUTE MODEL...
DON' YA THINK HER MOVEMENTS OUGHT BE A WEE BIT CUTESIER?
CUTESY, HOW SO..?
LISTENING TO THEM TALK ABOUT MY MODEL...
IS KINDA EMBARRASSING...
*Shirt: Youth

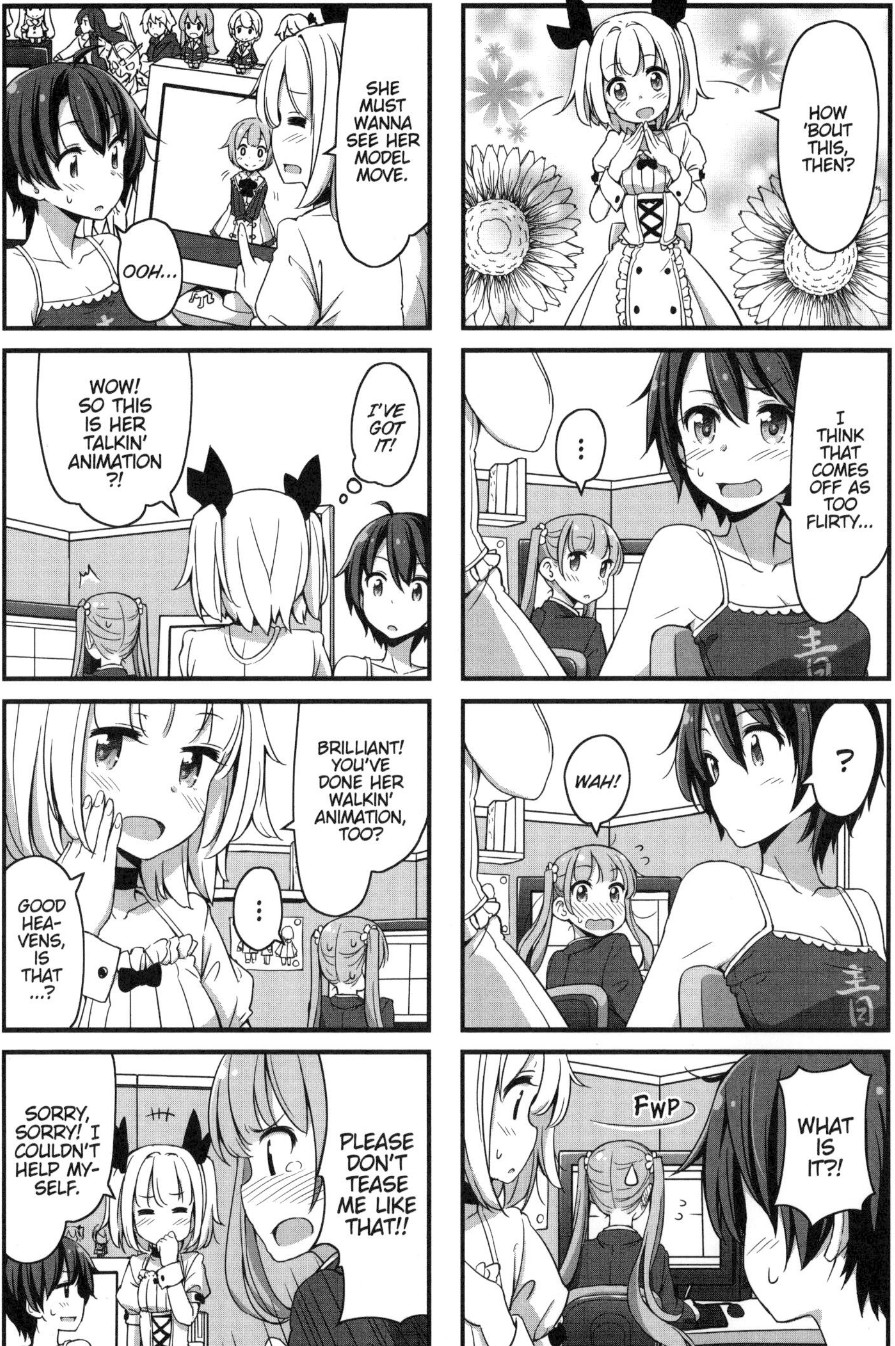
HOW 'BOUT THIS, THEN?
...
I THINK THAT COMES OFF AS TOO FLIRTY...
WAH!
?
FWP
WHAT IS IT?!
SHE MUST WANNA SEE HER MODEL MOVE.
OOH...
I'VE GOT IT!
WOW! SO THIS IS HER TALKIN' ANIMATION?!
BRILLIANT! YOU'VE DONE HER WALKIN' ANIMATION, TOO?
...
GOOD HEAVENS, IS THAT ...?
PLEASE DON'T TEASE ME LIKE THAT!!
SORRY, SORRY! I COULDN'T HELP MYSELF.

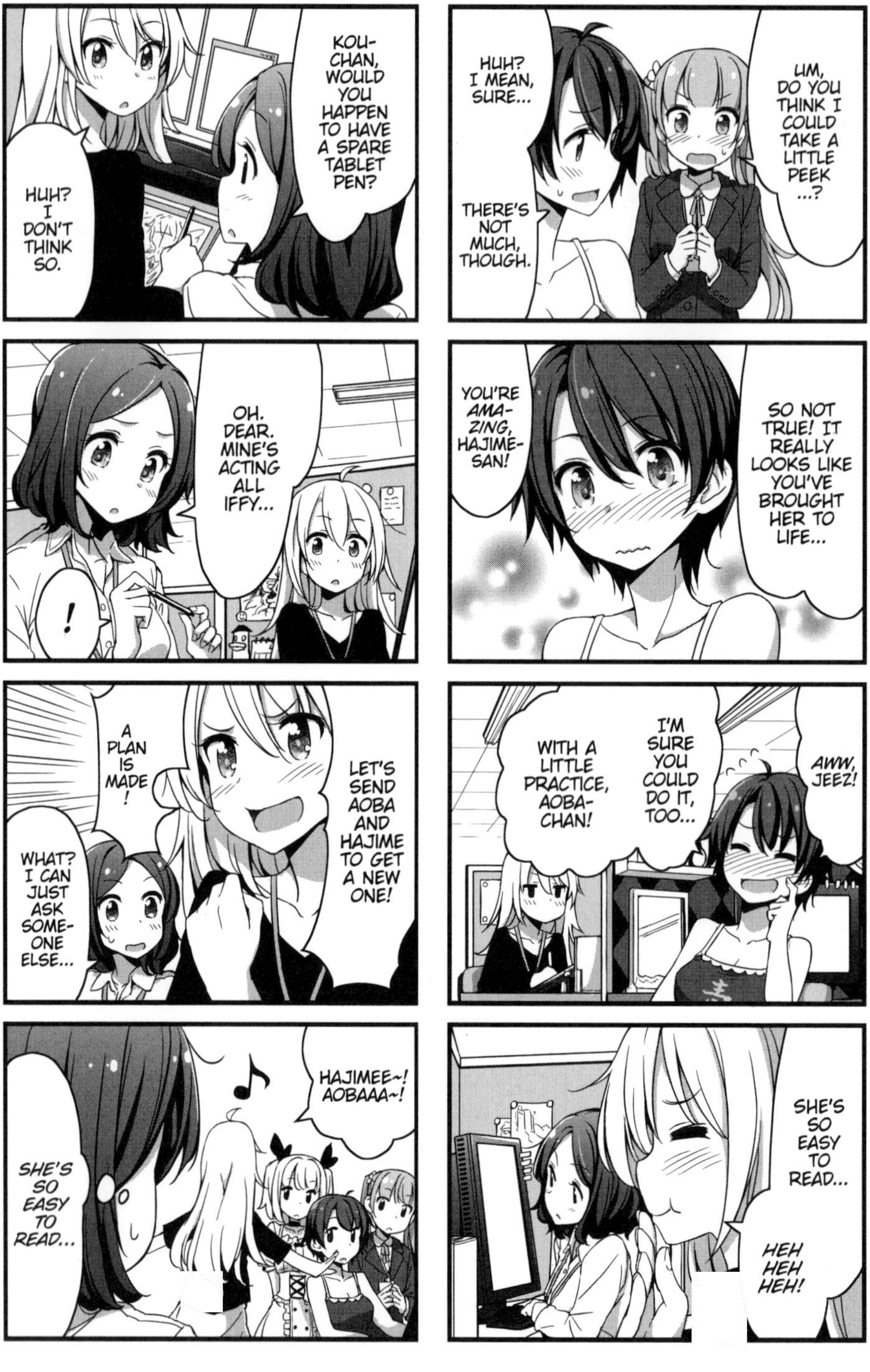
UM, DO YOU THINK I COULD TAKE A LITTLE PEEK...?
HUH? I MEAN, SURE...
THERE'S NOT MUCH, THOUGH.
SO NOT TRUE! IT REALLY LOOKS LIKE YOU'VE BROUGHT HER TO LIFE...
YOU'RE AMAZING, HAJIME-SAN!
AWW, JEEZ!
I'M SURE YOU COULD DO IT, TOO...
WITH A LITTLE PRACTICE, AOBA-CHAN!
SHE'S SO EASY TO READ...
HEH HEH HEH!
KOU-CHAN, WOULD YOU HAPPEN TO HAVE A SPARE TABLET PEN?
HUH? I DON'T THINK SO.
OH. DEAR. MINE'S ACTING ALL IFFY...
!
LET'S SEND AOBA AND HAJIME TO GET A NEW ONE!
A PLAN IS MADE!
WHAT? I CAN JUST ASK SOMEONE ELSE...
HAJIMEE~! AOBAAA~!
SHE'S SO EASY TO READ...

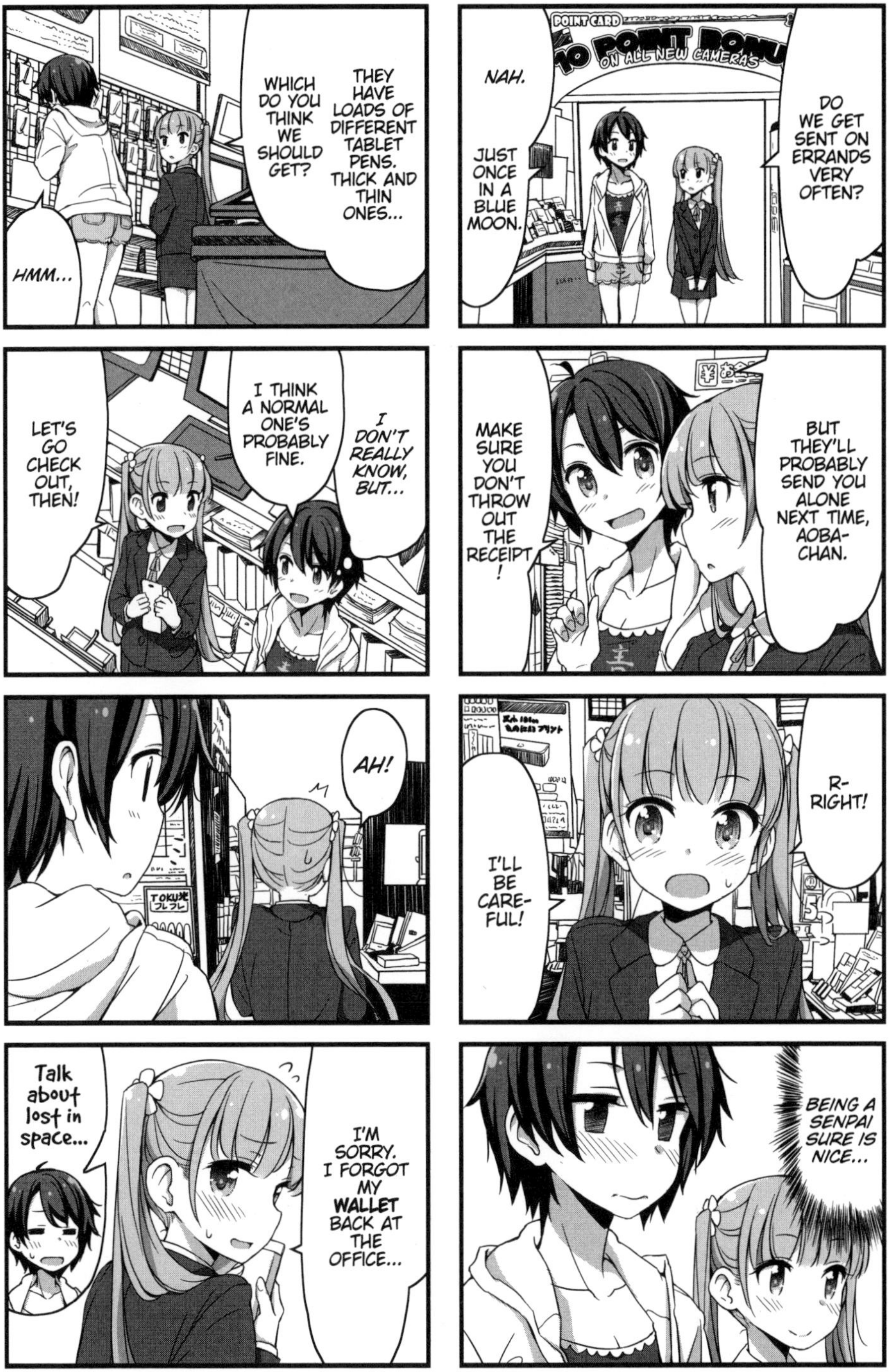
POINT CARD
ON ALL NEW CAMERAS
DO WE GET SENT ON ERRANDS VERY OFTEN?
NAH.
JUST ONCE IN A BLUE MOON.
THEY HAVE LOADS OF DIFFERENT TABLET PENS. THICK AND THIN ONES...
WHICH DO YOU THINK WE SHOULD GET?
HMM...
BUT THEY'LL PROBABLY SEND YOU ALONE NEXT TIME, AOBA-CHAN.
MAKE SURE YOU DON'T THROW OUT THE RECEIPT!
I DON'T REALLY KNOW, BUT...
I THINK A NORMAL ONE'S PROBABLY FINE.
LET'S GO CHECK OUT, THEN!
R-RIGHT!
I'LL BE CARE-FUL!
AH!
BEING A SENPAI SURE IS NICE...
I'M SORRY. I FORGOT MY **WALLET** BACK AT THE OFFICE...
Talk about lost in space...

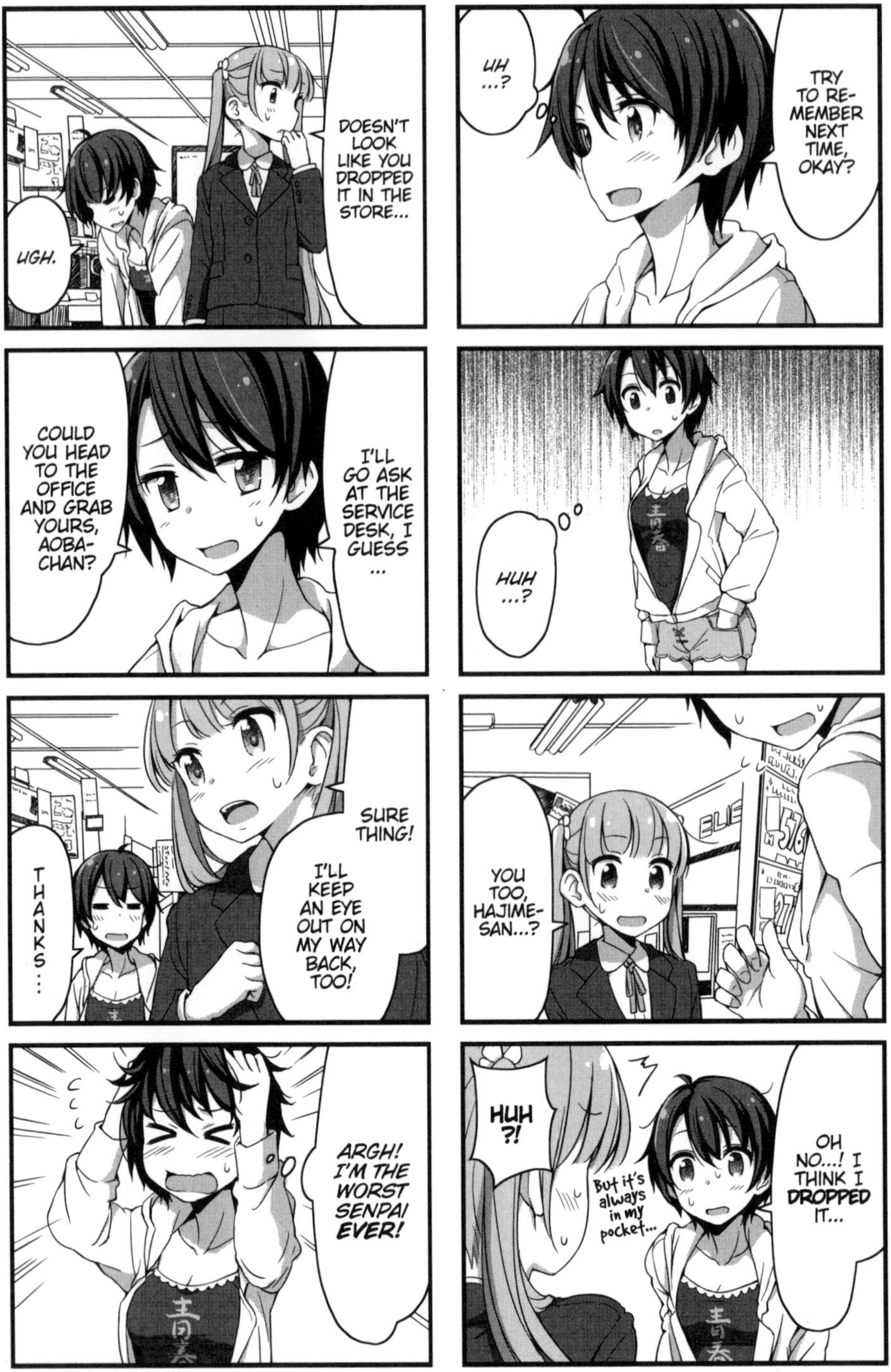
TRY TO RE-MEMBER NEXT TIME, OKAY?
UH ...?
DOESN'T LOOK LIKE YOU DROPPED IT IN THE STORE...
UGH.
HUH ...?
I'LL GO ASK AT THE SERVICE DESK, I GUESS ...
COULD YOU HEAD TO THE OFFICE AND GRAB YOURS, AOBA-CHAN?
YOU TOO, HAJIME-SAN...?
SURE THING!
I'LL KEEP AN EYE OUT ON MY WAY BACK, TOO!
THANKS...
OH NO...! I THINK I DROPPED IT...
HUH ?!
But it's always in my pocket...
ARGH! I'M THE WORST SENPAI EVER!

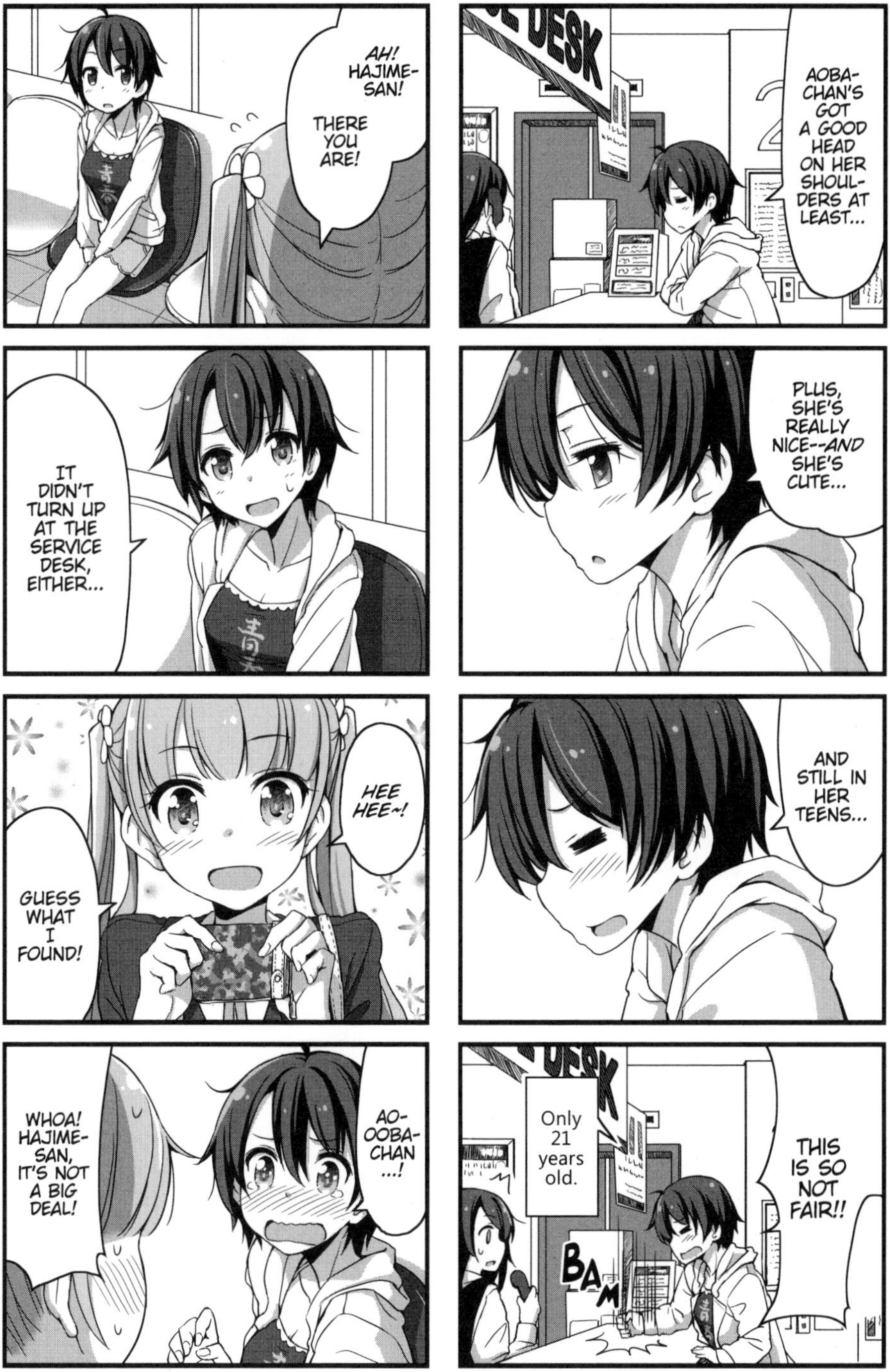
DESK
AOBA-CHAN'S GOT A GOOD HEAD ON HER SHOULDERS AT LEAST...
PLUS, SHE'S REALLY NICE--AND SHE'S CUTE...
AND STILL IN HER TEENS...
THIS IS SO NOT FAIR!!
Only 21 years old.
BAM
AH! HAJIME-SAN!
THERE YOU ARE!
IT DIDN'T TURN UP AT THE SERVICE DESK, EITHER...
HEE HEE~!
GUESS WHAT I FOUND!
AO-OOBA-CHAN...!
WHOA! HAJIME-SAN, IT'S NOT A BIG DEAL!

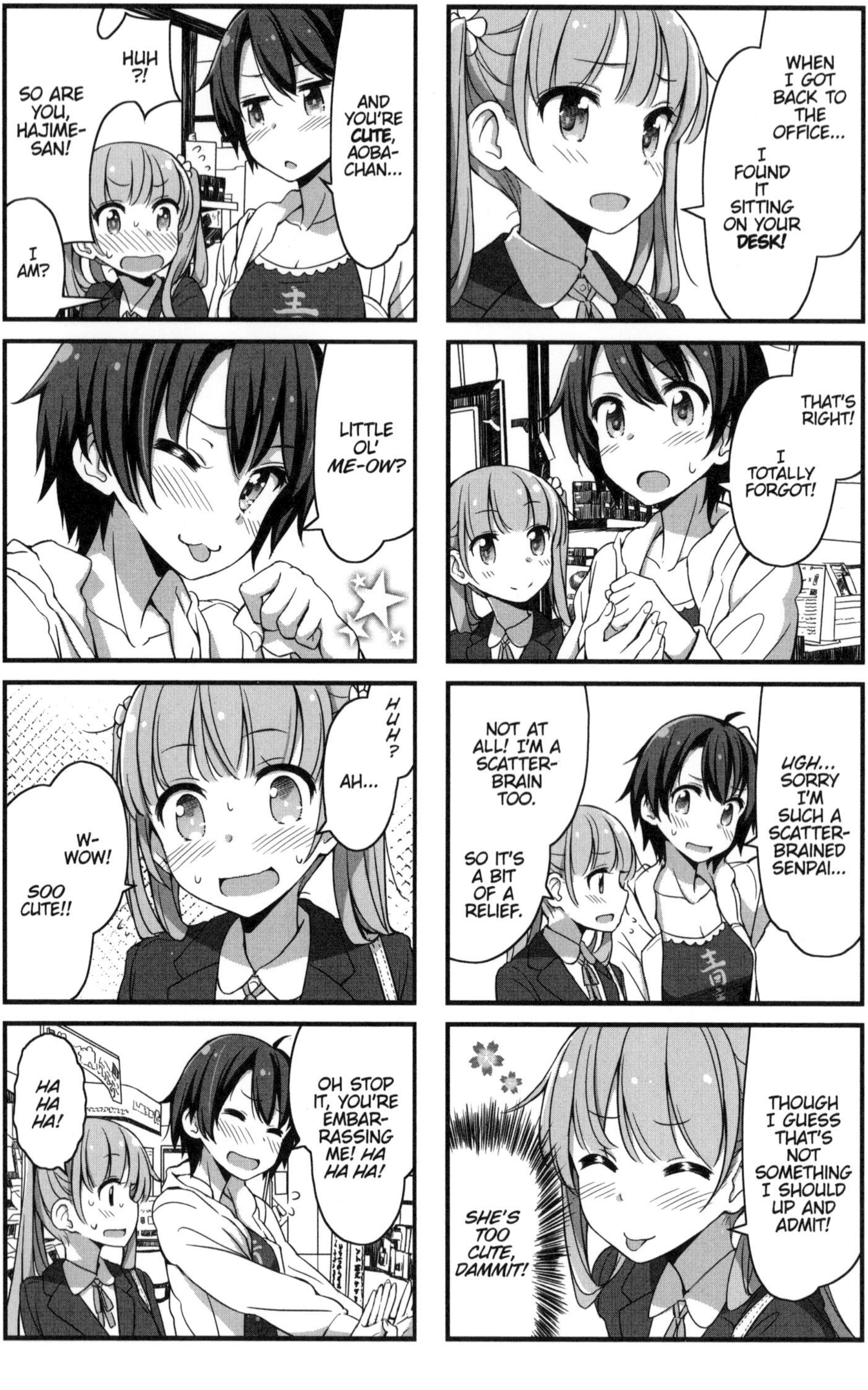
WHEN I GOT BACK TO THE OFFICE...
I FOUND IT SITTING ON YOUR **DESK!**
AND YOU'RE **CUTE,** AOBA-CHAN...
HUH ?!
SO ARE YOU, HAJIME-SAN!
I AM?
THAT'S RIGHT!
I TOTALLY FORGOT!
LITTLE OL' ME-OW?
UGH... SORRY I'M SUCH A SCATTER-BRAINED SENPAI...
NOT AT ALL! I'M A SCATTER-BRAIN TOO.
SO IT'S A BIT OF A RELIEF.
HUH?
AH...
W-WOW!
SOO CUTE!!
THOUGH I GUESS THAT'S NOT SOMETHING I SHOULD UP AND ADMIT!
SHE'S TOO CUTE, DAMMIT!
OH STOP IT, YOU'RE EMBARRASSING ME! HA HA HA!
HA HA HA!

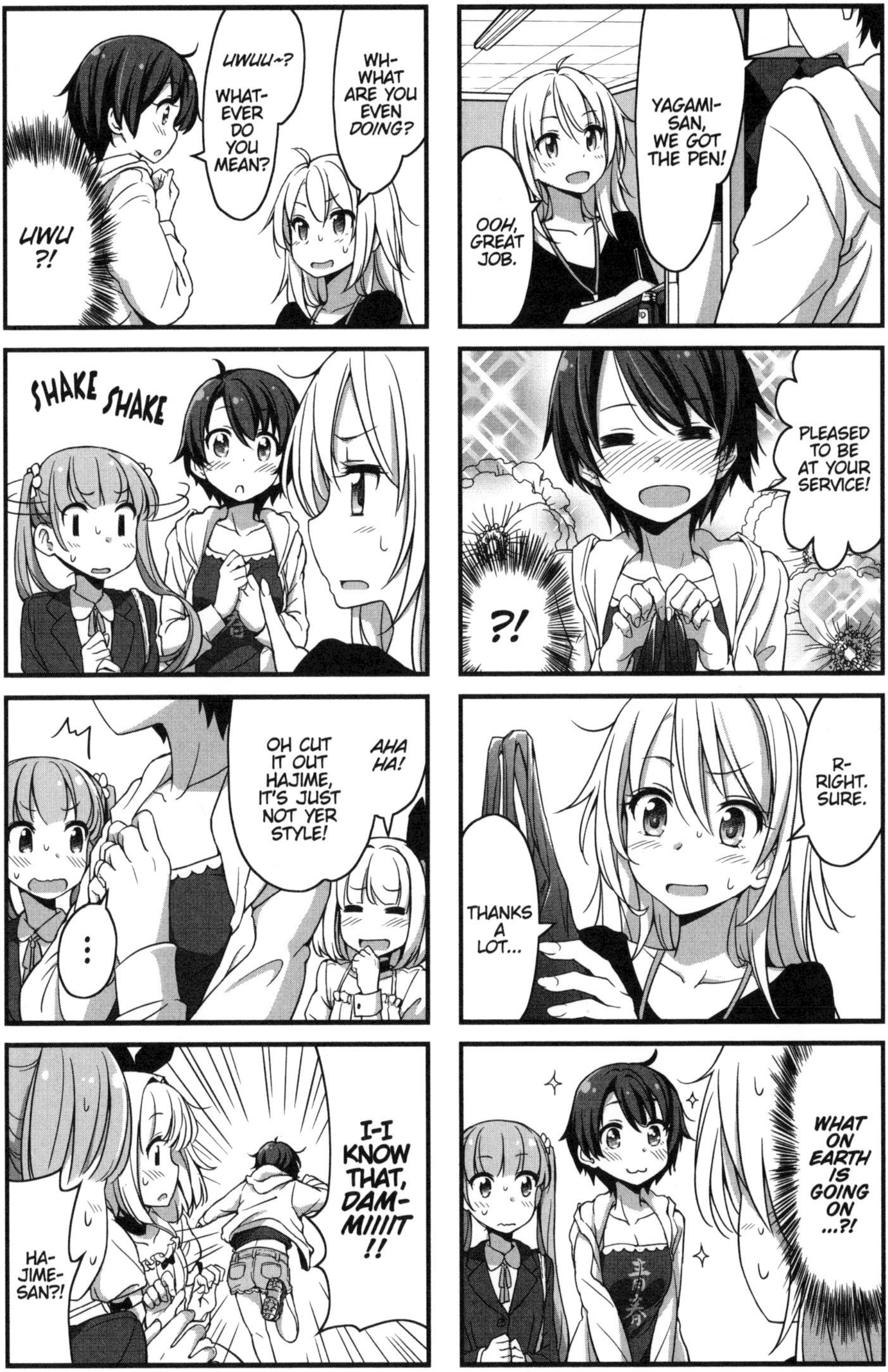
YAGAMI-SAN, WE GOT THE PEN!
OOH, GREAT JOB.
WH-WHAT ARE YOU EVEN DOING?
UWUU~? WHATEVER DO YOU MEAN?
UWU?!
PLEASED TO BE AT YOUR SERVICE!
?!
SHAKE SHAKE
R-RIGHT. SURE.
THANKS A LOT...
AHA HA!
OH CUT IT OUT HAJIME, IT'S JUST NOT YER STYLE!
...
WHAT ON EARTH IS GOING ON ...?!
I-I KNOW THAT, DAMMIIIIT!!
HAJIME-SAN?!

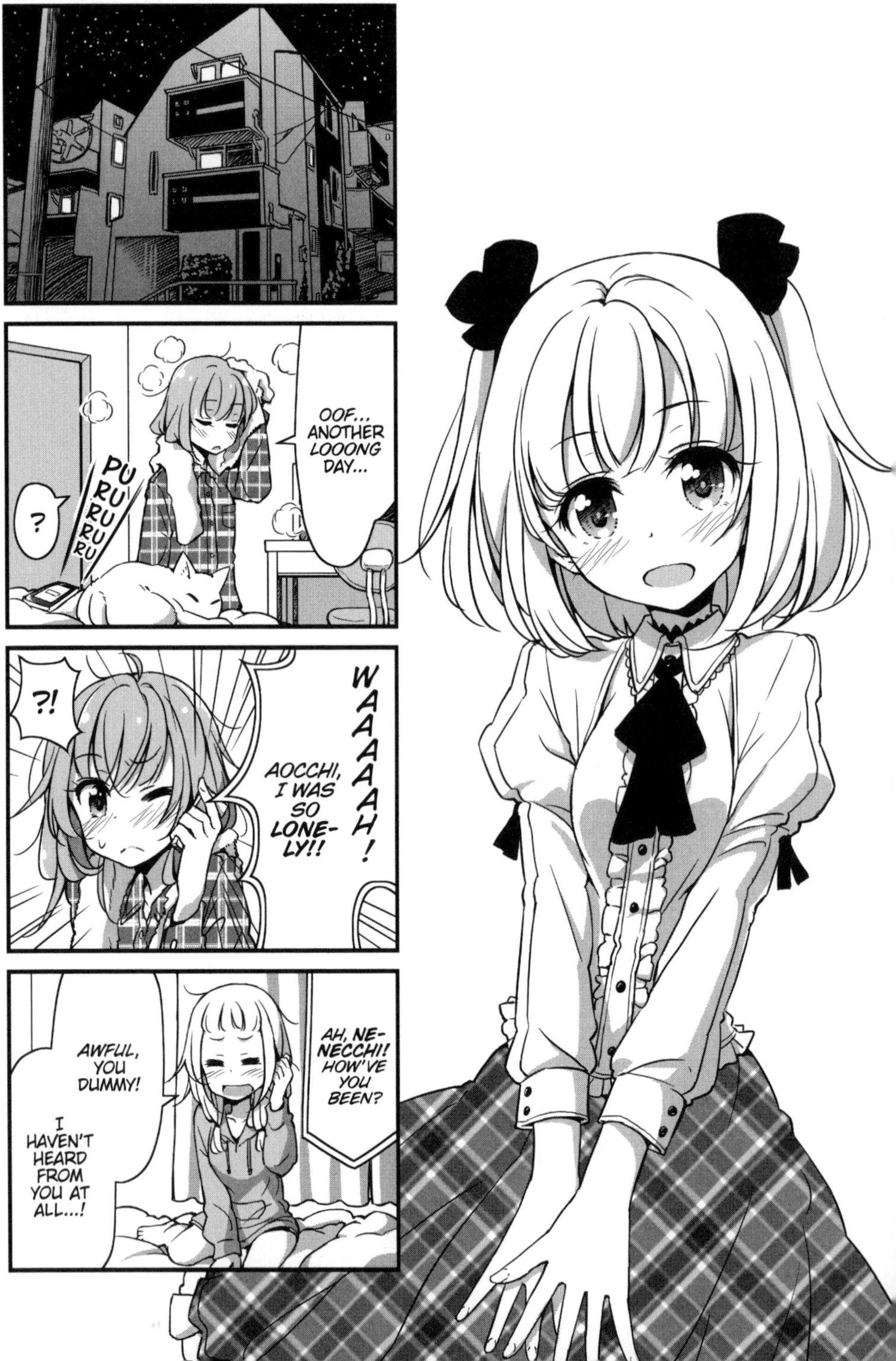
OOF... ANOTHER LOOONG DAY...
PURURURURU
?
WAAAAAAH!
AOCCHI, I WAS SO LONE-LY!!
?!
AH, NE-NECCHI! HOW'VE YOU BEEN?
AWFUL, YOU DUMMY!
I HAVEN'T HEARD FROM YOU AT ALL...!

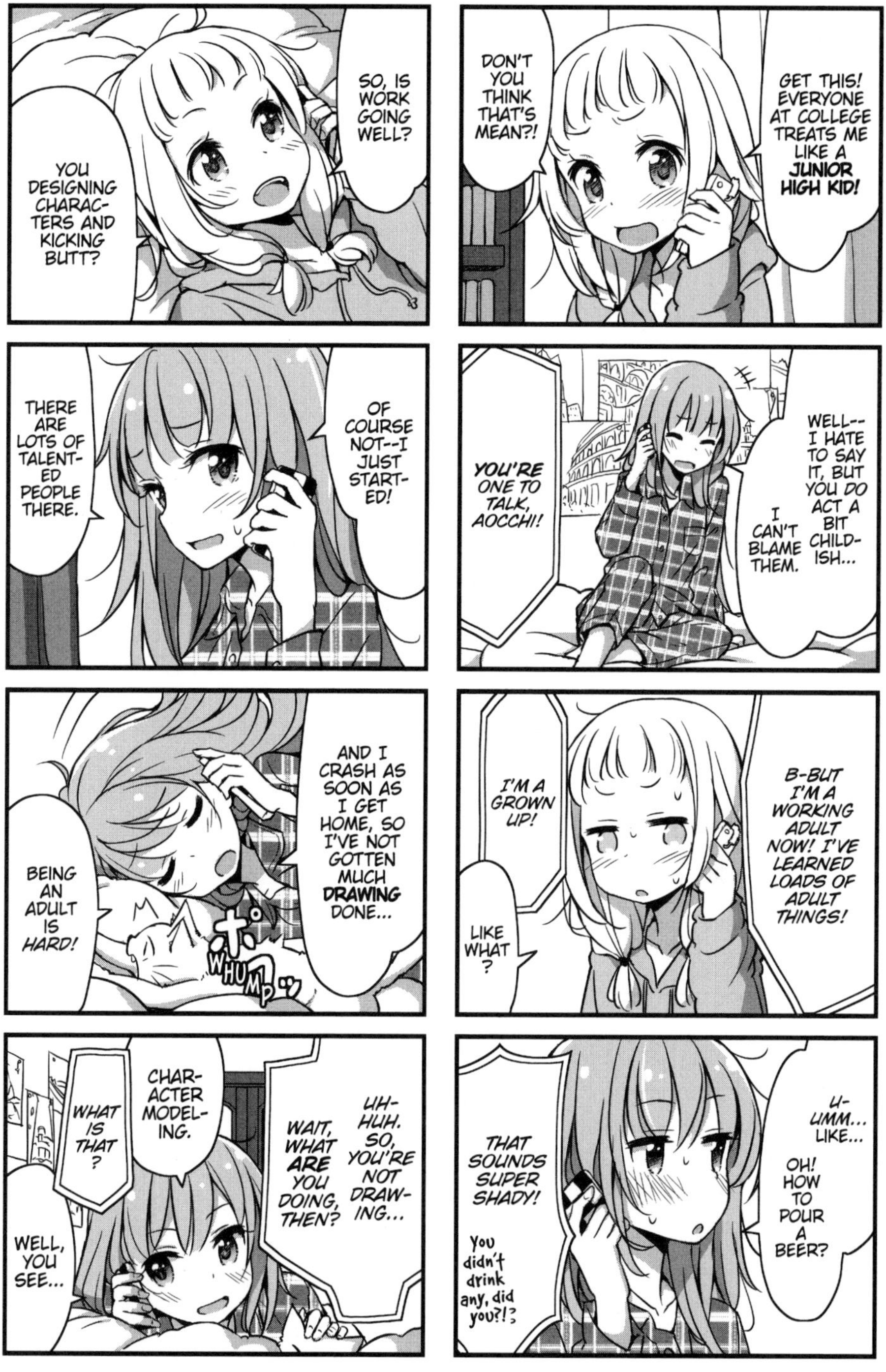
GET THIS! EVERYONE AT COLLEGE TREATS ME LIKE A **JUNIOR HIGH KID!**
DON'T YOU THINK THAT'S MEAN?!
SO, IS WORK GOING WELL?
YOU DESIGNING CHARACTERS AND KICKING BUTT?
WELL-- I HATE TO SAY IT, BUT YOU DO ACT A BIT CHILDISH...
I CAN'T BLAME THEM.
YOU'RE *ONE TO TALK, AOCCHI!*
OF COURSE NOT--I JUST STARTED!
THERE ARE LOTS OF TALENTED PEOPLE THERE.
B-BUT I'M A WORKING ADULT NOW! I'VE LEARNED LOADS OF ADULT THINGS!
I'M A GROWN UP!
LIKE WHAT?
AND I CRASH AS SOON AS I GET HOME, SO I'VE NOT GOTTEN MUCH **DRAWING** DONE...
WHUMP
BEING AN ADULT IS *HARD!*
U-UMM... LIKE...
OH! HOW TO POUR A BEER?
THAT SOUNDS SUPER SHADY!
You didn't drink any, did you?!
UH-HUH. SO, YOU'RE NOT DRAWING...
WAIT, WHAT ***ARE*** *YOU DOING, THEN?*
CHARACTER MODELING.
WHAT IS THAT?
WELL, YOU SEE...

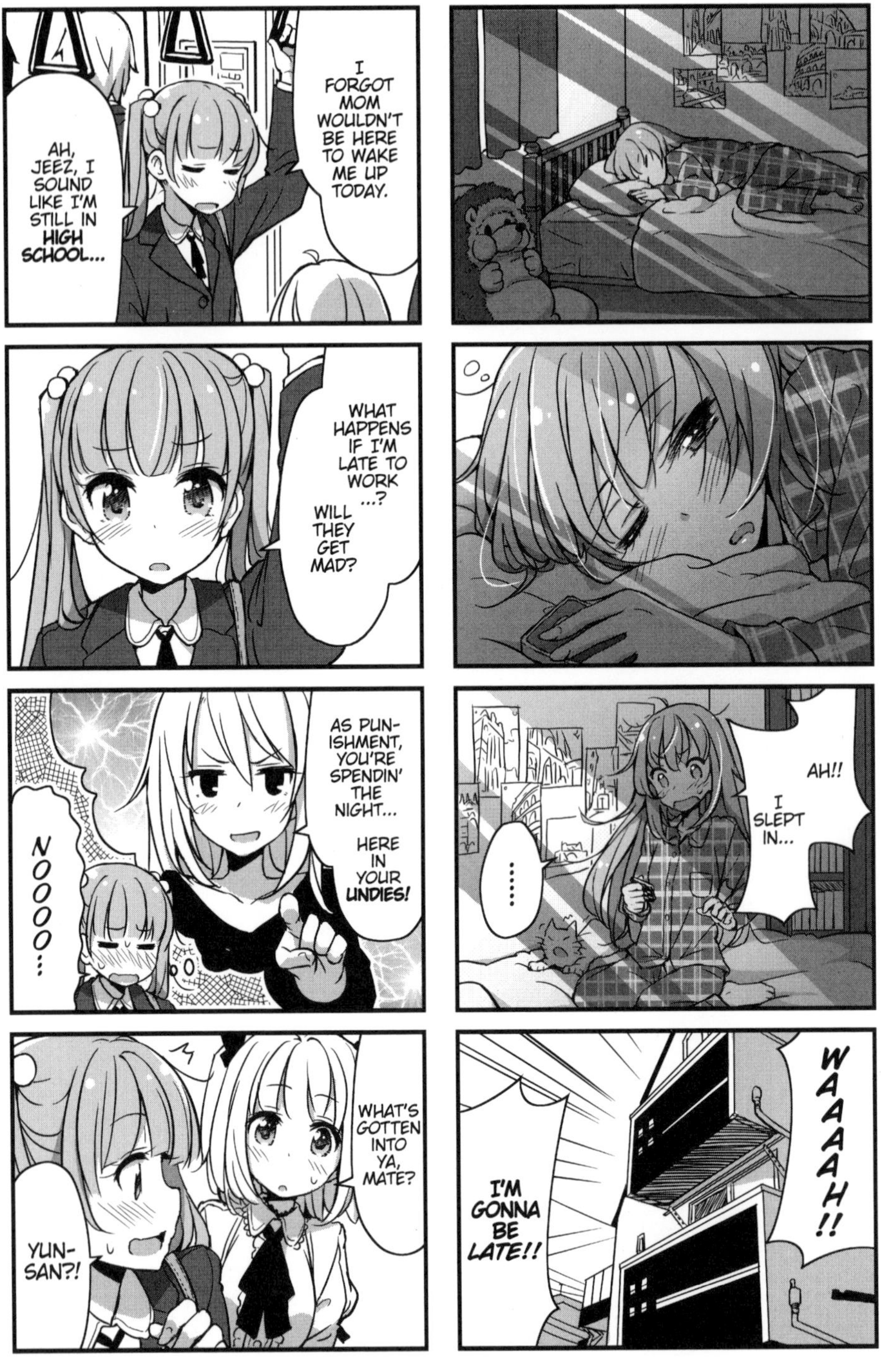
AH!!
I SLEPT IN...
......
WAAAAAH!!
I'M GONNA BE LATE!!
I FORGOT MOM WOULDN'T BE HERE TO WAKE ME UP TODAY.
AH, JEEZ, I SOUND LIKE I'M STILL IN HIGH SCHOOL...
WHAT HAPPENS IF I'M LATE TO WORK ...?
WILL THEY GET MAD?
AS PUN-ISHMENT, YOU'RE SPENDIN' THE NIGHT...
HERE IN YOUR UNDIES!
NOOOOO...
WHAT'S GOTTEN INTO YA, MATE?
YUN-SAN?!

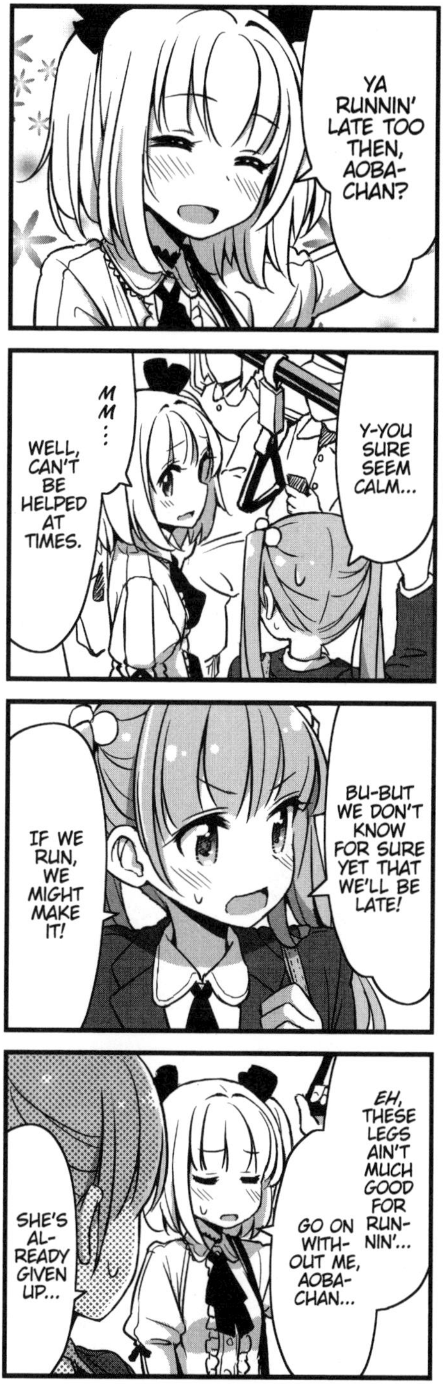
YA RUNNIN' LATE TOO THEN, AOBA-CHAN?
Y-YOU SURE SEEM CALM...
MM...
WELL, CAN'T BE HELPED AT TIMES.
BU-BUT WE DON'T KNOW FOR SURE YET THAT WE'LL BE LATE!
IF WE RUN, WE MIGHT MAKE IT!
EH, THESE LEGS AIN'T MUCH GOOD FOR RUN-NIN'...
GO ON WITH-OUT ME, AOBA-CHAN...
SHE'S AL-READY GIVEN UP...
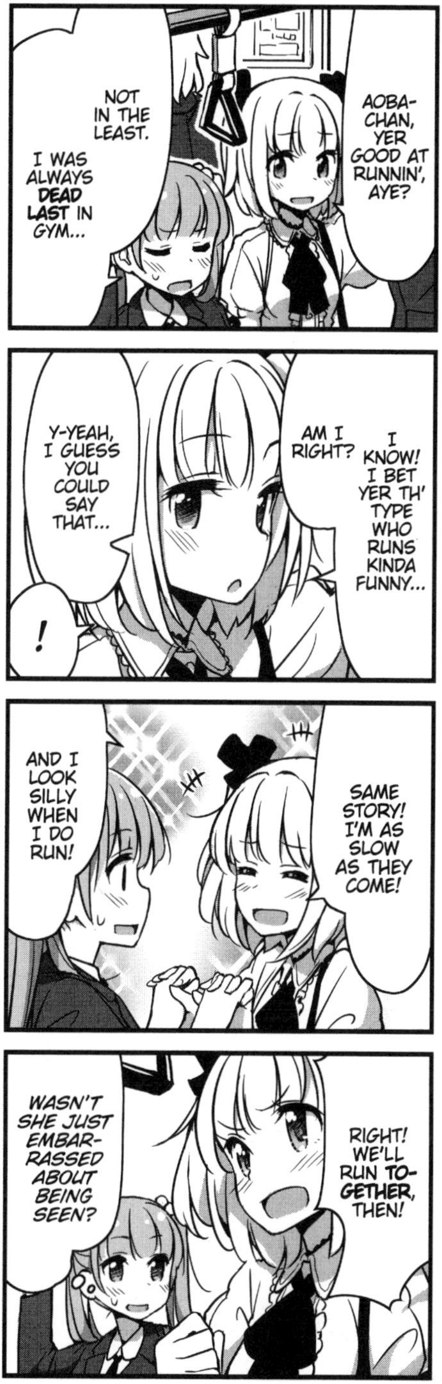
AOBA-CHAN, YER GOOD AT RUNNIN', AYE?
NOT IN THE LEAST.
I WAS ALWAYS **DEAD LAST** IN GYM...
I KNOW! I BET YER TH' TYPE WHO RUNS KINDA FUNNY...
AM I RIGHT?
Y-YEAH, I GUESS YOU COULD SAY THAT...
!
SAME STORY! I'M AS SLOW AS THEY COME!
AND I LOOK SILLY WHEN I DO RUN!
RIGHT! WE'LL RUN **TO-GETHER**, THEN!
WASN'T SHE JUST EMBAR-RASSED ABOUT BEING SEEN?

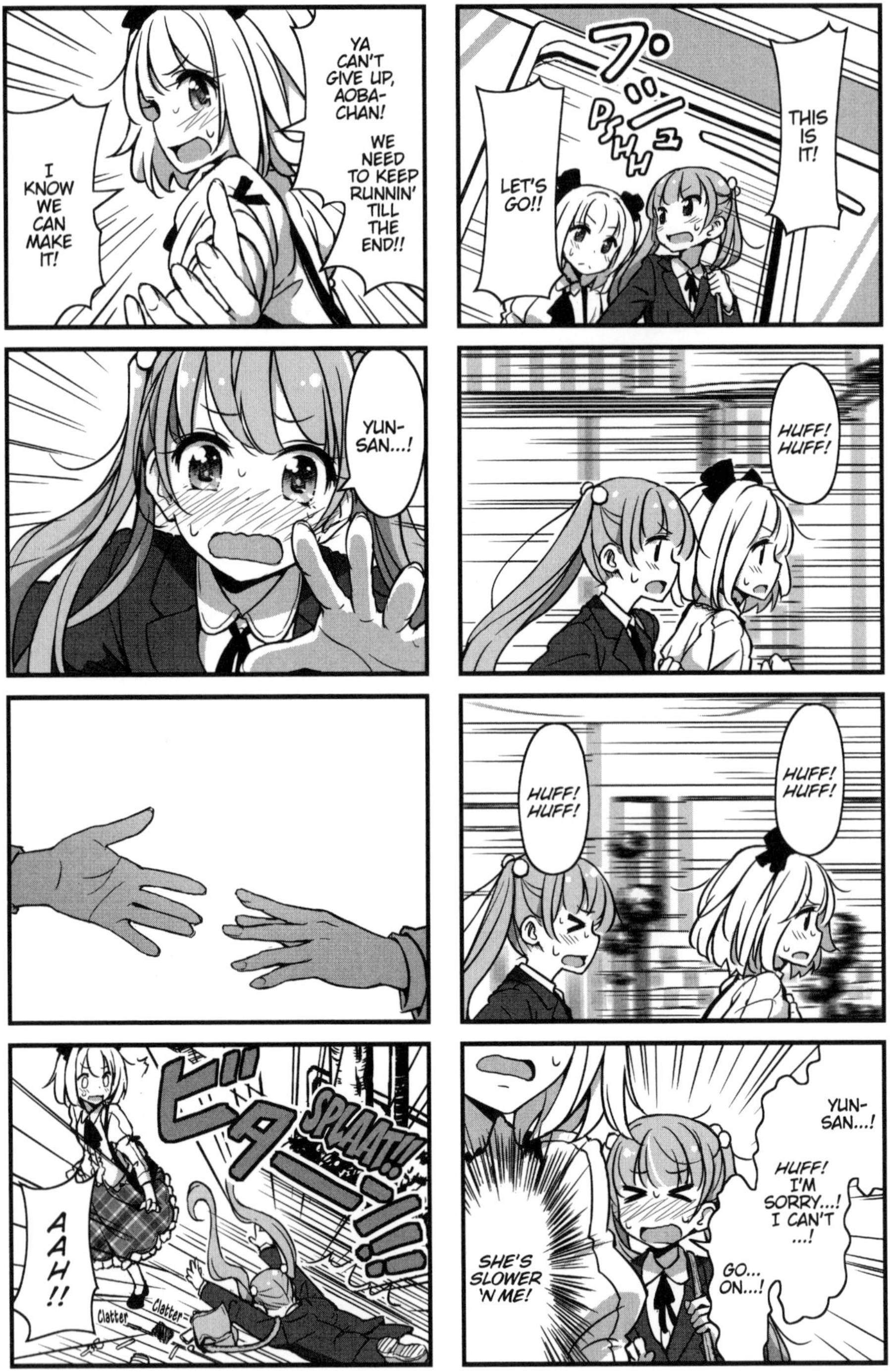
THIS IS IT!
PSHHH
LET'S GO!!
YA CAN'T GIVE UP, AOBA-CHAN!
WE NEED TO KEEP RUNNIN' TILL THE END!!
I KNOW WE CAN MAKE IT!
HUFF! HUFF!
YUN-SAN...!
HUFF! HUFF!
HUFF! HUFF!
YUN-SAN...!
HUFF! I'M SORRY...! I CAN'T ...!
GO... ON...!
SHE'S SLOWER 'N ME!
SPLAAAT!!
AAH!!
Clatter
Clatter

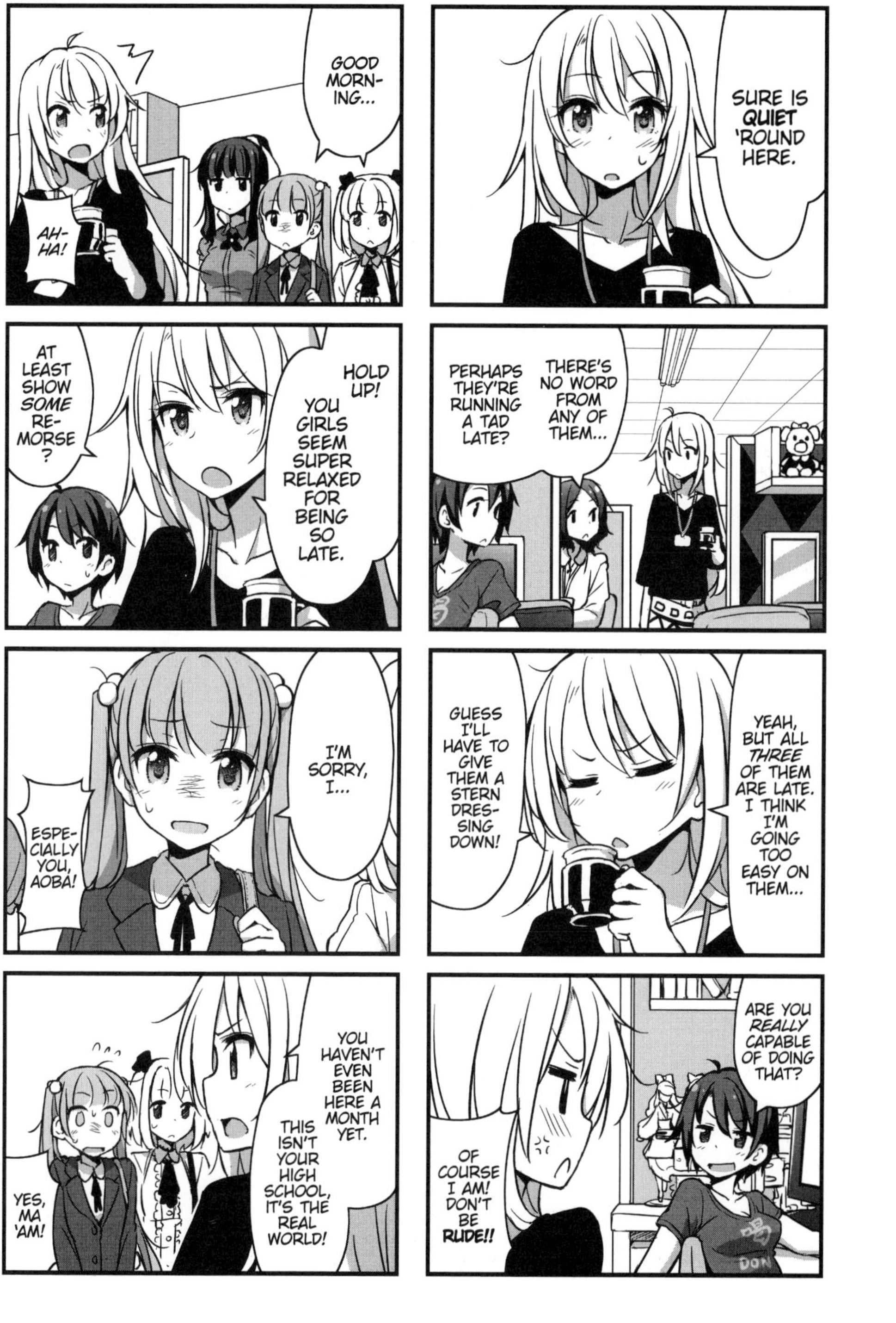
SURE IS QUIET 'ROUND HERE.
GOOD MORN-ING...
AH-HA!
THERE'S NO WORD FROM ANY OF THEM...
PERHAPS THEY'RE RUNNING A TAD LATE?
HOLD UP! YOU GIRLS SEEM SUPER RELAXED FOR BEING SO LATE.
AT LEAST SHOW SOME RE-MORSE?
YEAH, BUT ALL THREE OF THEM ARE LATE. I THINK I'M GOING TOO EASY ON THEM...
GUESS I'LL HAVE TO GIVE THEM A STERN DRES-SING DOWN!
I'M SORRY, I...
ESPE-CIALLY YOU, AOBA!
ARE YOU REALLY CAPABLE OF DOING THAT?
OF COURSE I AM! DON'T BE RUDE!!
YOU HAVEN'T EVEN BEEN HERE A MONTH YET.
THIS ISN'T YOUR HIGH SCHOOL, IT'S THE REAL WORLD!
YES, MA'AM!

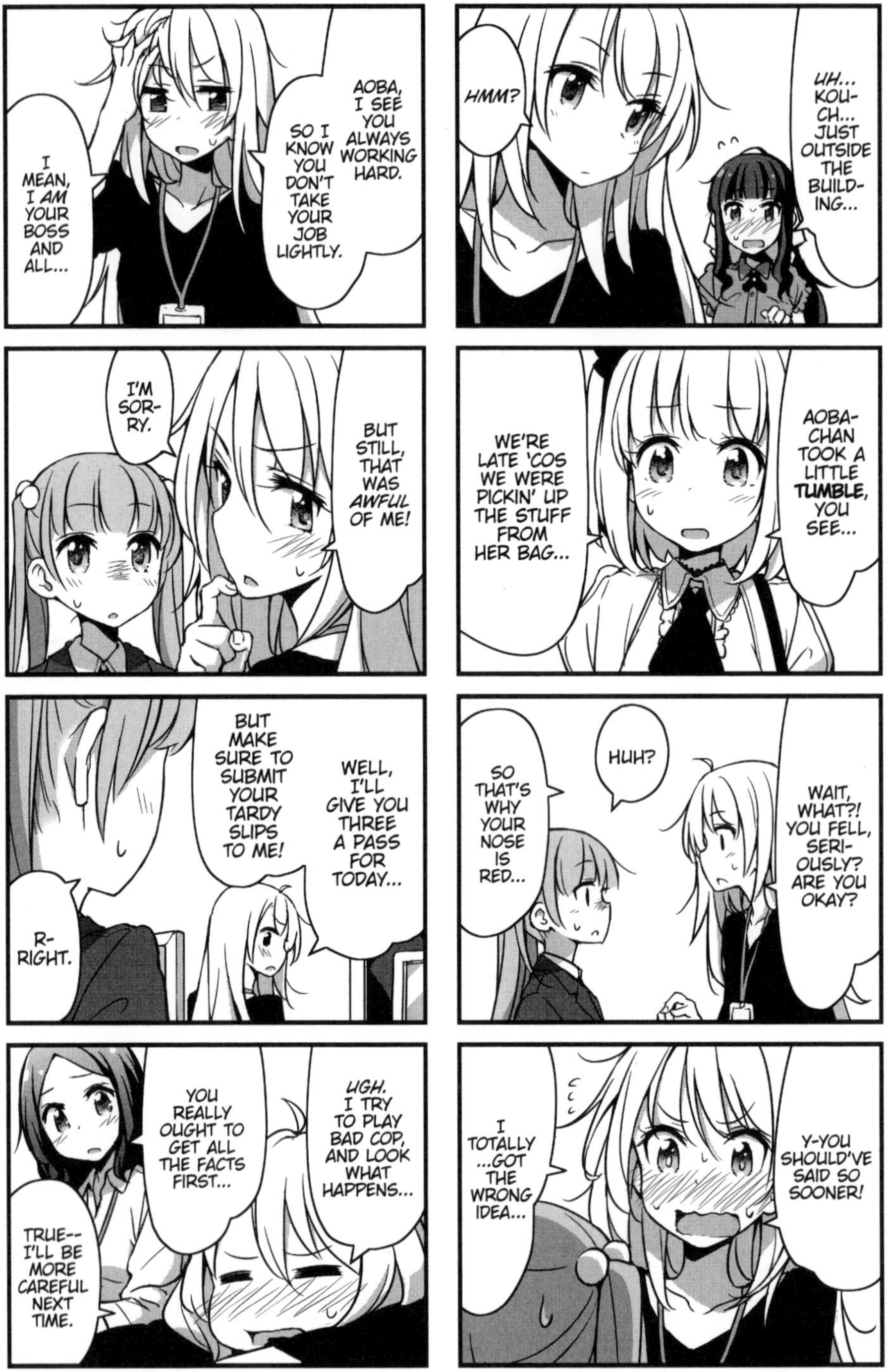
UH... KOUCH... JUST OUTSIDE THE BUILDING...
HMM?
AOBA, I SEE YOU ALWAYS WORKING HARD.
SO I KNOW YOU DON'T TAKE YOUR JOB LIGHTLY.
I MEAN, I *AM* YOUR BOSS AND ALL...
AOBA-CHAN TOOK A LITTLE **TUMBLE**, YOU SEE...
WE'RE LATE 'COS WE WERE PICKIN' UP THE STUFF FROM HER BAG...
BUT STILL, THAT WAS *AWFUL* OF ME!
I'M SORRY.
WAIT, WHAT?! YOU FELL, SERIOUSLY? ARE YOU OKAY?
HUH?
SO THAT'S WHY YOUR NOSE IS RED...
WELL, I'LL GIVE YOU THREE A PASS FOR TODAY...
BUT MAKE SURE TO SUBMIT YOUR TARDY SLIPS TO ME!
R-RIGHT.
Y-YOU SHOULD'VE SAID SO SOONER!
I TOTALLY ...GOT THE WRONG IDEA...
UGH. I TRY TO PLAY BAD COP, AND LOOK WHAT HAPPENS...
YOU REALLY OUGHT TO GET ALL THE FACTS FIRST...
TRUE-- I'LL BE MORE CAREFUL NEXT TIME.

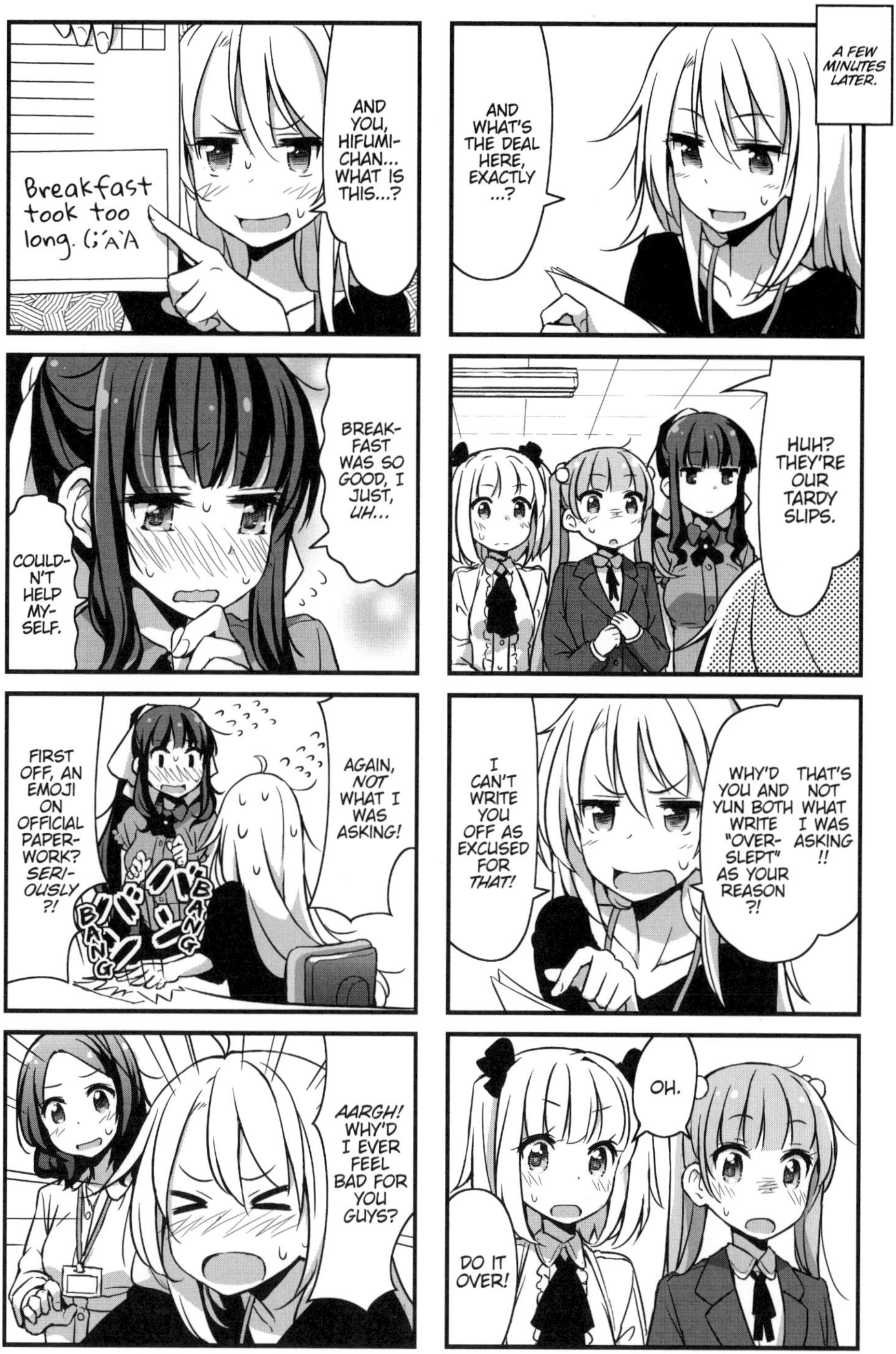
A FEW MINUTES LATER.
AND WHAT'S THE DEAL HERE, EXACTLY ...?
HUH? THEY'RE OUR TARDY SLIPS.
THAT'S NOT WHAT I WAS ASKING !!
WHY'D YOU AND YUN BOTH WRITE "OVER-SLEPT" AS YOUR REASON ?!
I CAN'T WRITE YOU OFF AS EXCUSED FOR THAT!
OH.
DO IT OVER!
AND YOU, HIFUMI-CHAN... WHAT IS THIS...?
Breakfast took too long. (;´A`A)
BREAK-FAST WAS SO GOOD, I JUST, UH...
COULD-N'T HELP MY-SELF.
AGAIN, NOT WHAT I WAS ASKING!
BANG BANG BANG
FIRST OFF, AN EMOJI ON OFFICIAL PAPER-WORK? SERI-OUSLY ?!
AARGH! WHY'D I EVER FEEL BAD FOR YOU GUYS?

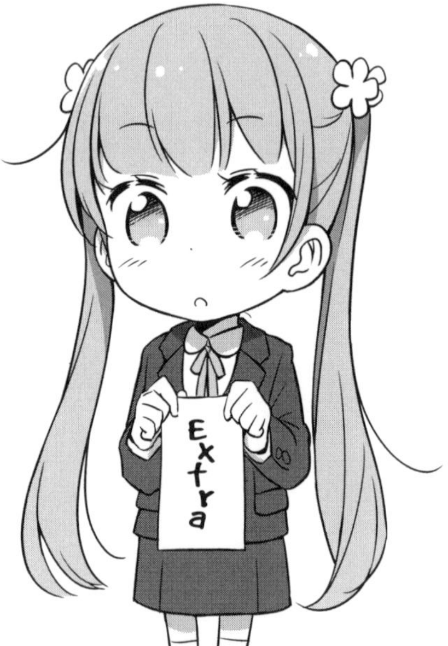
Extra

Days Off?

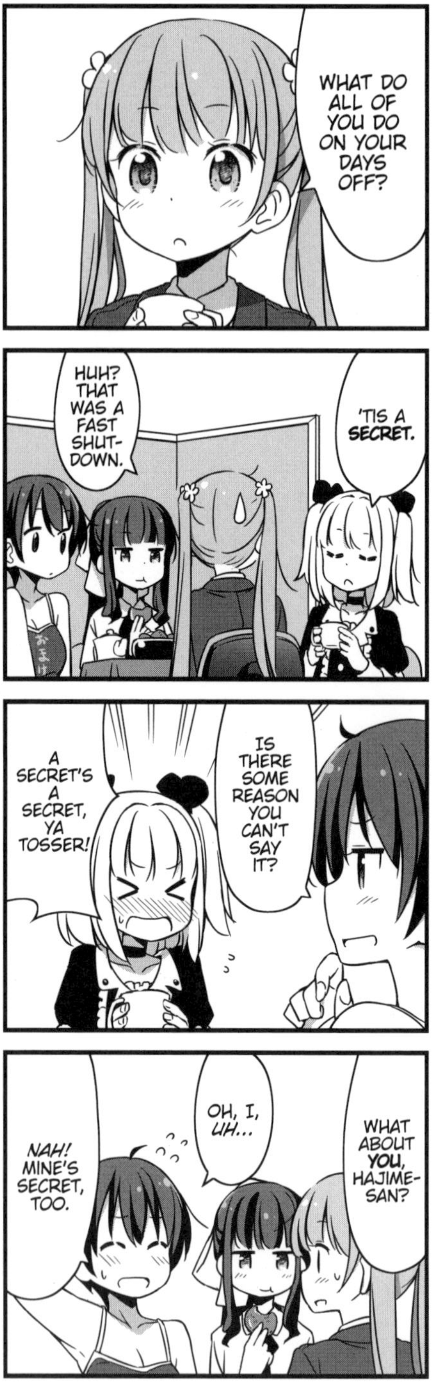
WHAT DO ALL OF YOU DO ON YOUR DAYS OFF?
'TIS A **SECRET.**
HUH? THAT WAS A FAST SHUT-DOWN.
IS THERE SOME REASON YOU CAN'T SAY IT?
A SECRET'S A SECRET, YA TOSSER!
WHAT ABOUT **YOU**, HAJIME-SAN?
OH, I, *UH...*
NAH! MINE'S SECRET, TOO.

Yun's Day Off

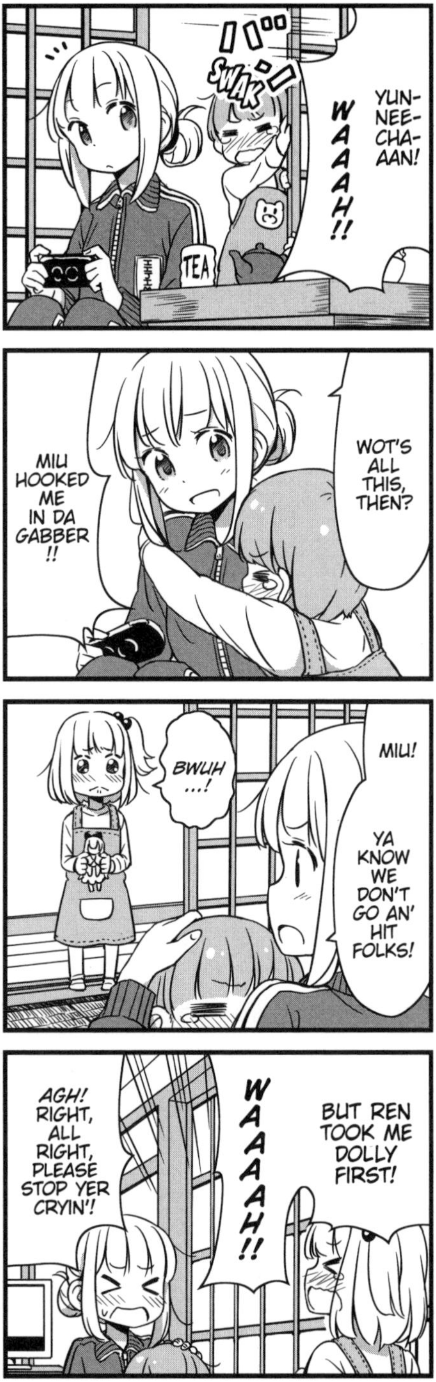
YUN-NEE-CHA-AAN!
WAAAAH!!
SWAK
TEA
WOT'S ALL THIS, THEN?
MIU HOOKED ME IN DA GABBER!!
MIU!
YA KNOW WE DON'T GO AN' HIT FOLKS!
BWUH...!
BUT REN TOOK ME DOLLY FIRST!
WAAAAAH!!
AGH! RIGHT, ALL RIGHT, PLEASE STOP YER CRYIN'!

Hajime's Day Off

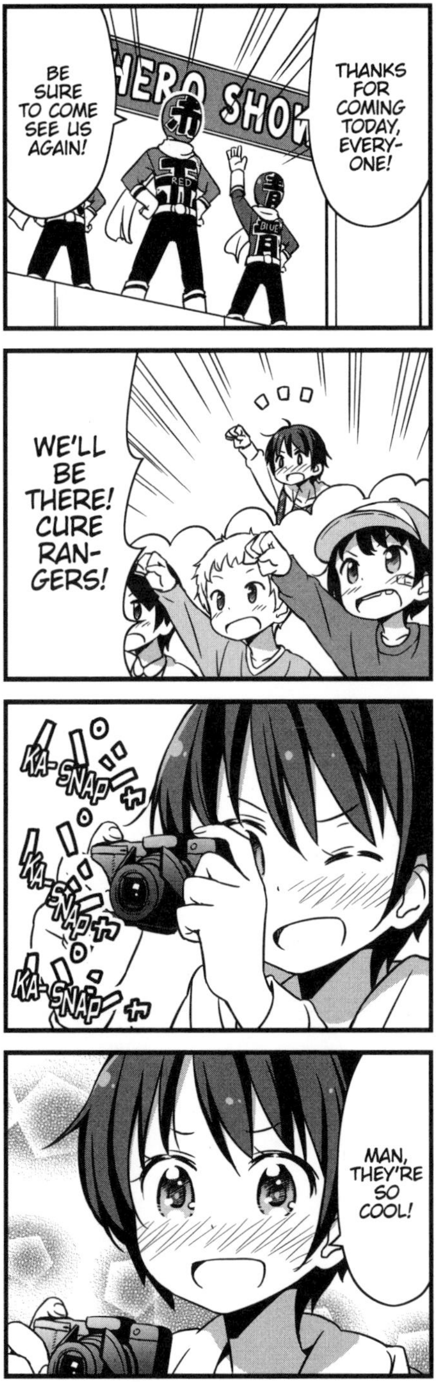
THANKS FOR COMING TODAY, EVERY-ONE!
HERO SHOW
RED
BLUE
BE SURE TO COME SEE US AGAIN!
WE'LL BE THERE! CURE RAN-GERS!
KA-SNAP
KA-SNAP
KA-SNAP
MAN, THEY'RE SO COOL!

NEW GAME!

NEW GAME!

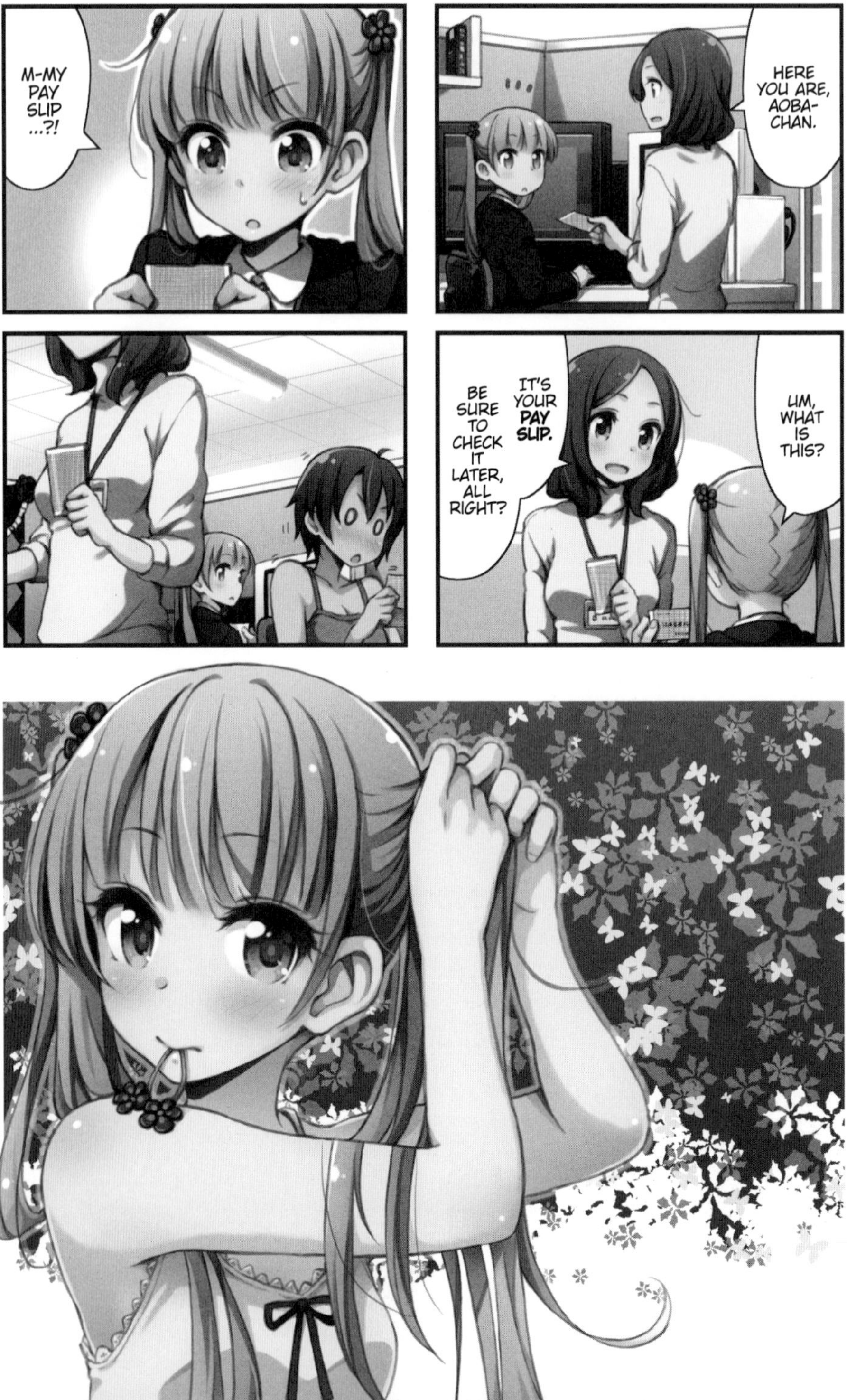
HERE YOU ARE, AOBA-CHAN.
M-MY PAY SLIP ...?!
UM, WHAT IS THIS?
IT'S YOUR **PAY SLIP.**
BE SURE TO CHECK IT LATER, ALL RIGHT?

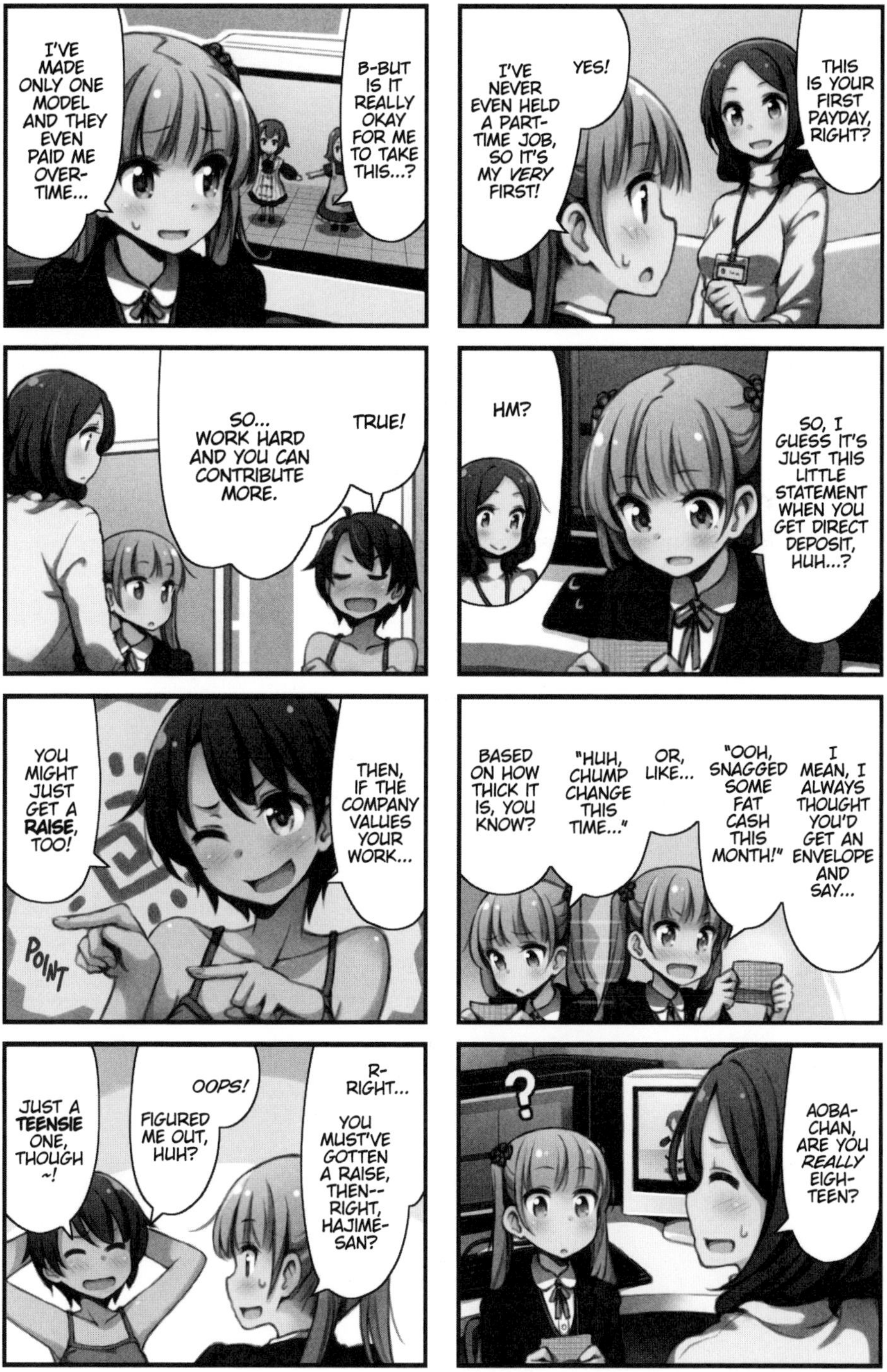
THIS IS YOUR FIRST PAYDAY, RIGHT?
YES!
I'VE NEVER EVEN HELD A PART-TIME JOB, SO IT'S MY *VERY* FIRST!
B-BUT IS IT REALLY OKAY FOR ME TO TAKE THIS...?
I'VE MADE ONLY ONE MODEL AND THEY EVEN PAID ME OVERTIME...
SO, I GUESS IT'S JUST THIS LITTLE STATEMENT WHEN YOU GET DIRECT DEPOSIT, HUH...?
HM?
TRUE!
SO... WORK HARD AND YOU CAN CONTRIBUTE MORE.
I MEAN, I ALWAYS THOUGHT YOU'D GET AN ENVELOPE AND SAY...
"OOH, SNAGGED SOME FAT CASH THIS MONTH!"
OR, LIKE...
"HUH, CHUMP CHANGE THIS TIME..."
BASED ON HOW THICK IT IS, YOU KNOW?
THEN, IF THE COMPANY VALUES YOUR WORK...
YOU MIGHT JUST GET A **RAISE**, TOO!
POINT
AOBA-CHAN, ARE YOU *REALLY* EIGHTEEN?
?
R-RIGHT... YOU MUST'VE GOTTEN A RAISE, THEN--RIGHT, HAJIME-SAN?
OOPS!
FIGURED ME OUT, HUH?
JUST A **TEENSIE** ONE, THOUGH~!

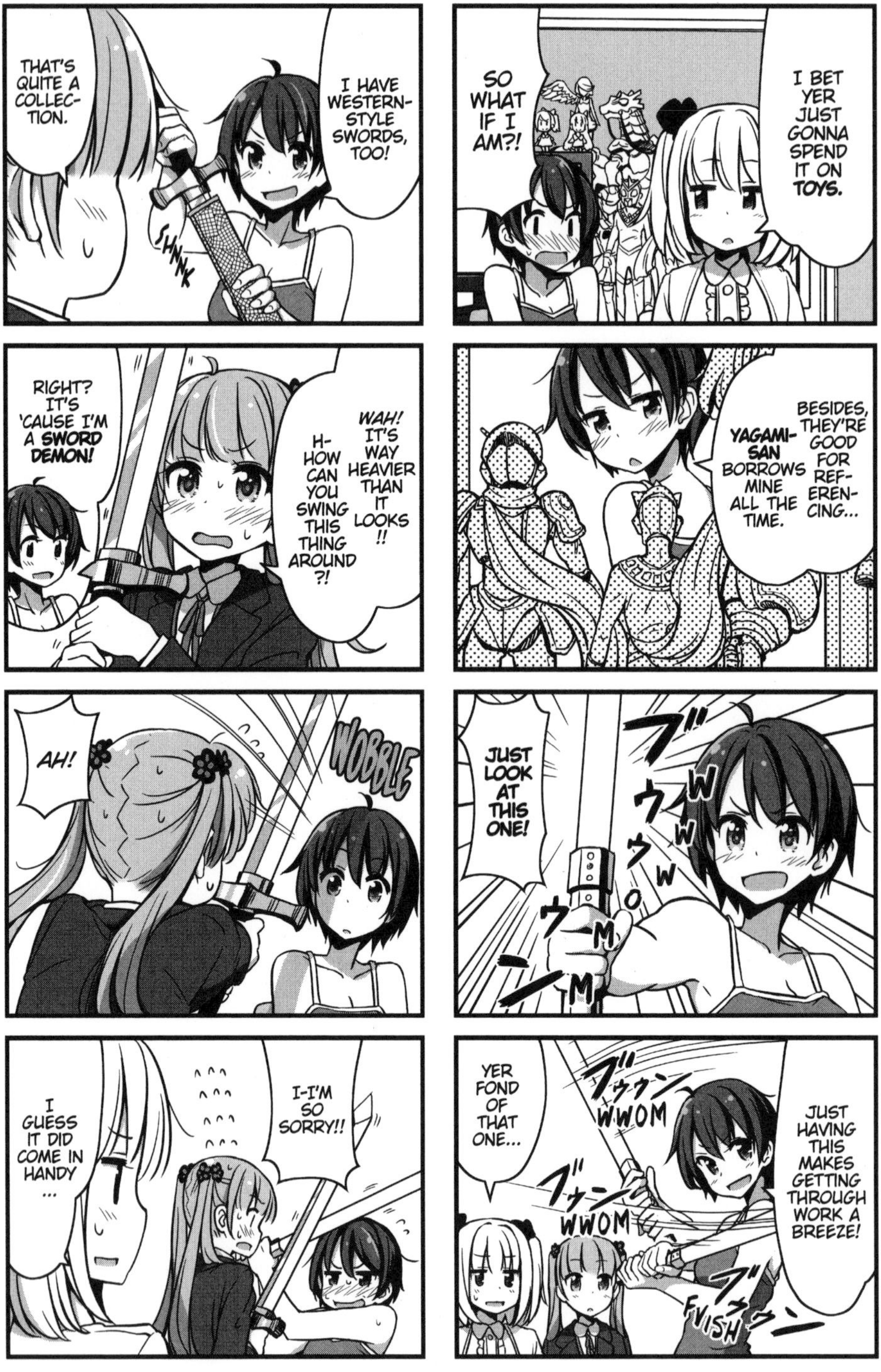
I BET YER JUST GONNA SPEND IT ON **TOYS.**
SO WHAT IF I AM?!
I HAVE WESTERN-STYLE SWORDS, TOO!
SHNNK
THAT'S QUITE A COLLECTION.
BESIDES, THEY'RE GOOD FOR REFERENCING...
YAGAMI-SAN BORROWS MINE ALL THE TIME.
WAH! IT'S WAY HEAVIER THAN IT LOOKS!!
H-HOW CAN YOU SWING THIS THING AROUND?!
RIGHT? IT'S 'CAUSE I'M A **SWORD DEMON!**
JUST LOOK AT THIS ONE!
WWWWOMM
WOBBLE
AH!
JUST HAVING THIS MAKES GETTING THROUGH WORK A BREEZE!
WWOM
WWOM
FWISH
YER FOND OF THAT ONE...
I-I'M SO SORRY!!
I GUESS IT DID COME IN HANDY...

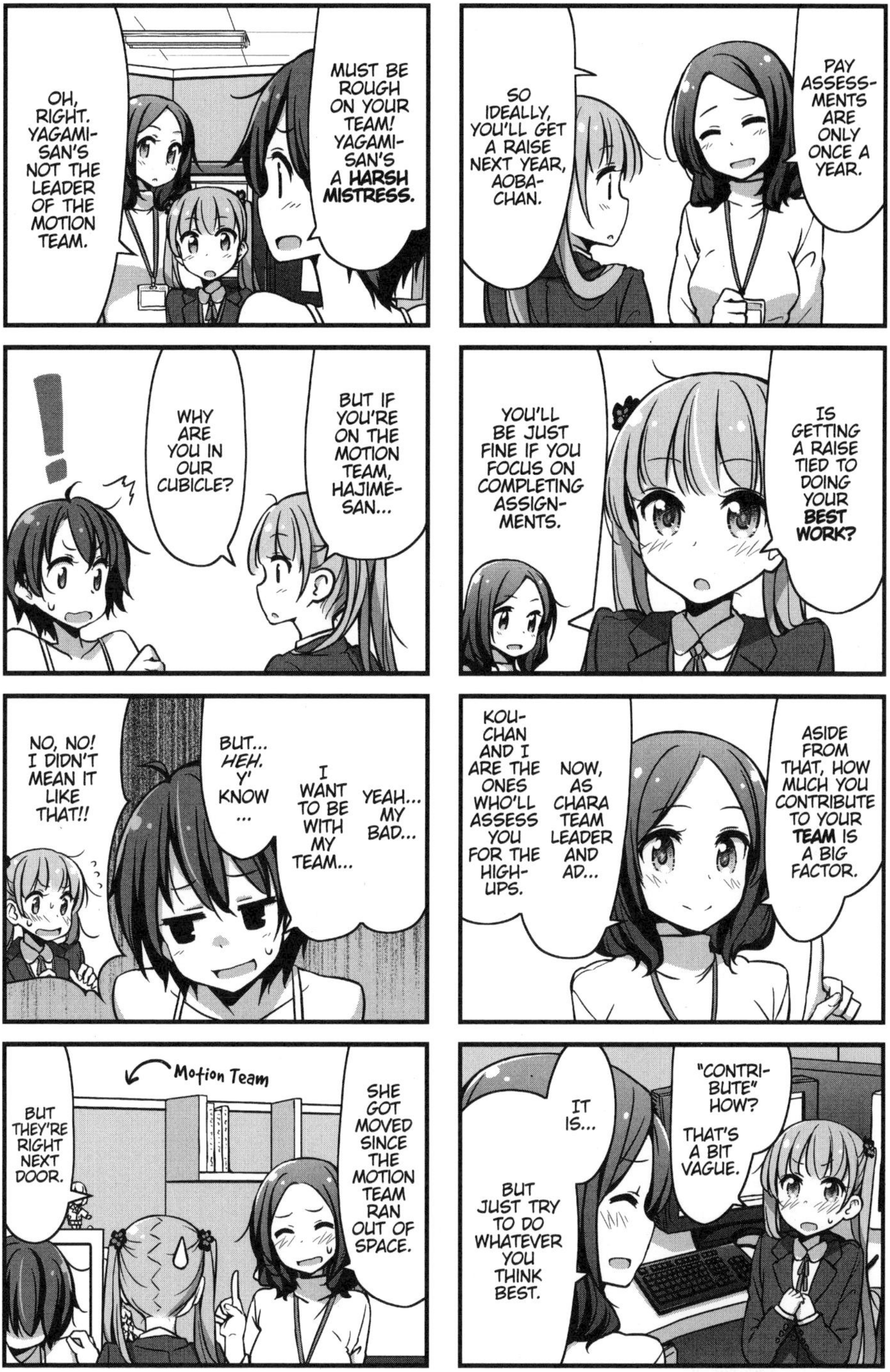
PAY ASSESSMENTS ARE ONLY ONCE A YEAR.
SO IDEALLY, YOU'LL GET A RAISE NEXT YEAR, AOBA-CHAN.
MUST BE ROUGH ON YOUR TEAM! YAGAMI-SAN'S A **HARSH MISTRESS.**
OH, RIGHT. YAGAMI-SAN'S NOT THE LEADER OF THE MOTION TEAM.
IS GETTING A RAISE TIED TO DOING YOUR **BEST WORK?**
YOU'LL BE JUST FINE IF YOU FOCUS ON COMPLETING ASSIGNMENTS.
BUT IF YOU'RE ON THE MOTION TEAM, HAJIME-SAN...
WHY ARE YOU IN OUR CUBICLE?
!
ASIDE FROM THAT, HOW MUCH YOU CONTRIBUTE TO YOUR **TEAM** IS A BIG FACTOR.
NOW, AS CHARA TEAM LEADER AND AD...
KOU-CHAN AND I ARE THE ONES WHO'LL ASSESS YOU FOR THE HIGH-UPS.
YEAH... MY BAD...
I WANT TO BE WITH MY TEAM...
BUT... *HEH.* Y' KNOW ...
NO, NO! I DIDN'T MEAN IT LIKE THAT!!
"CONTRIBUTE" HOW?
THAT'S A BIT VAGUE.
IT IS...
BUT JUST TRY TO DO WHATEVER YOU THINK BEST.
SHE GOT MOVED SINCE THE MOTION TEAM RAN OUT OF SPACE.
Motion Team
BUT THEY'RE RIGHT NEXT DOOR.

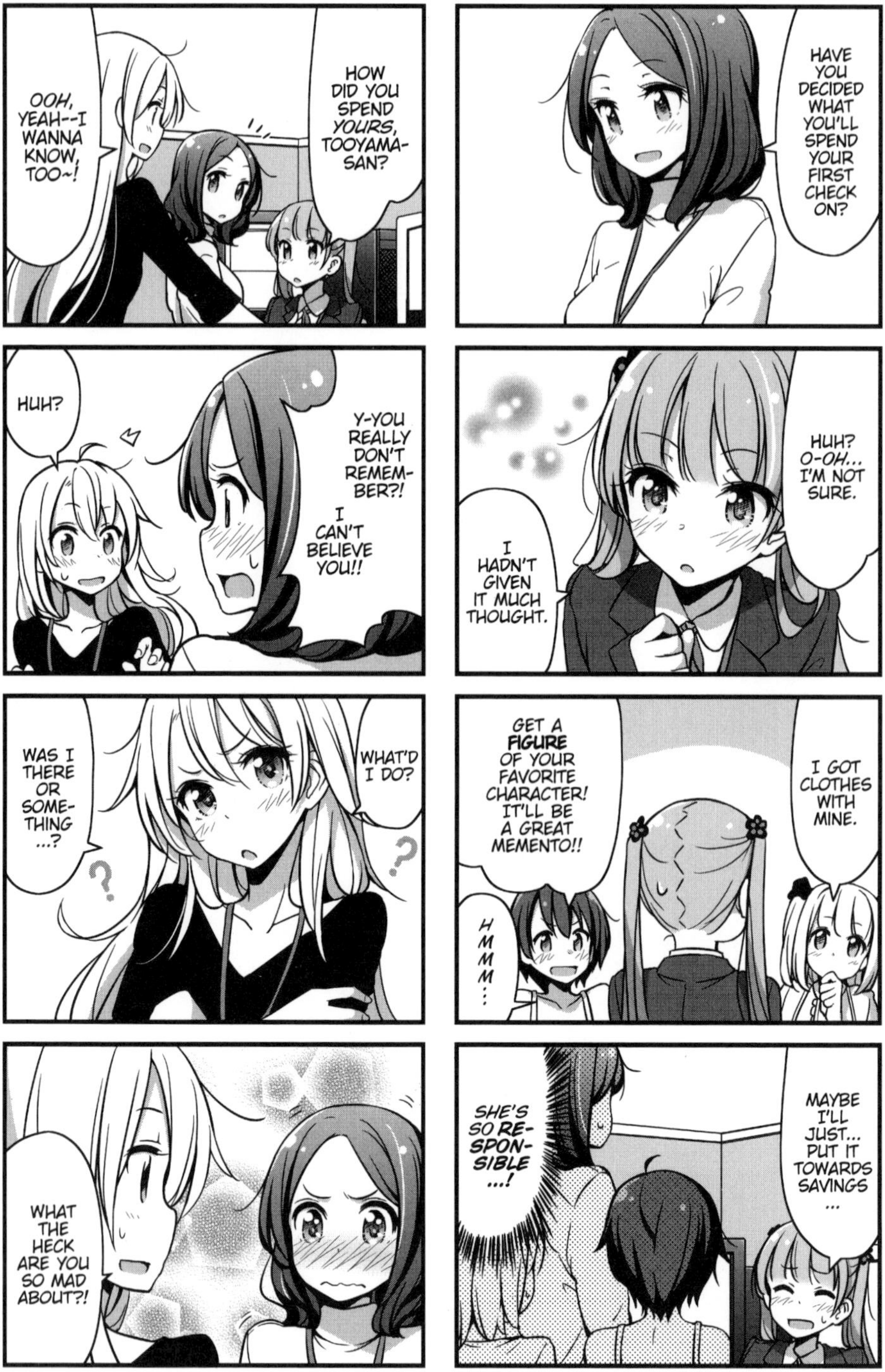
HAVE YOU DECIDED WHAT YOU'LL SPEND YOUR FIRST CHECK ON?
HUH? O-OH... I'M NOT SURE.
I HADN'T GIVEN IT MUCH THOUGHT.
I GOT CLOTHES WITH MINE.
GET A **FIGURE** OF YOUR FAVORITE CHARACTER! IT'LL BE A GREAT MEMENTO!!
HMMM...
MAYBE I'LL JUST... PUT IT TOWARDS SAVINGS...
SHE'S SO RESPONSIBLE...!
HOW DID YOU SPEND *YOURS*, TOOYAMA-SAN?
OOH, YEAH--I WANNA KNOW, TOO~!
Y-YOU REALLY DON'T REMEMBER?!
I CAN'T BELIEVE YOU!!
HUH?
WHAT'D I DO?
WAS I THERE OR SOMETHING...?
WHAT THE HECK ARE YOU SO MAD ABOUT?!

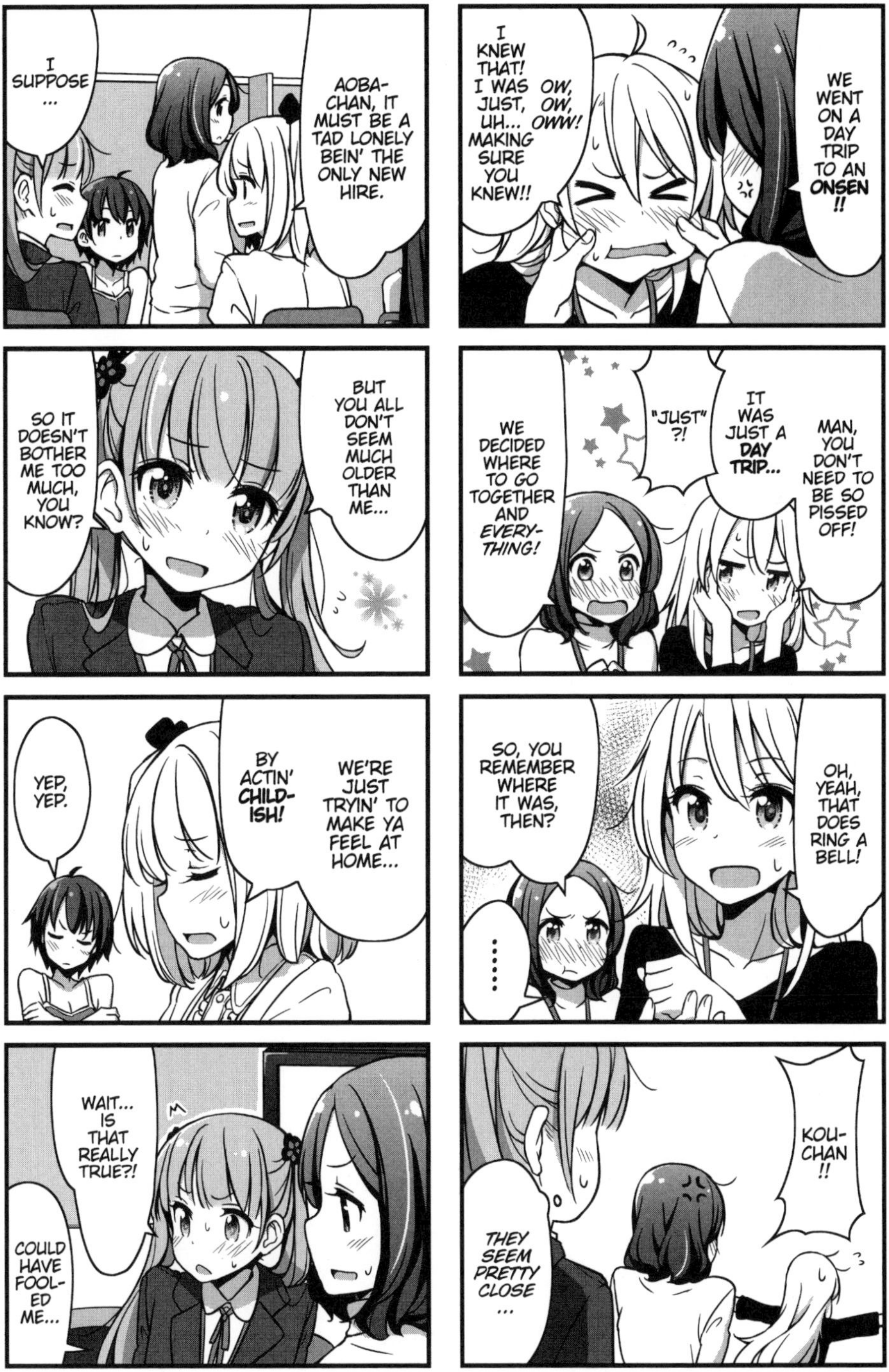
WE WENT ON A DAY TRIP TO AN **ONSEN**!!
OW, OW, *OWW!*
I KNEW THAT! I WAS JUST, UH... MAKING SURE YOU KNEW!!
AOBA-CHAN, IT MUST BE A TAD LONELY BEIN' THE ONLY NEW HIRE.
I SUPPOSE...
MAN, YOU DON'T NEED TO BE SO PISSED OFF!
IT WAS JUST A **DAY TRIP...**
"JUST"?!
WE DECIDED WHERE TO GO TOGETHER AND *EVERY-THING!*
BUT YOU ALL DON'T SEEM MUCH OLDER THAN ME...
SO IT DOESN'T BOTHER ME TOO MUCH, YOU KNOW?
OH, YEAH, THAT DOES RING A BELL!
SO, YOU REMEMBER WHERE IT WAS, THEN?
......
WE'RE JUST TRYIN' TO MAKE YA FEEL AT HOME...
BY ACTIN' **CHILD-ISH!**
YEP, YEP.
KOU-CHAN!!
THEY SEEM PRETTY CLOSE...
WAIT... IS THAT REALLY TRUE?!
COULD HAVE FOOL-ED ME...

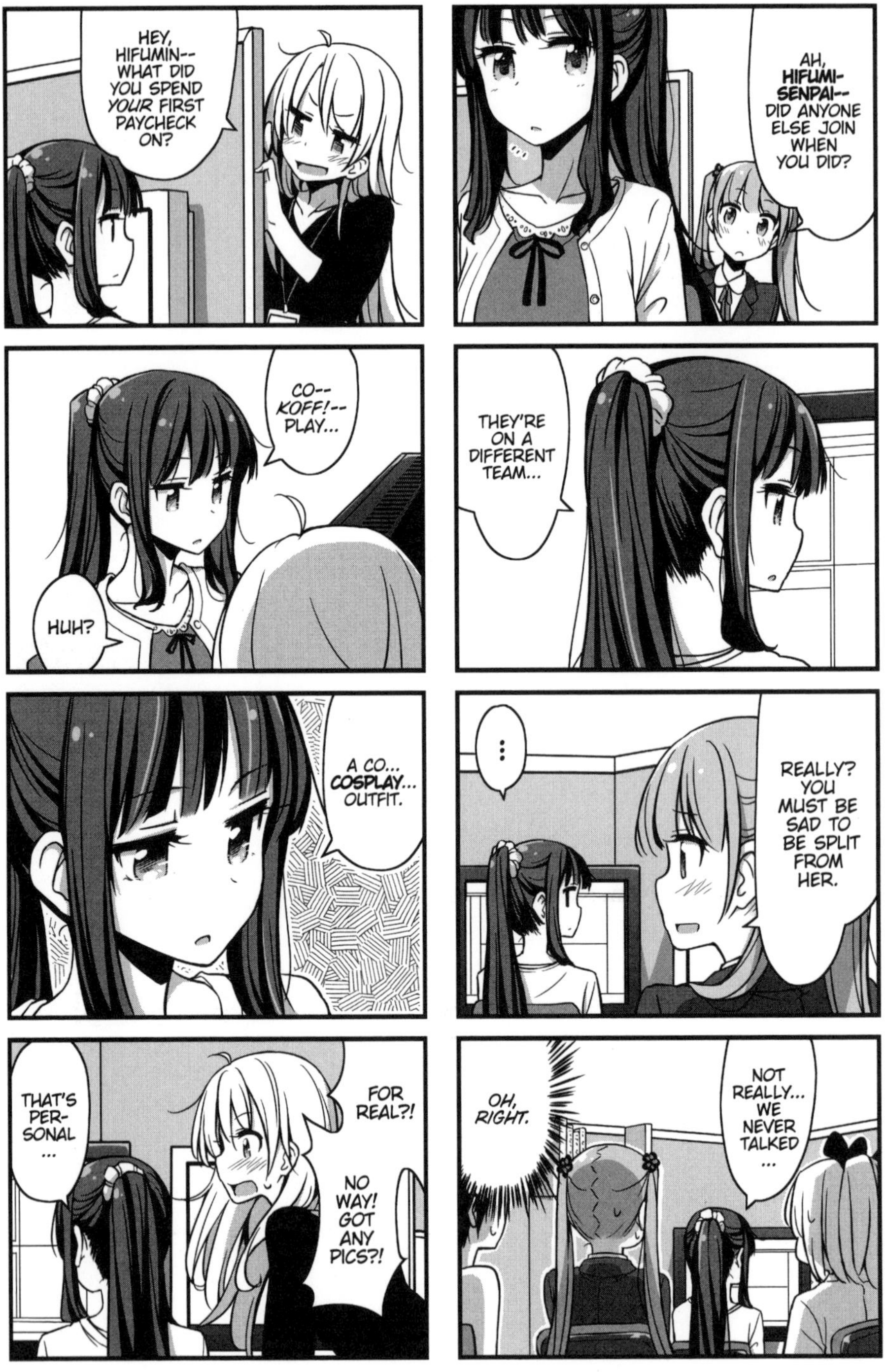
AH, HIFUMI-SENPAI-- DID ANYONE ELSE JOIN WHEN YOU DID?
...
THEY'RE ON A DIFFERENT TEAM...
...
REALLY? YOU MUST BE SAD TO BE SPLIT FROM HER.
NOT REALLY... WE NEVER TALKED...
OH, RIGHT.
HEY, HIFUMIN-- WHAT DID YOU SPEND YOUR FIRST PAYCHECK ON?
CO-- KOFF!-- PLAY...
HUH?
A CO... COSPLAY... OUTFIT.
FOR REAL?!
NO WAY! GOT ANY PICS?!
THAT'S PERSONAL...

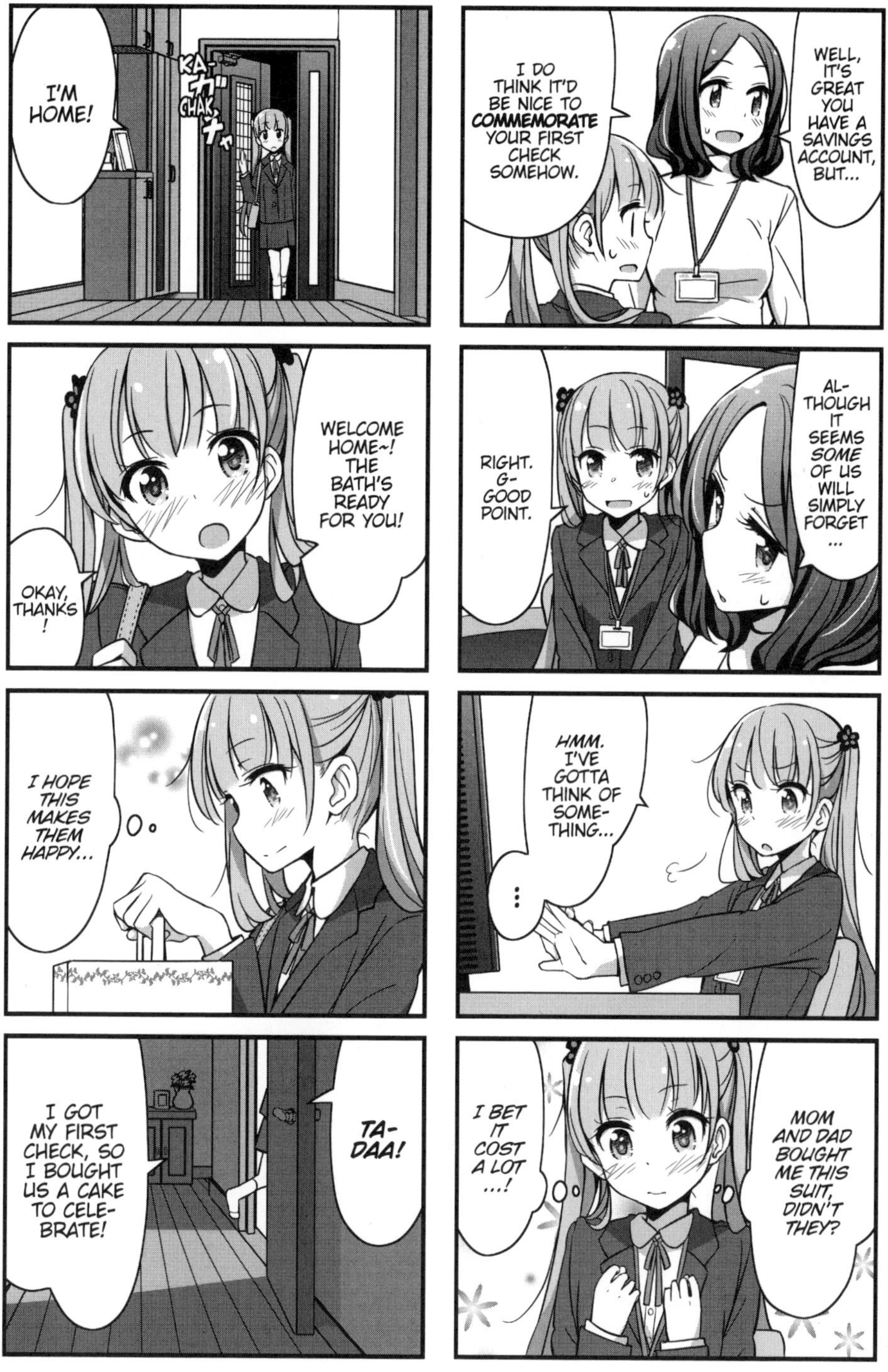
WELL, IT'S GREAT YOU HAVE A SAVINGS ACCOUNT, BUT...
I DO THINK IT'D BE NICE TO **COMMEMORATE** YOUR FIRST CHECK SOMEHOW.
AL-THOUGH IT SEEMS *SOME* OF US WILL SIMPLY FORGET ...
RIGHT. G-GOOD POINT.
HMM. I'VE GOTTA THINK OF SOME-THING...
...
MOM AND DAD BOUGHT ME THIS SUIT, DIDN'T THEY?
I BET IT COST A LOT ...!
KA-CHAK
ガチャ
I'M HOME!
WELCOME HOME~! THE BATH'S READY FOR YOU!
OKAY, THANKS!
I HOPE THIS MAKES THEM HAPPY...
TA-DAA!
I GOT MY FIRST CHECK, SO I BOUGHT US A CAKE TO CELE-BRATE!

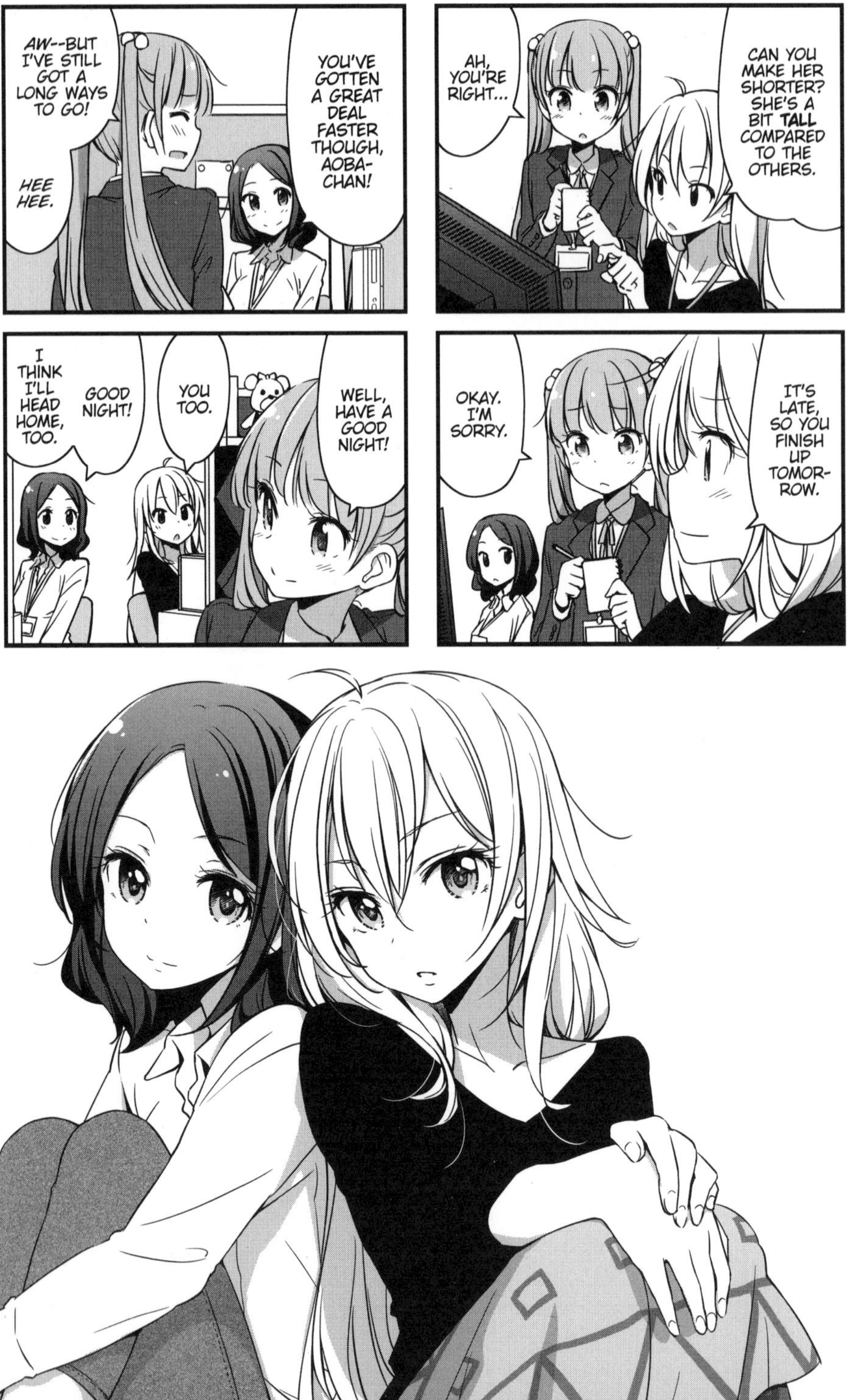
CAN YOU MAKE HER SHORTER? SHE'S A BIT **TALL** COMPARED TO THE OTHERS.
AH, YOU'RE RIGHT...
IT'S LATE, SO YOU FINISH UP TOMOR-ROW.
OKAY. I'M SORRY.
YOU'VE GOTTEN A GREAT DEAL FASTER THOUGH, AOBA-CHAN!
AW--BUT I'VE STILL GOT A LONG WAYS TO GO!
HEE HEE.
WELL, HAVE A GOOD NIGHT!
YOU TOO.
GOOD NIGHT!
I THINK I'LL HEAD HOME, TOO.

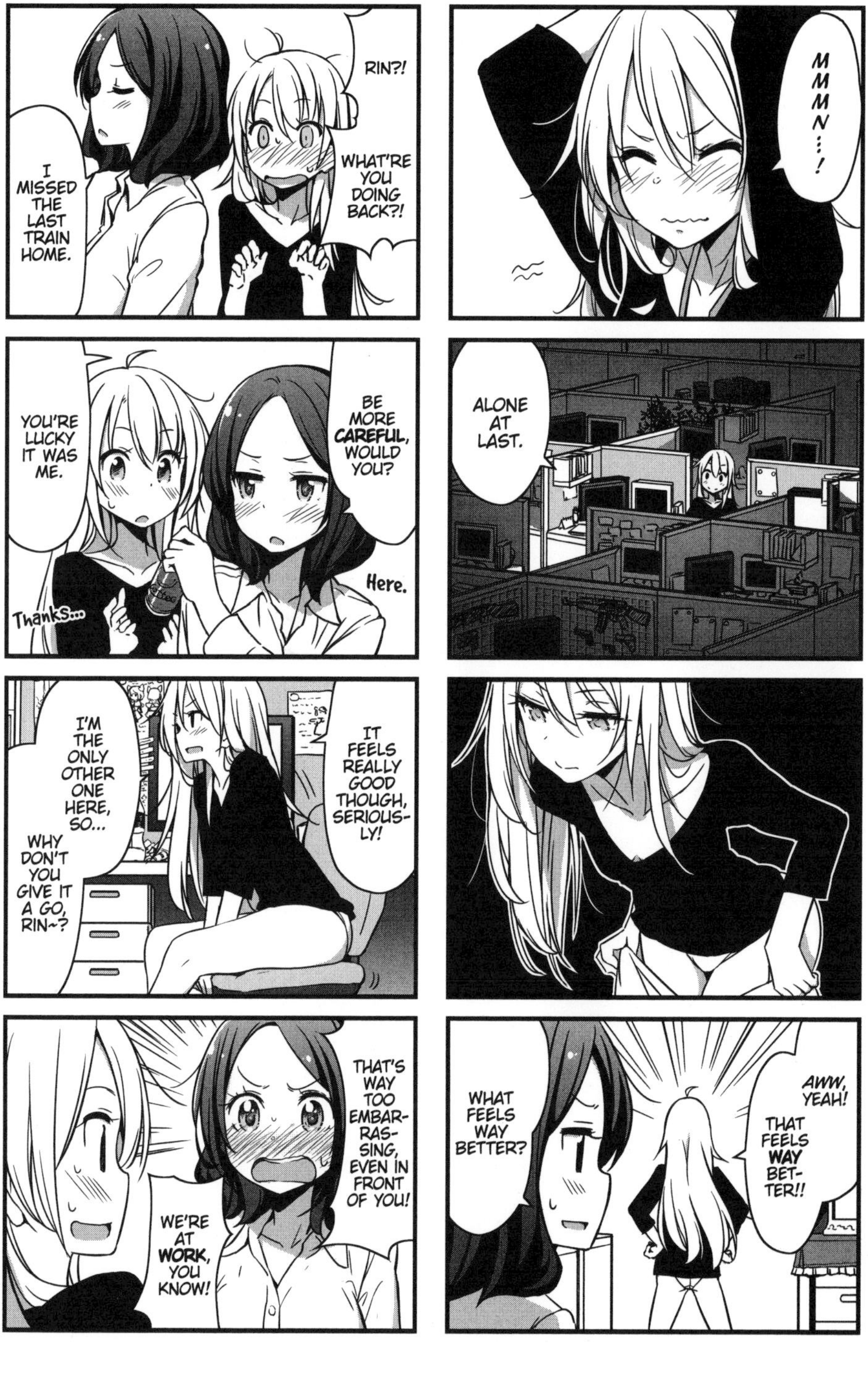
MMMN...!
ALONE AT LAST.
AWW, YEAH! THAT FEELS **WAY** BETTER!!
WHAT FEELS WAY BETTER?
RIN?! WHAT'RE YOU DOING BACK?!
I MISSED THE LAST TRAIN HOME.
BE MORE **CAREFUL**, WOULD YOU?
Here.
YOU'RE LUCKY IT WAS ME.
Thanks...
IT FEELS REALLY GOOD THOUGH, SERIOUSLY!
I'M THE ONLY OTHER ONE HERE, SO... WHY DON'T YOU GIVE IT A GO, RIN~?
THAT'S WAY TOO EMBARRASSING, EVEN IN FRONT OF YOU!
WE'RE AT **WORK**, YOU KNOW!

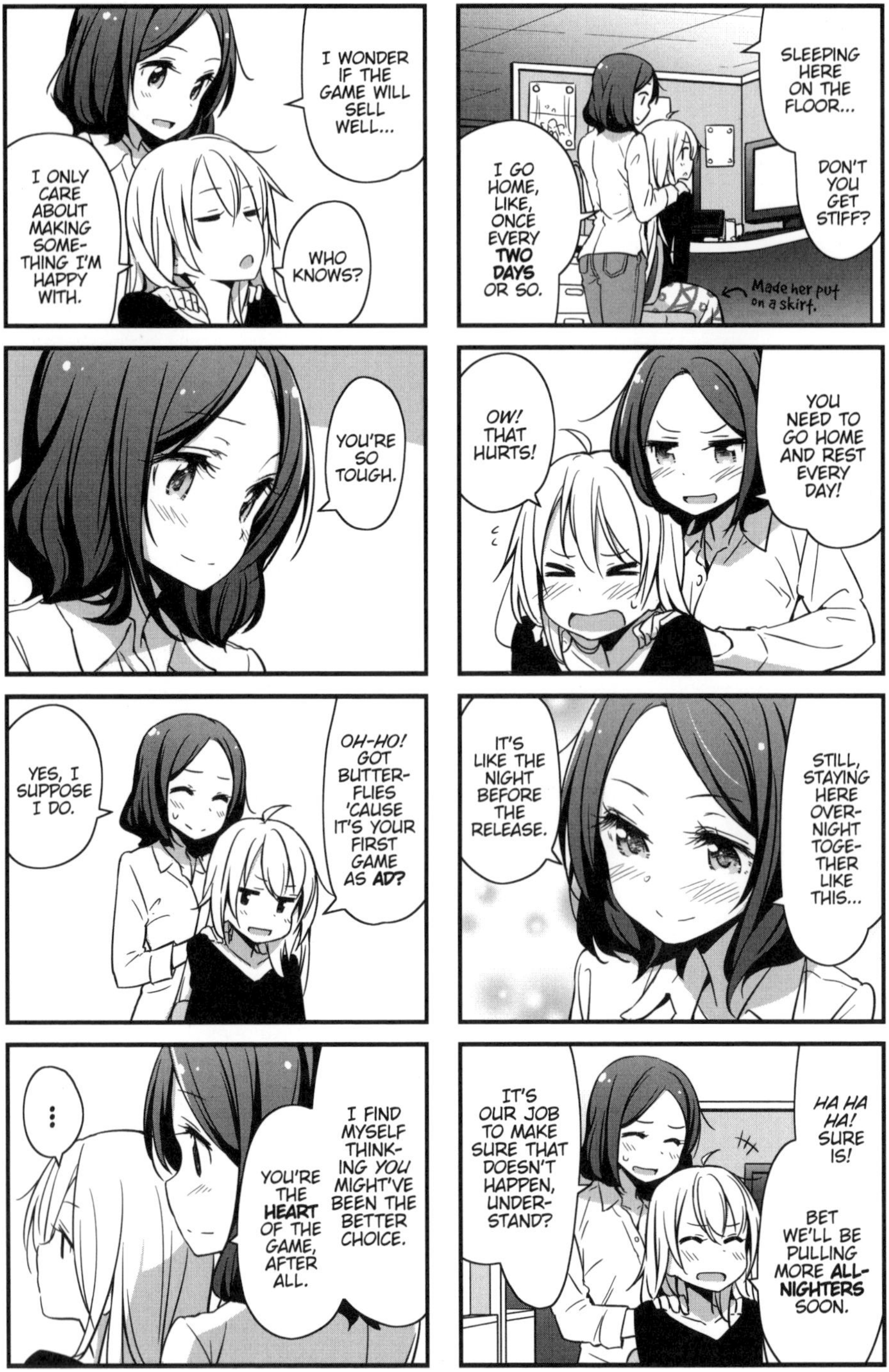
SLEEPING HERE ON THE FLOOR...
DON'T YOU GET STIFF?
I GO HOME, LIKE, ONCE EVERY **TWO DAYS** OR SO.
Made her put on a skirt.
YOU NEED TO GO HOME AND REST EVERY DAY!
OW! THAT HURTS!
STILL, STAYING HERE OVERNIGHT TOGETHER LIKE THIS...
IT'S LIKE THE NIGHT BEFORE THE RELEASE.
HA HA HA! SURE IS!
BET WE'LL BE PULLING MORE **ALL-NIGHTERS** SOON.
IT'S OUR JOB TO MAKE SURE THAT DOESN'T HAPPEN, UNDERSTAND?
I WONDER IF THE GAME WILL SELL WELL...
WHO KNOWS?
I ONLY CARE ABOUT MAKING SOMETHING I'M HAPPY WITH.
YOU'RE SO TOUGH.
OH-HO! GOT BUTTERFLIES 'CAUSE IT'S YOUR FIRST GAME AS **AD?**
YES, I SUPPOSE I DO.
I FIND MYSELF THINKING *YOU* MIGHT'VE BEEN THE BETTER CHOICE.
YOU'RE THE **HEART** OF THE GAME, AFTER ALL.
...

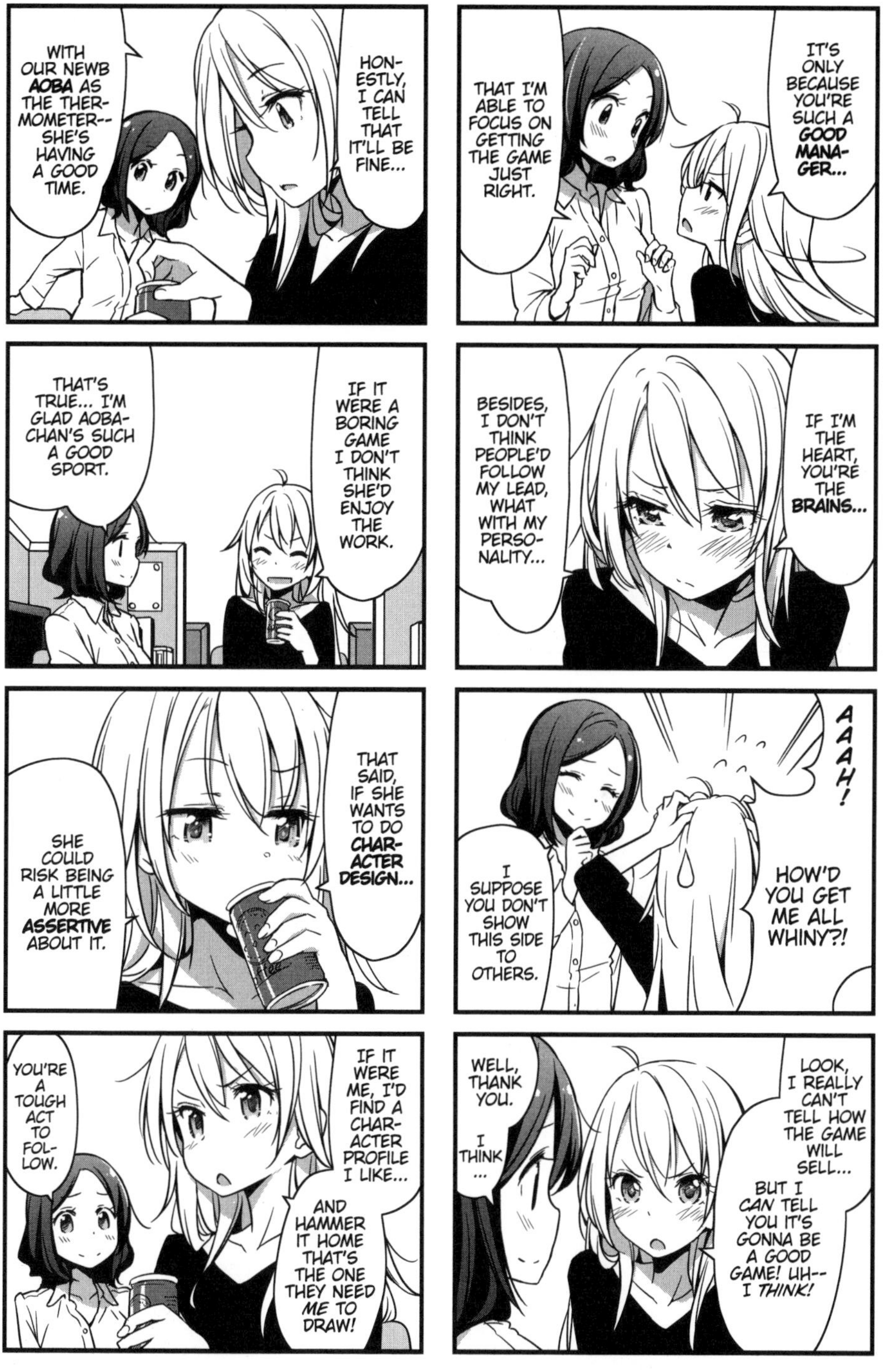
IT'S ONLY BECAUSE YOU'RE SUCH A **GOOD MANAGER...**
THAT I'M ABLE TO FOCUS ON GETTING THE GAME JUST RIGHT.
HONESTLY, I CAN TELL THAT IT'LL BE FINE...
WITH OUR NEWB **AOBA** AS THE THERMOMETER-- SHE'S HAVING A GOOD TIME.
IF I'M THE HEART, YOU'RE THE **BRAINS...**
BESIDES, I DON'T THINK PEOPLE'D FOLLOW MY LEAD, WHAT WITH MY PERSONALITY...
IF IT WERE A BORING GAME I DON'T THINK SHE'D ENJOY THE WORK.
THAT'S TRUE... I'M GLAD AOBA-CHAN'S SUCH A GOOD SPORT.
AAAH!
HOW'D YOU GET ME ALL WHINY?!
I SUPPOSE YOU DON'T SHOW THIS SIDE TO OTHERS.
THAT SAID, IF SHE WANTS TO DO **CHARACTER DESIGN...**
SHE COULD RISK BEING A LITTLE MORE **ASSERTIVE** ABOUT IT.
LOOK, I REALLY CAN'T TELL HOW THE GAME WILL SELL...
BUT I *CAN* TELL YOU IT'S GONNA BE A GOOD GAME! UH-- I *THINK!*
WELL, THANK YOU.
I THINK...
IF IT WERE ME, I'D FIND A CHARACTER PROFILE I LIKE...
AND HAMMER IT HOME THAT'S THE ONE THEY NEED *ME* TO DRAW!
YOU'RE A TOUGH ACT TO FOLLOW.

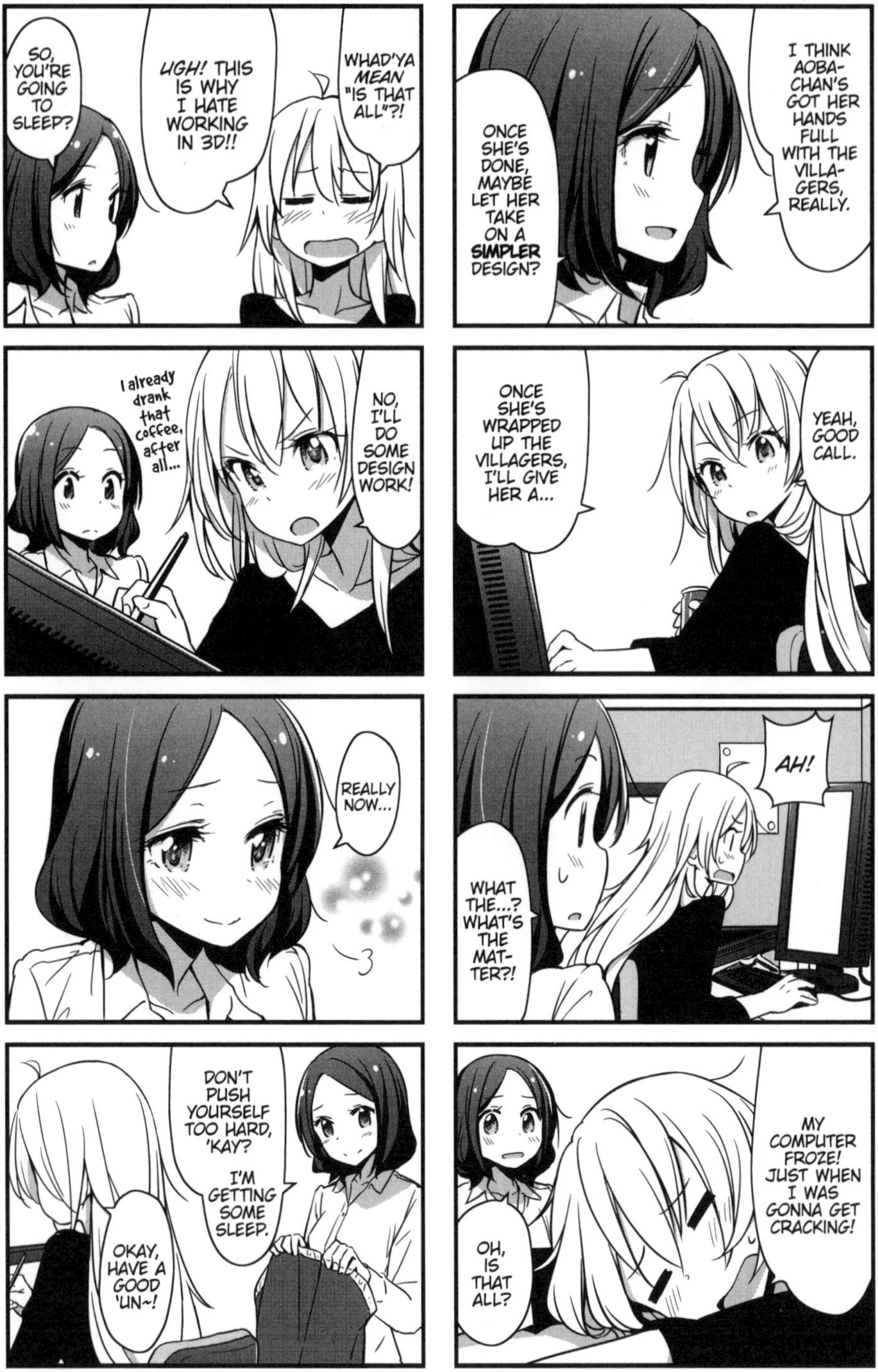
I THINK AOBA-CHAN'S GOT HER HANDS FULL WITH THE VILLAGERS, REALLY.
ONCE SHE'S DONE, MAYBE LET HER TAKE ON A **SIMPLER** DESIGN?
YEAH, GOOD CALL.
ONCE SHE'S WRAPPED UP THE VILLAGERS, I'LL GIVE HER A...
AH!
WHAT THE...? WHAT'S THE MATTER?!
MY COMPUTER FROZE! JUST WHEN I WAS GONNA GET CRACKING!
OH, IS THAT ALL?
WHAD'YA *MEAN* "IS THAT ALL"?!
UGH! THIS IS WHY I HATE WORKING IN 3D!!
SO, YOU'RE GOING TO SLEEP?
NO, I'LL DO SOME DESIGN WORK!
I already drank that coffee, after all...
REALLY NOW...
DON'T PUSH YOURSELF TOO HARD, 'KAY?
I'M GETTING SOME SLEEP.
OKAY, HAVE A GOOD 'UN~!

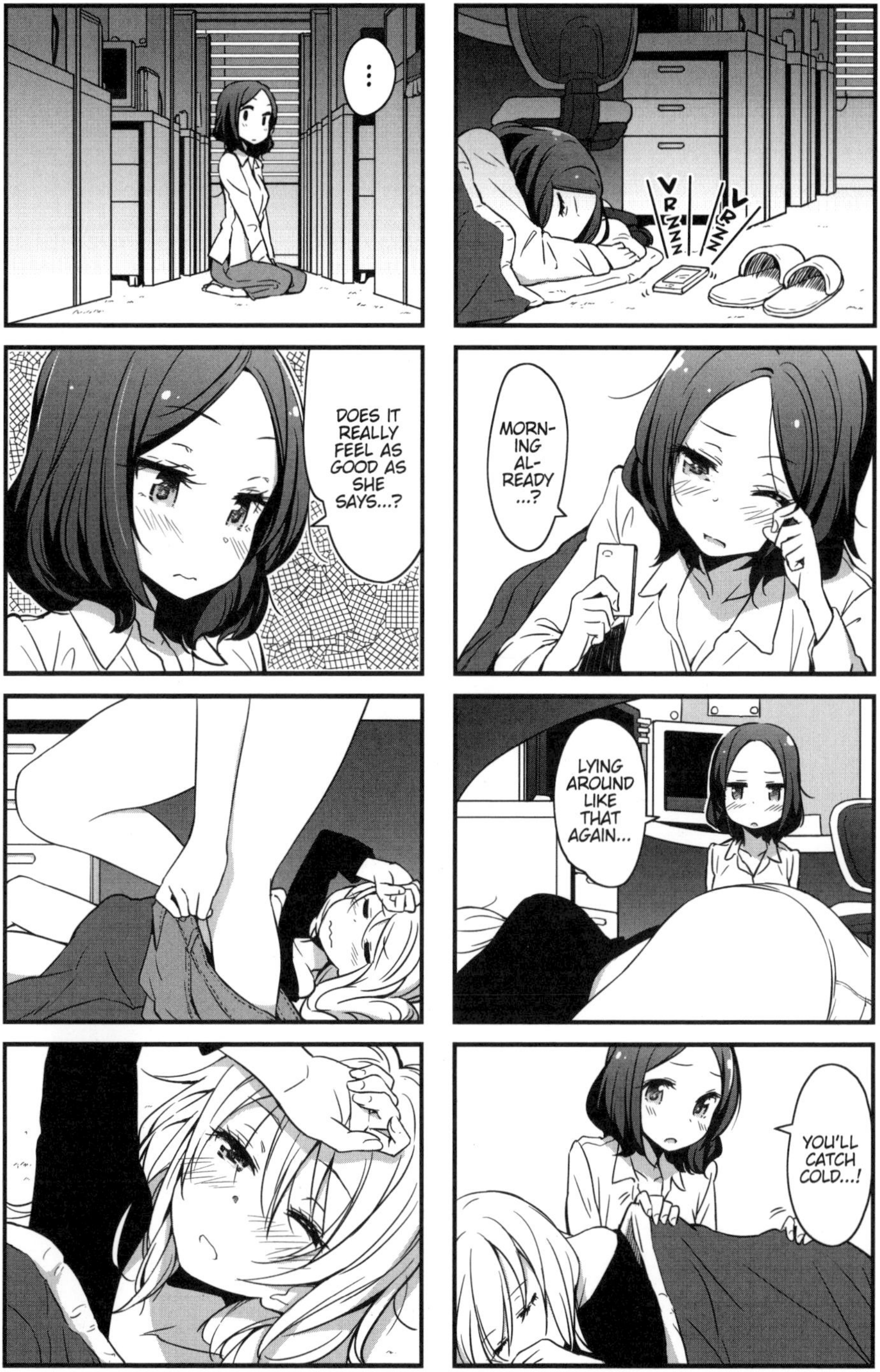
VRZZZ
VRNN
...
MORN-ING AL-READY ...?
DOES IT REALLY FEEL AS GOOD AS SHE SAYS...?
LYING AROUND LIKE THAT AGAIN...
YOU'LL CATCH COLD...!

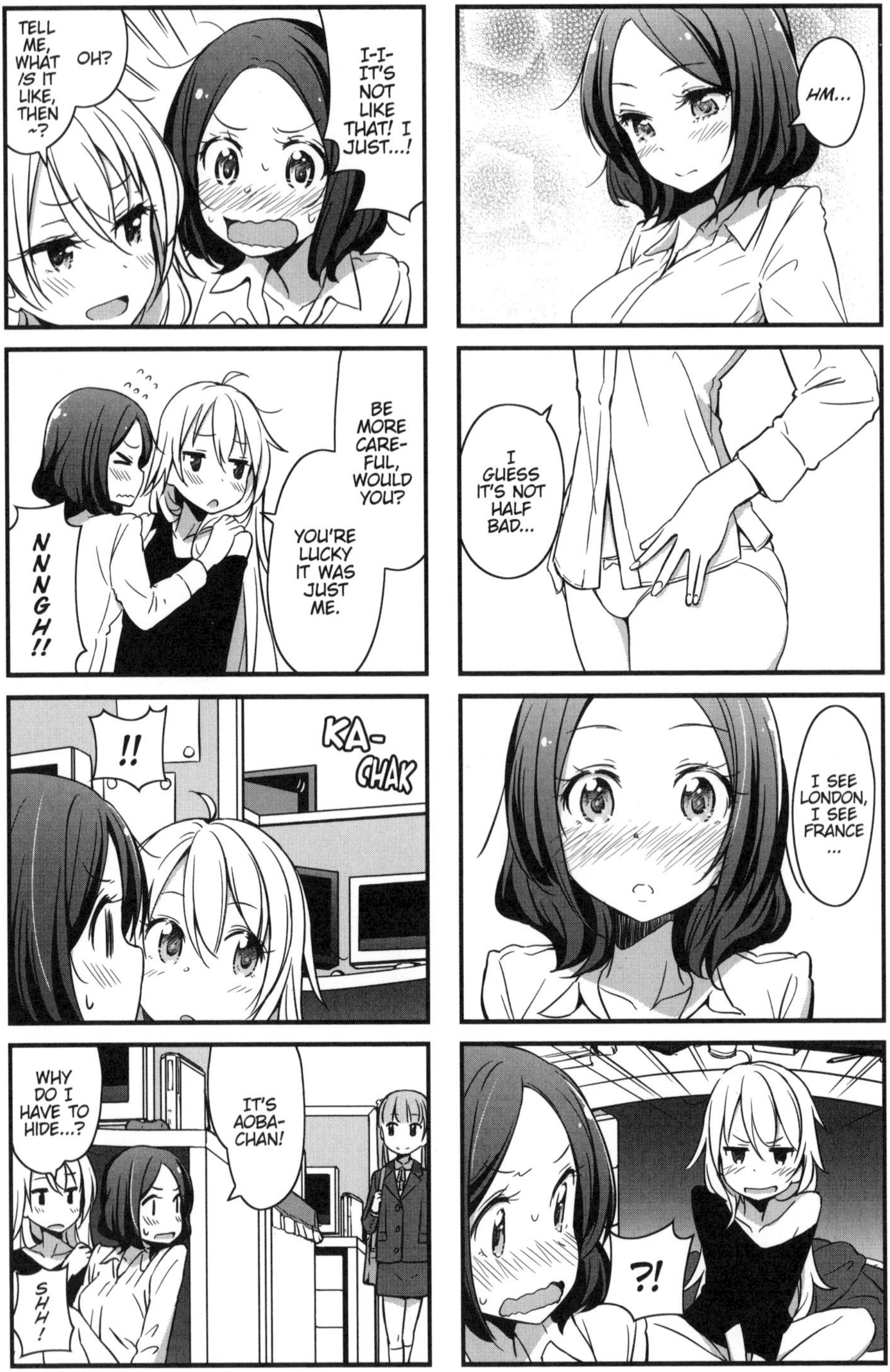
HM...
I-I-IT'S NOT LIKE THAT! I JUST...!
OH?
TELL ME, WHAT IS IT LIKE, THEN~?
I GUESS IT'S NOT HALF BAD...
BE MORE CAREFUL, WOULD YOU?
YOU'RE LUCKY IT WAS JUST ME.
NNNGH!!
I SEE LONDON, I SEE FRANCE...
KA-CHAK
!!
?!
IT'S AOBA-CHAN!
WHY DO I HAVE TO HIDE...?
SHH!

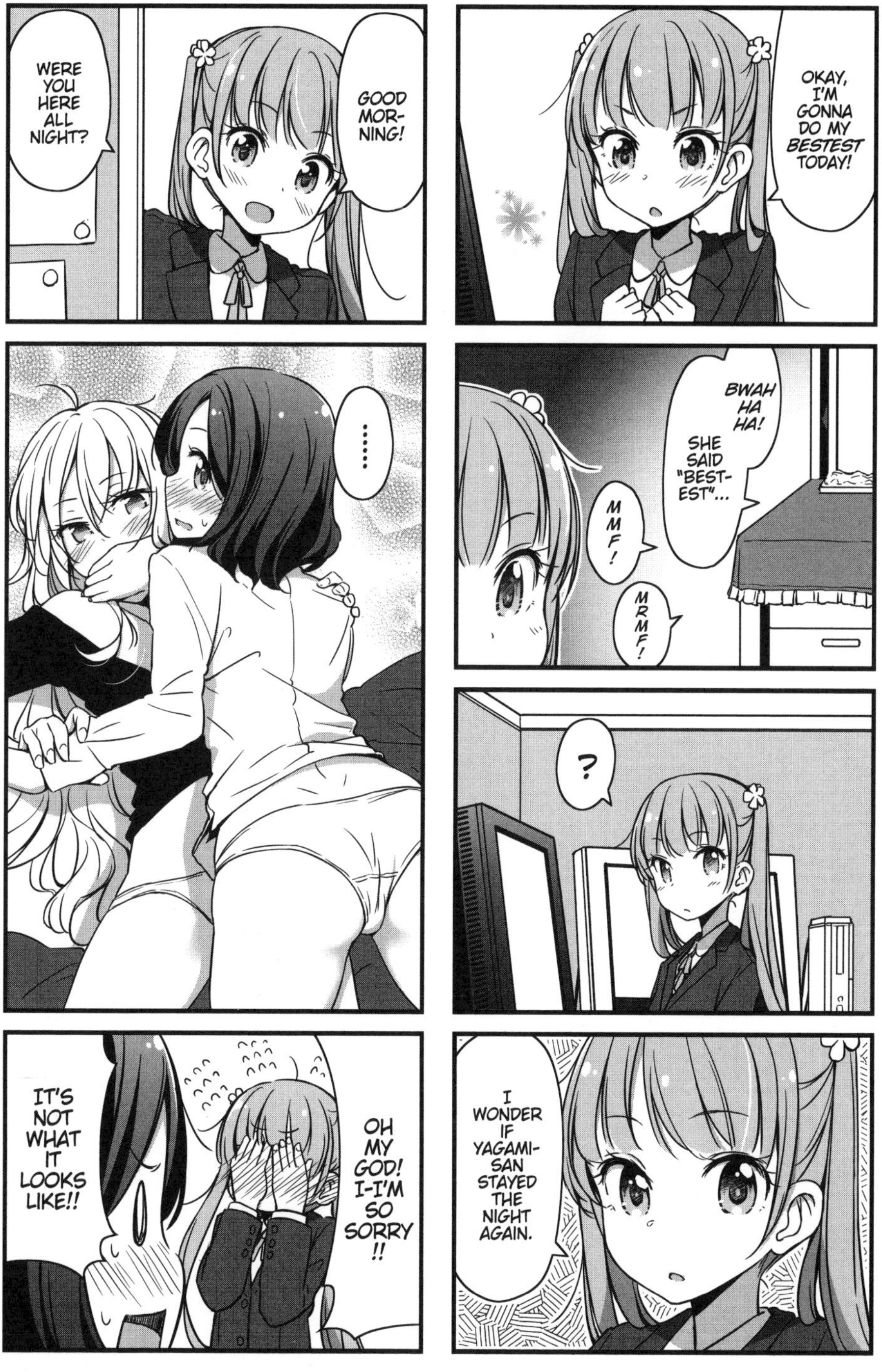
OKAY, I'M GONNA DO MY BESTEST TODAY!
BWAH HA HA!
SHE SAID "BEST-EST"...
MMF!
MRMF!
?
I WONDER IF YAGAMI-SAN STAYED THE NIGHT AGAIN.
GOOD MORN-ING!
WERE YOU HERE ALL NIGHT?
......
OH MY GOD! I-I'M SO SORRY !!
IT'S NOT WHAT IT LOOKS LIKE!!

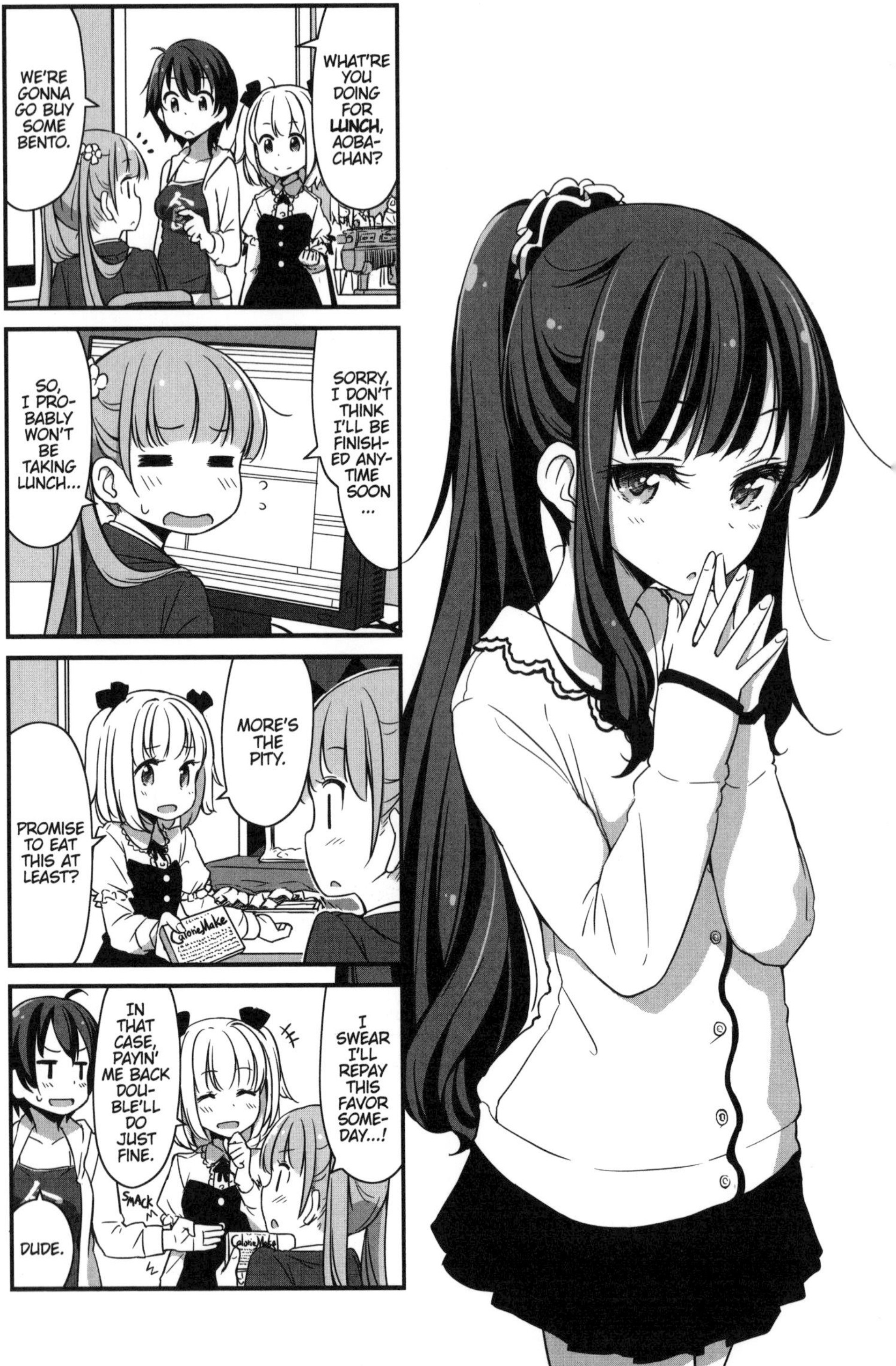
WHAT'RE YOU DOING FOR **LUNCH**, AOBA-CHAN?
WE'RE GONNA GO BUY SOME BENTO.
SORRY, I DON'T THINK I'LL BE FINISHED ANYTIME SOON...
SO, I PROBABLY WON'T BE TAKING LUNCH...
MORE'S THE PITY.
PROMISE TO EAT THIS AT LEAST?
CalorieMake
I SWEAR I'LL REPAY THIS FAVOR SOMEDAY...!
IN THAT CASE, PAYIN' ME BACK DOUBLE'LL DO JUST FINE.
SMACK
CalorieMake
DUDE.

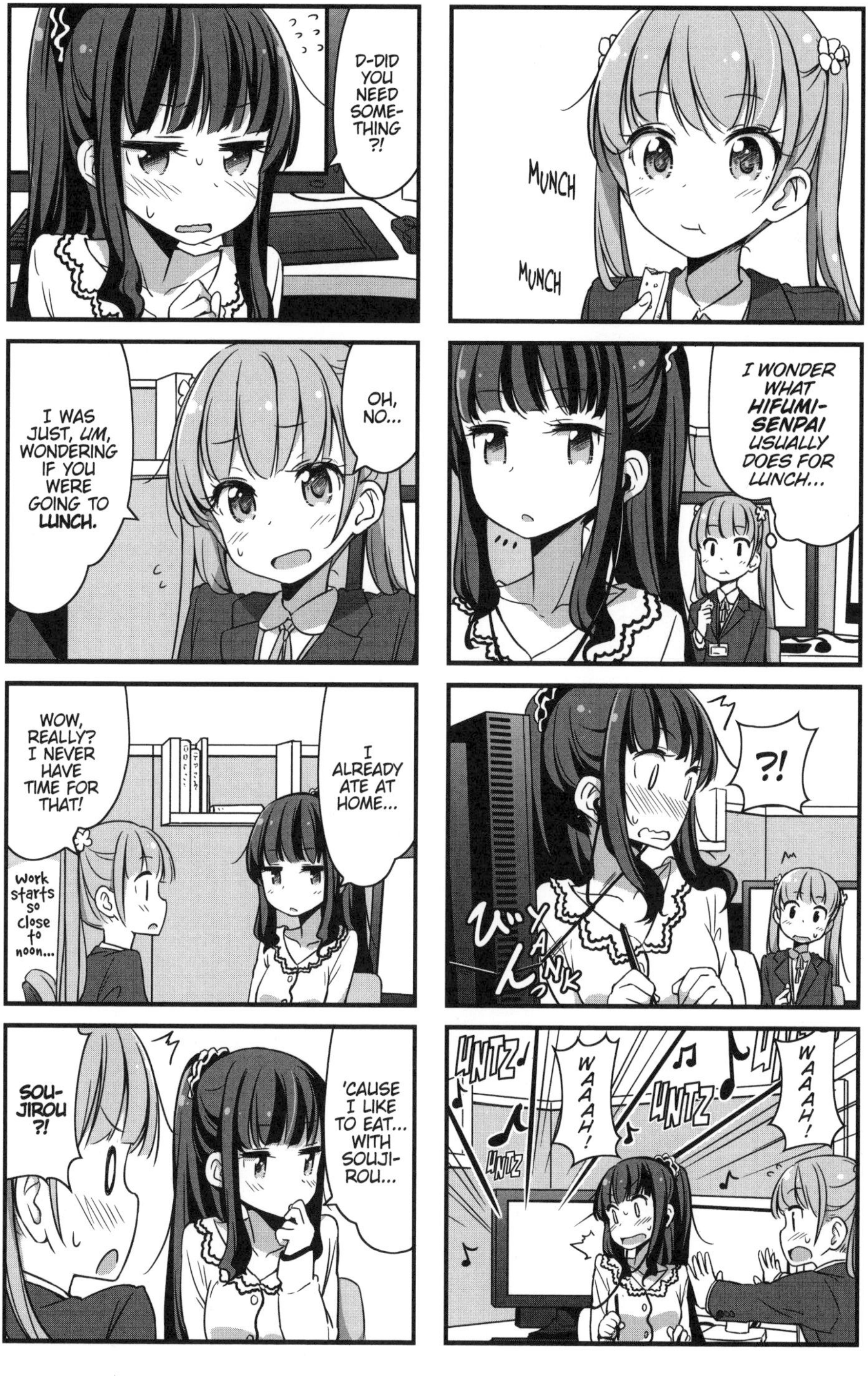
MUNCH
MUNCH
D-DID YOU NEED SOMETHING?!
I WONDER WHAT HIFUMI-SENPAI USUALLY DOES FOR LUNCH...
OH, NO...
I WAS JUST, UM, WONDERING IF YOU WERE GOING TO LUNCH.
?!
YANK
I ALREADY ATE AT HOME...
WOW, REALLY? I NEVER HAVE TIME FOR THAT!
Work starts so close to noon...
WAAAH!
WAAAH!
UNTZ
UNTZ
UNTZ
'CAUSE I LIKE TO EAT... WITH SOUJIROU...
SOUJIROU?!

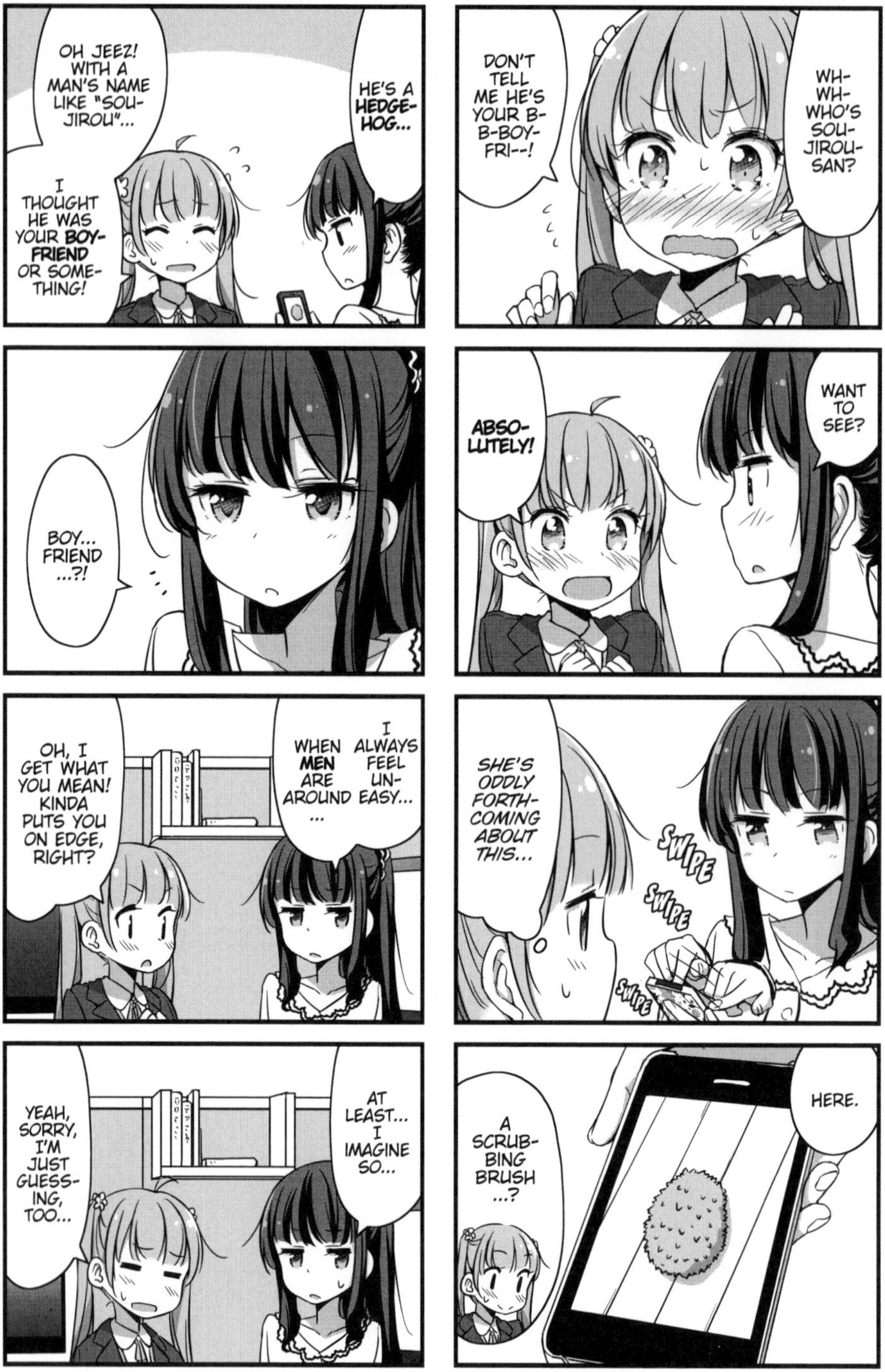
WH-WH-WHO'S SOU-JIROU-SAN?
DON'T TELL ME HE'S YOUR B-B-BOY-FRI--!
HE'S A **HEDGEHOG...**
OH JEEZ! WITH A MAN'S NAME LIKE "SOUJIROU"...
I THOUGHT HE WAS YOUR **BOYFRIEND** OR SOMETHING!
WANT TO SEE?
ABSOLUTELY!
BOY... FRIEND ...?!
SHE'S ODDLY FORTHCOMING ABOUT THIS...
SWIPE
SWIPE
SWIPE
I ALWAYS FEEL UNEASY... WHEN **MEN** ARE AROUND ...
OH, I GET WHAT YOU MEAN! KINDA PUTS YOU ON EDGE, RIGHT?
HERE.
A SCRUBBING BRUSH ...?
AT LEAST... I IMAGINE SO...
YEAH, SORRY, I'M JUST GUESSING, TOO...

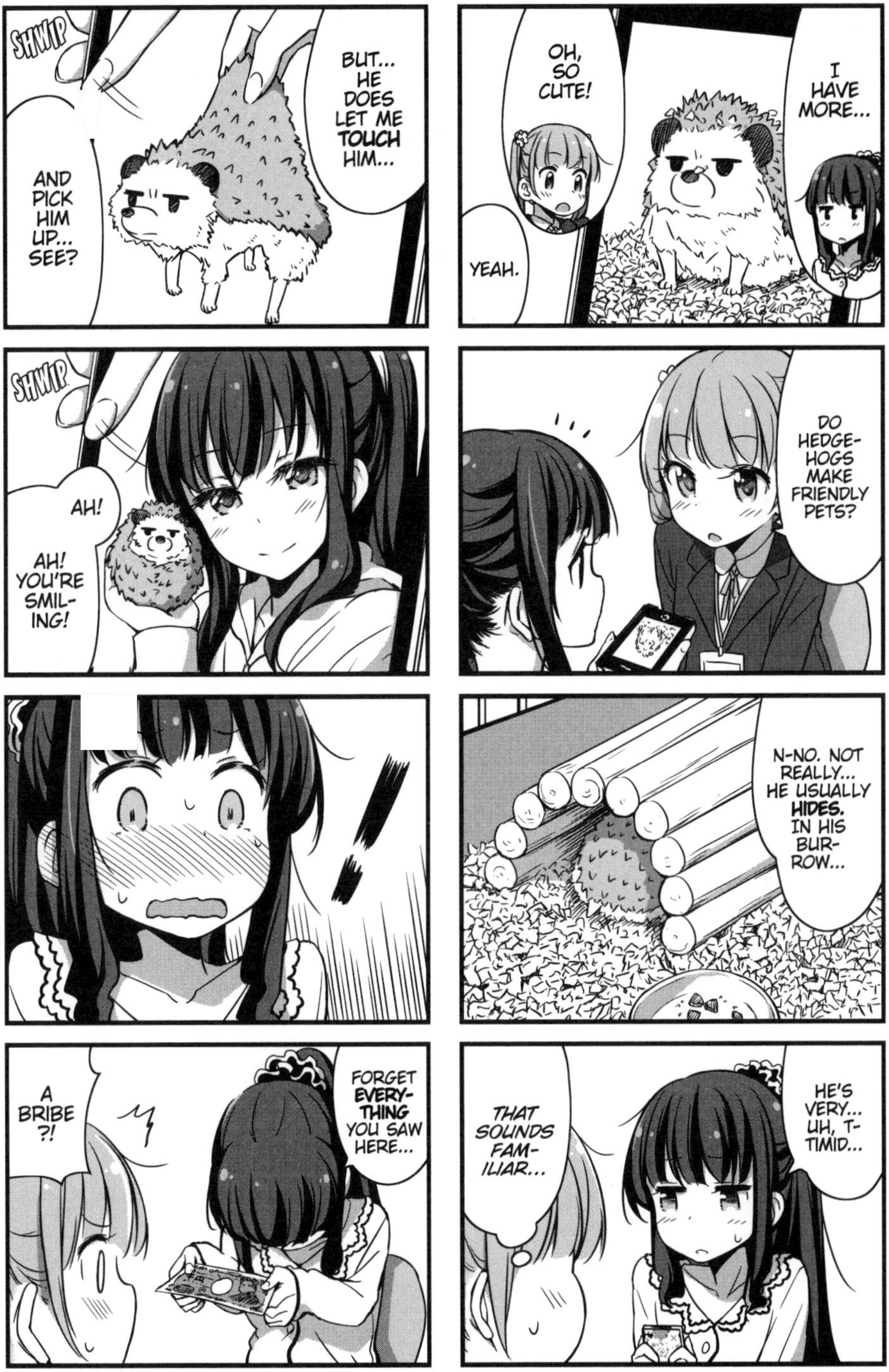
I HAVE MORE...
OH, SO CUTE!
YEAH.
SHWIP
BUT... HE DOES LET ME TOUCH HIM...
AND PICK HIM UP... SEE?
DO HEDGEHOGS MAKE FRIENDLY PETS?
SHWIP
AH!
AH! YOU'RE SMILING!
N-NO. NOT REALLY... HE USUALLY HIDES. IN HIS BURROW...
!
HE'S VERY... UH, T-TIMID...
THAT SOUNDS FAMILIAR...
FORGET EVERYTHING YOU SAW HERE...
A BRIBE?!

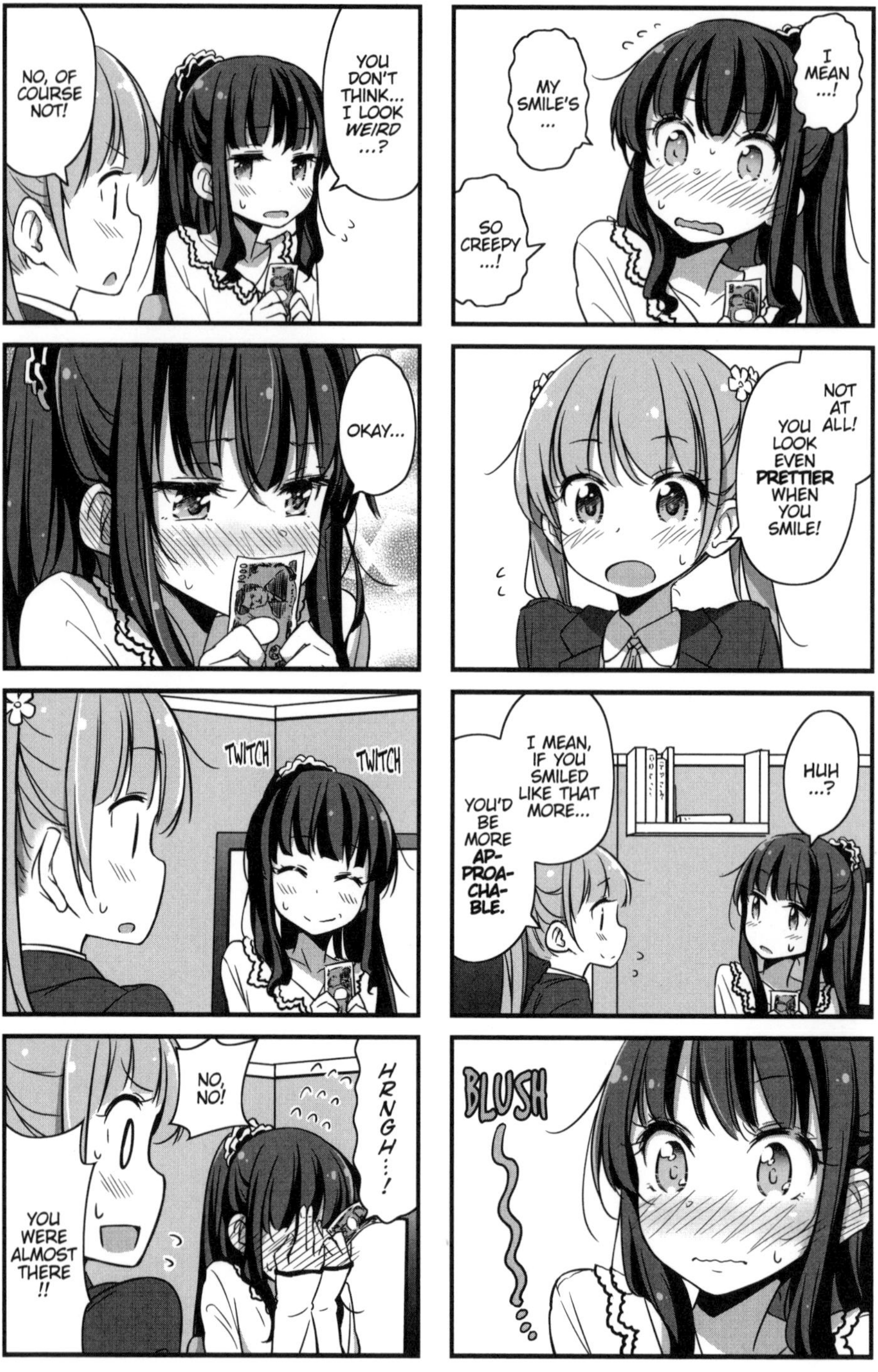
I MEAN ...!
MY SMILE'S ...
SO CREEPY ...!
YOU DON'T THINK... I LOOK *WEIRD* ...?
NO, OF COURSE NOT!
NOT AT ALL! YOU LOOK EVEN **PRETTIER** WHEN YOU SMILE!
OKAY...
HUH ...?
I MEAN, IF YOU SMILED LIKE THAT MORE...
YOU'D BE MORE **AP-PROA-CHA-BLE.**
TWITCH
TWITCH
BLUSH
HRNGH...!
NO, NO!
YOU WERE ALMOST THERE !!

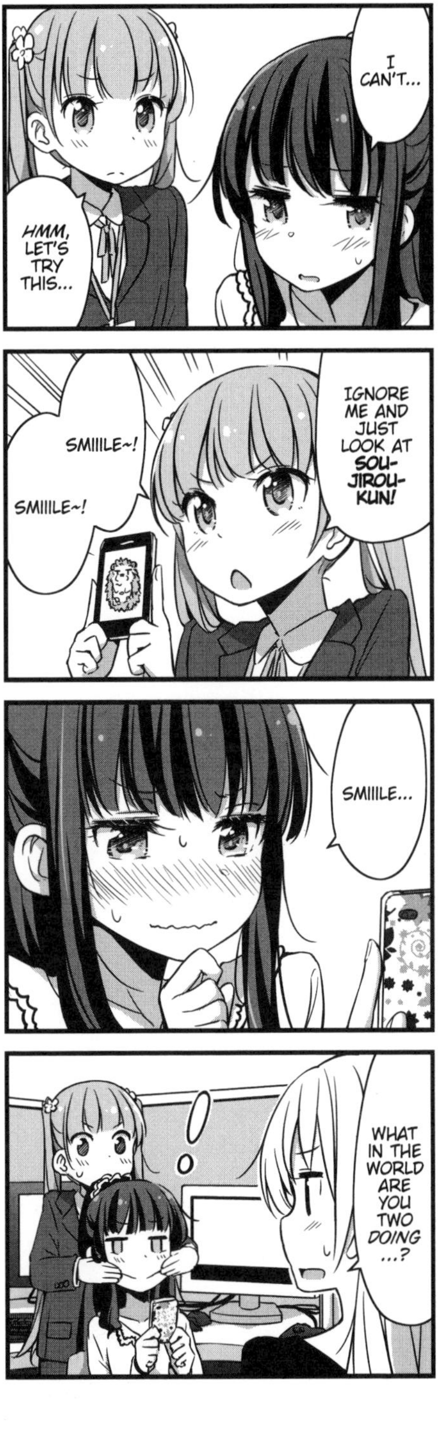
I CAN'T...
HMM, LET'S TRY THIS...
IGNORE ME AND JUST LOOK AT SOUJIROU-KUN!
SMIIILE~!
SMIIILE~!
SMIIILE...
WHAT IN THE WORLD ARE YOU TWO DOING...?

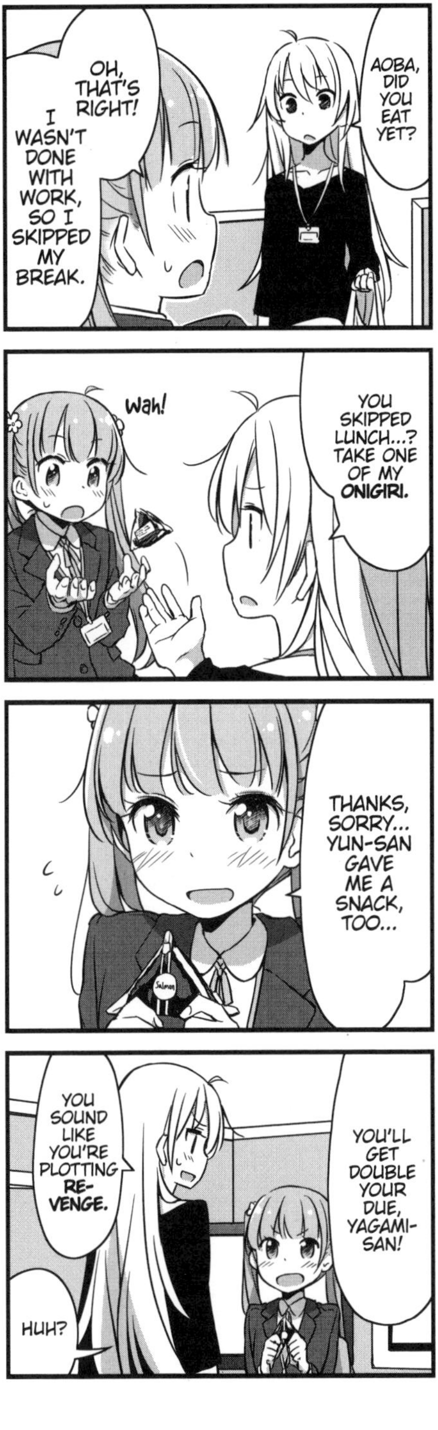
AOBA, DID YOU EAT YET?
OH, THAT'S RIGHT! I WASN'T DONE WITH WORK, SO I SKIPPED MY BREAK.
YOU SKIPPED LUNCH...? TAKE ONE OF MY ONIGIRI.
Wah!
THANKS, SORRY... YUN-SAN GAVE ME A SNACK, TOO...
Salmon
YOU'LL GET DOUBLE YOUR DUE, YAGAMI-SAN!
YOU SOUND LIKE YOU'RE PLOTTING RE-VENGE.
HUH?

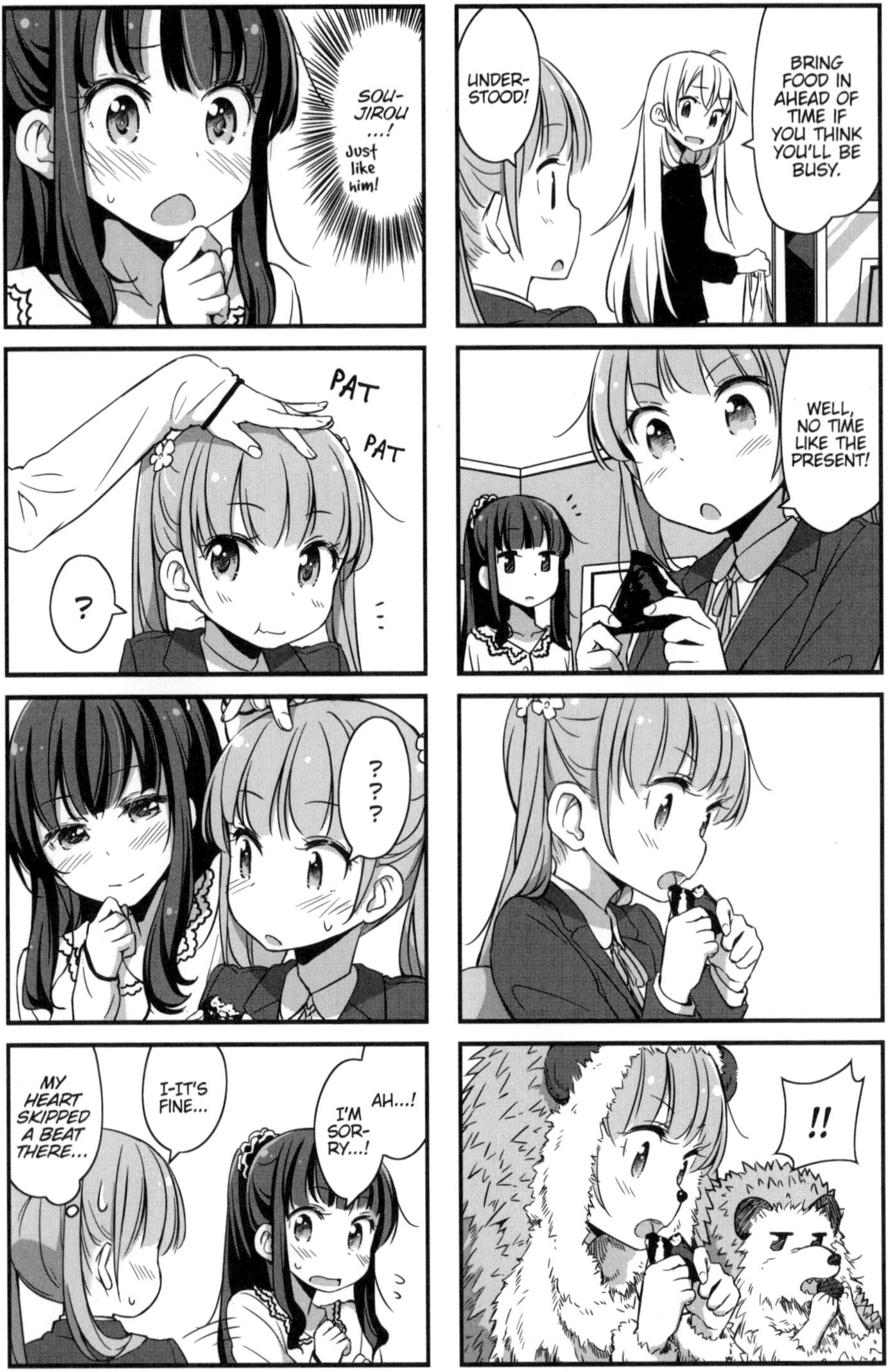
BRING FOOD IN AHEAD OF TIME IF YOU THINK YOU'LL BE BUSY.
UNDER-STOOD!
WELL, NO TIME LIKE THE PRESENT!
!!
SOU-JIROU ...!
Just like him!
PAT
PAT
?
?·?·?
AH...! I'M SOR-RY...!
I-IT'S FINE...
MY HEART SKIPPED A BEAT THERE...

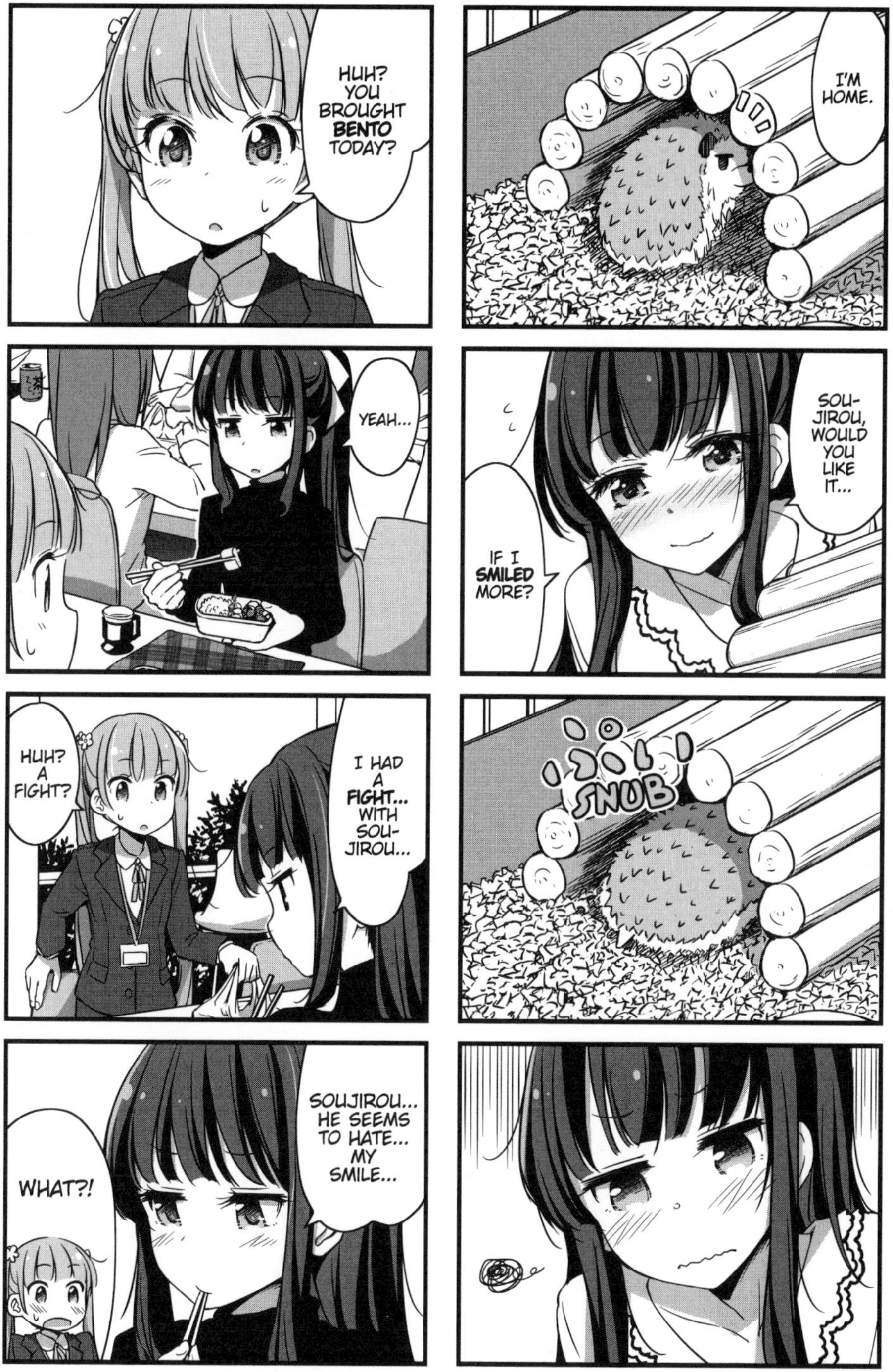
I'M HOME.
SOU-JIROU, WOULD YOU LIKE IT...
IF I SMILED MORE?
SNUB
HUH? YOU BROUGHT BENTO TODAY?
YEAH...
I HAD A FIGHT... WITH SOU-JIROU...
HUH? A FIGHT?
SOUJIROU... HE SEEMS TO HATE... MY SMILE...
WHAT?!

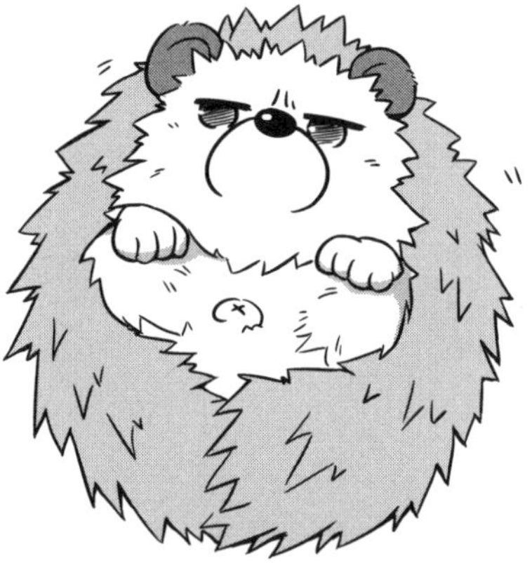

Hifumi's Day Off

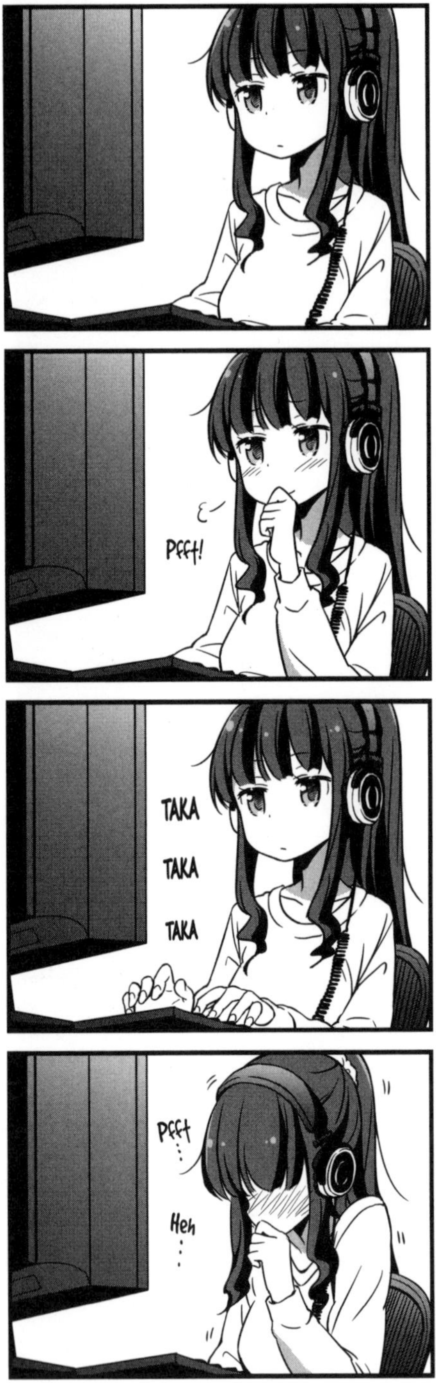
Pfft!
TAKA
TAKA
TAKA
Pfft...
Heh...

Kou's Day Off

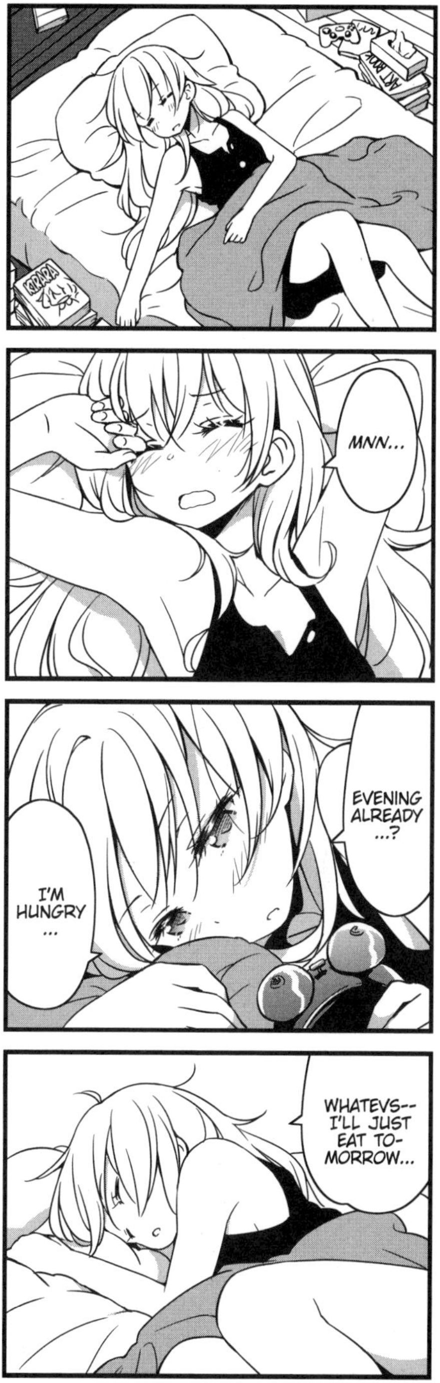
KIRARA
MNN...
EVENING ALREADY ...?
I'M HUNGRY ...
WHATEVS-- I'LL JUST EAT TO-MORROW...

Rin's Day Off

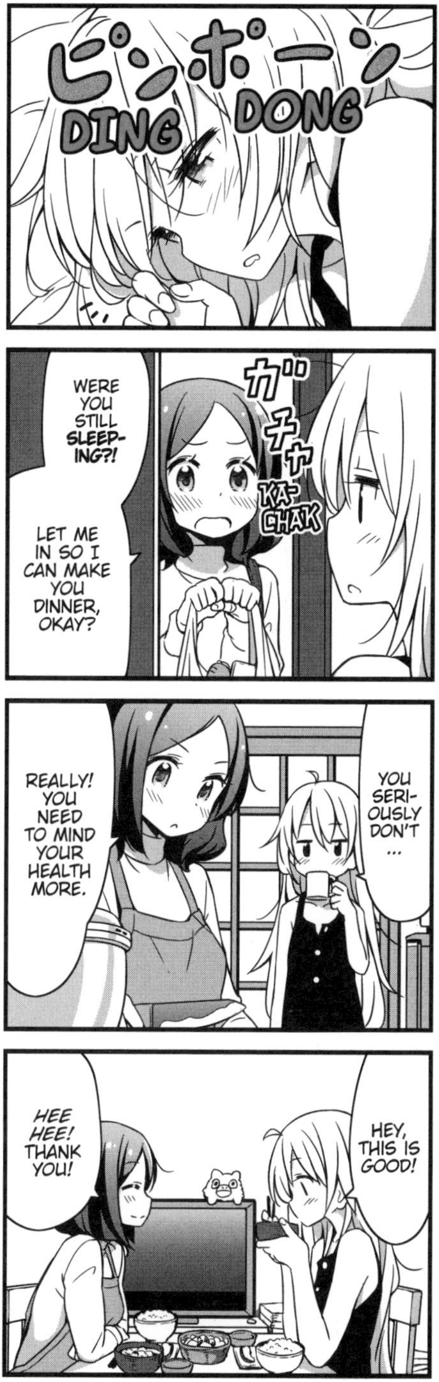
ピンポーン
DING DONG
ガチャ
KA-CHAK
WERE YOU STILL SLEEP-ING?!
LET ME IN SO I CAN MAKE YOU DINNER, OKAY?
YOU SERI-OUSLY DON'T ...
REALLY! YOU NEED TO MIND YOUR HEALTH MORE.
HEY, THIS IS GOOD!
HEE HEE! THANK YOU!

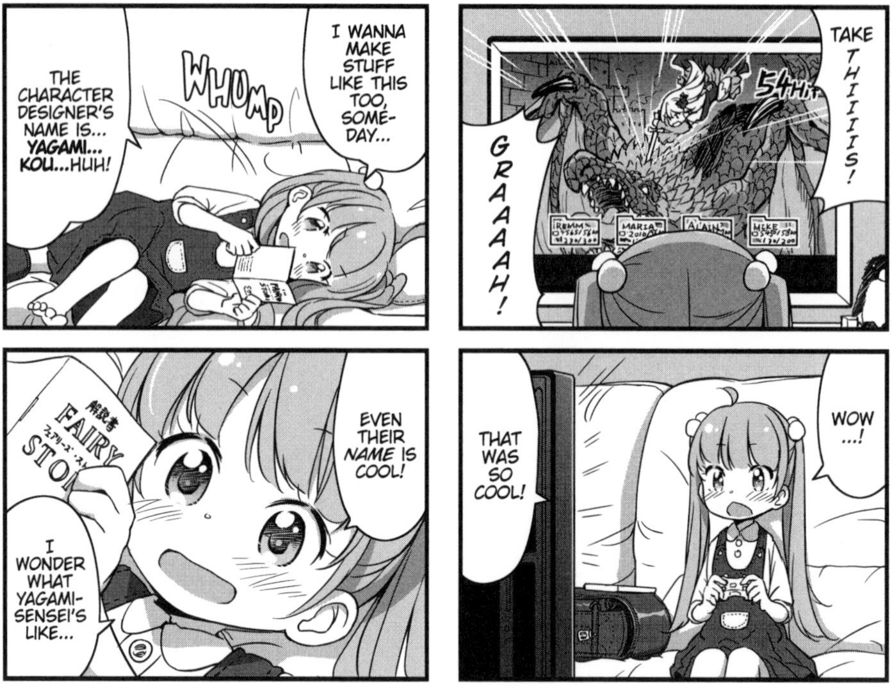
TAKE THIIIIS!
54Hit
GRAAAAH!
I WANNA MAKE STUFF LIKE THIS TOO, SOME-DAY...
WHUMP
THE CHARACTER DESIGNER'S NAME IS... YAGAMI... KOU...HUH!
WOW ...!
THAT WAS SO COOL!
EVEN THEIR *NAME* IS COOL!
I WONDER WHAT YAGAMI-SENSEI'S LIKE...

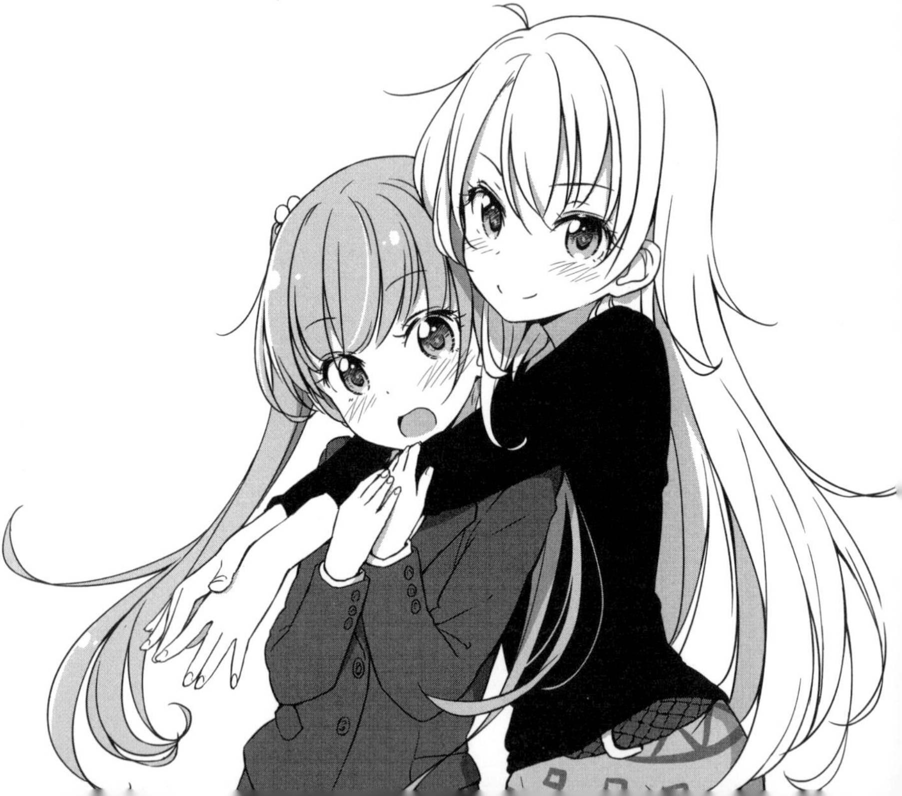

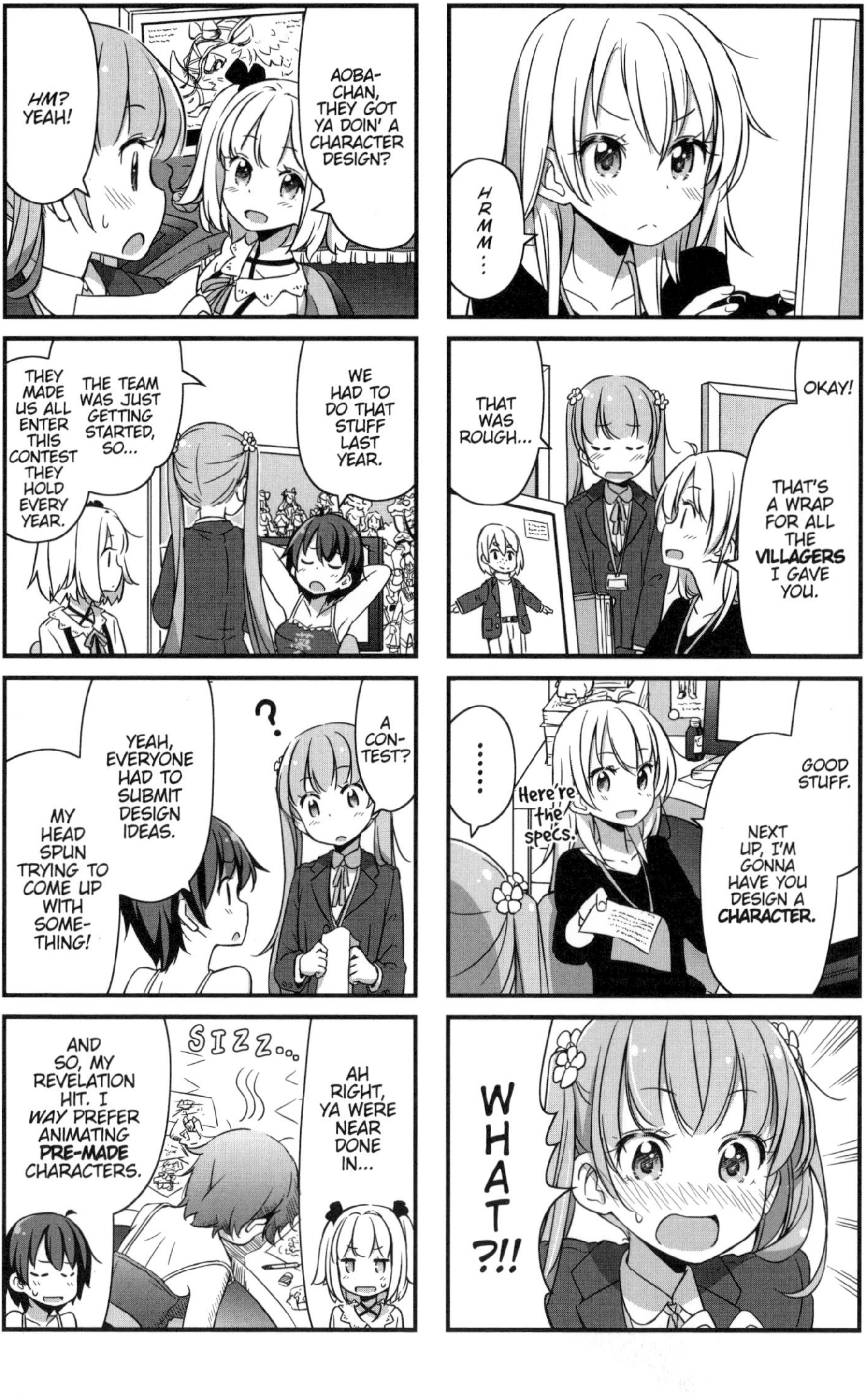
HRMM...
OKAY!
THAT'S A WRAP FOR ALL THE **VILLAGERS** I GAVE YOU.
THAT WAS ROUGH...
GOOD STUFF.
NEXT UP, I'M GONNA HAVE YOU DESIGN A **CHARACTER.**
Here're the specs.
......
WHAT?!!
AOBA-CHAN, THEY GOT YA DOIN' A CHARACTER DESIGN?
HM? YEAH!
WE HAD TO DO THAT STUFF LAST YEAR.
THE TEAM WAS JUST GETTING STARTED, SO...
THEY MADE US ALL ENTER THIS CONTEST THEY HOLD EVERY YEAR.
A CON-TEST?
?
YEAH, EVERYONE HAD TO SUBMIT DESIGN IDEAS.
MY HEAD SPUN TRYING TO COME UP WITH SOME-THING!
AH RIGHT, YA WERE NEAR DONE IN...
SIZZ...
AND SO, MY REVELATION HIT. I *WAY* PREFER ANIMATING **PRE-MADE** CHARACTERS.

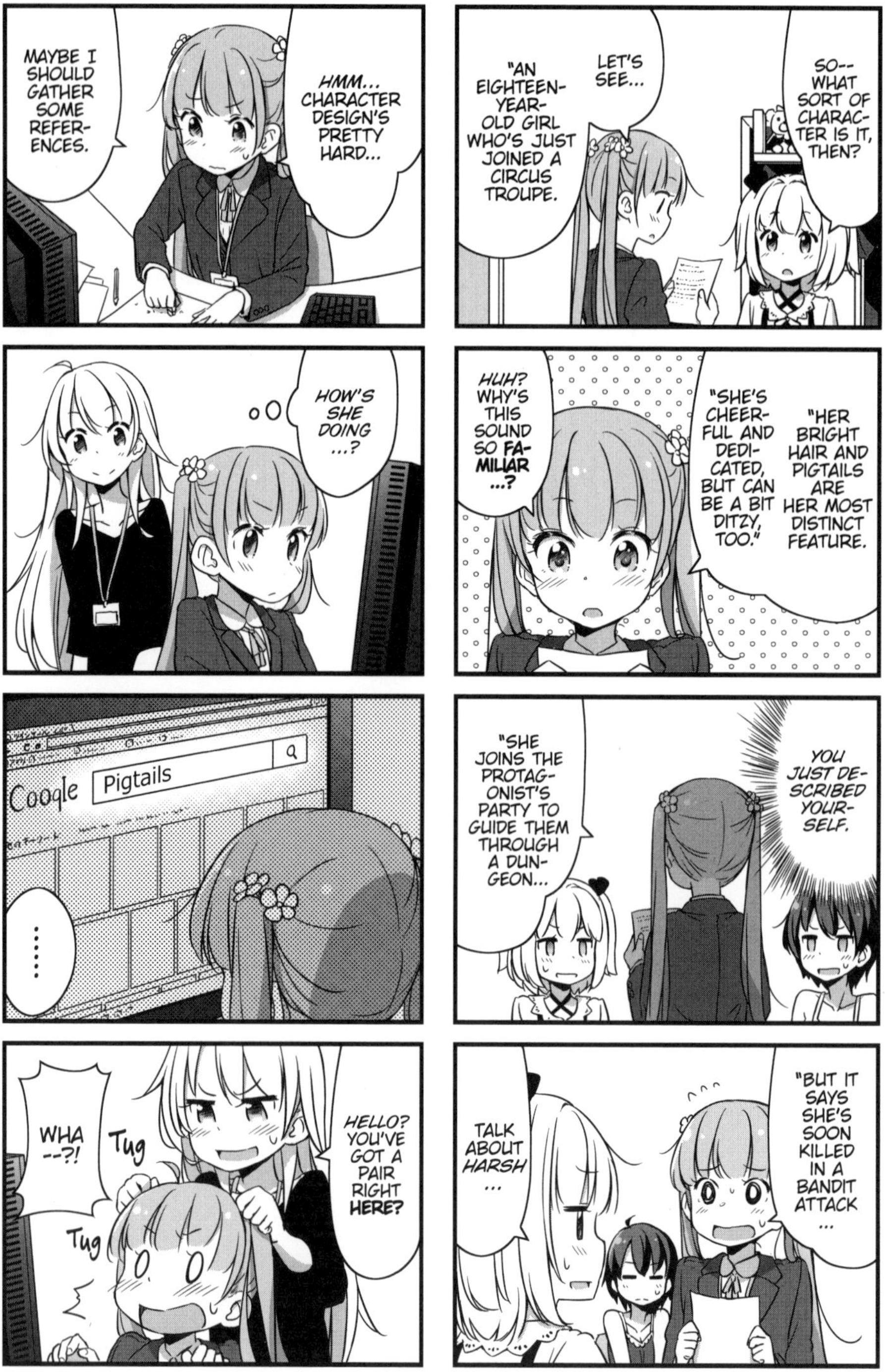
SO--WHAT SORT OF CHARACTER IS IT, THEN?
LET'S SEE...
"AN EIGHTEEN-YEAR-OLD GIRL WHO'S JUST JOINED A CIRCUS TROUPE.
"HER BRIGHT HAIR AND PIGTAILS ARE HER MOST DISTINCT FEATURE.
"SHE'S CHEERFUL AND DEDICATED, BUT CAN BE A BIT DITZY, TOO."
HUH? WHY'S THIS SOUND SO FAMILIAR...?
YOU JUST DESCRIBED YOURSELF.
"SHE JOINS THE PROTAGONIST'S PARTY TO GUIDE THEM THROUGH A DUNGEON...
"BUT IT SAYS SHE'S SOON KILLED IN A BANDIT ATTACK...
TALK ABOUT HARSH...
HMM... CHARACTER DESIGN'S PRETTY HARD...
MAYBE I SHOULD GATHER SOME REFERENCES.
HOW'S SHE DOING...?
Coogle
Pigtails
......
HELLO? YOU'VE GOT A PAIR RIGHT HERE?
Tug
WHA--?!
Tug

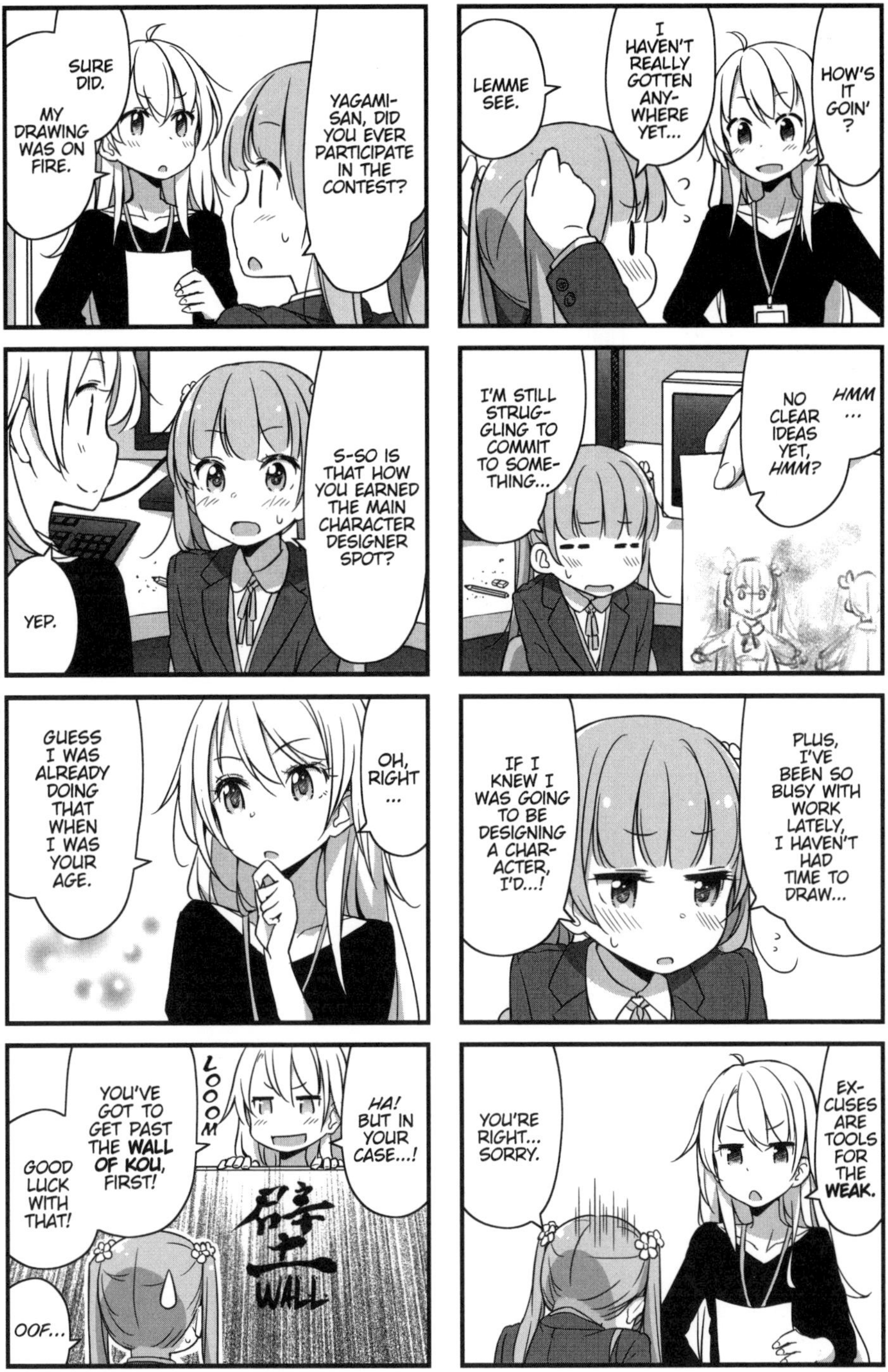
HOW'S IT GOIN'?
I HAVEN'T REALLY GOTTEN ANYWHERE YET...
LEMME SEE.
HMM...
NO CLEAR IDEAS YET, HMM?
I'M STILL STRUGGLING TO COMMIT TO SOMETHING...
PLUS, I'VE BEEN SO BUSY WITH WORK LATELY, I HAVEN'T HAD TIME TO DRAW...
IF I KNEW I WAS GOING TO BE DESIGNING A CHARACTER, I'D...!
EXCUSES ARE TOOLS FOR THE **WEAK.**
YOU'RE RIGHT... SORRY.
YAGAMI-SAN, DID YOU EVER PARTICIPATE IN THE CONTEST?
SURE DID.
MY DRAWING WAS ON FIRE.
S-SO IS THAT HOW YOU EARNED THE MAIN CHARACTER DESIGNER SPOT?
YEP.
OH, RIGHT...
GUESS I WAS ALREADY DOING THAT WHEN I WAS YOUR AGE.
HA! BUT IN YOUR CASE...!
LOOOOM
YOU'VE GOT TO GET PAST THE **WALL OF KOU,** FIRST!
GOOD LUCK WITH THAT!
壁
WALL
OOF...

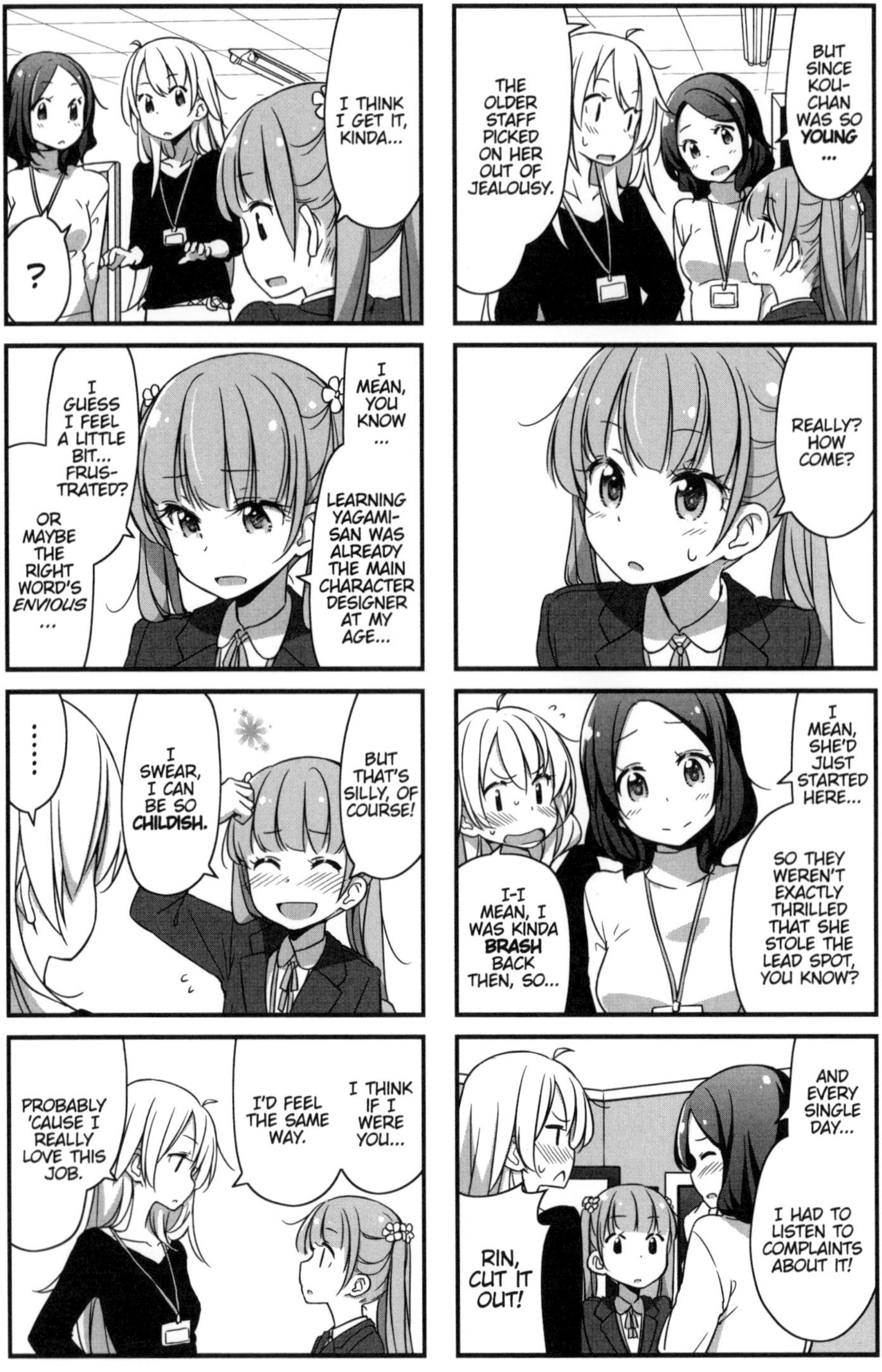
BUT SINCE KOU-CHAN WAS SO YOUNG ...
THE OLDER STAFF PICKED ON HER OUT OF JEALOUSY.
I THINK I GET IT, KINDA...
?
REALLY? HOW COME?
I MEAN, YOU KNOW ...
LEARNING YAGAMI-SAN WAS ALREADY THE MAIN CHARACTER DESIGNER AT MY AGE...
I GUESS I FEEL A LITTLE BIT... FRUSTRATED?
OR MAYBE THE RIGHT WORD'S *ENVIOUS* ...
I MEAN, SHE'D JUST STARTED HERE...
SO THEY WEREN'T EXACTLY THRILLED THAT SHE STOLE THE LEAD SPOT, YOU KNOW?
I-I MEAN, I WAS KINDA **BRASH** BACK THEN, SO...
BUT THAT'S SILLY, OF COURSE!
I SWEAR, I CAN BE SO **CHILDISH.**
......
AND EVERY SINGLE DAY...
I HAD TO LISTEN TO COMPLAINTS ABOUT IT!
RIN, CUT IT OUT!
I THINK IF I WERE YOU...
I'D FEEL THE SAME WAY.
PROBABLY 'CAUSE I REALLY LOVE THIS JOB.

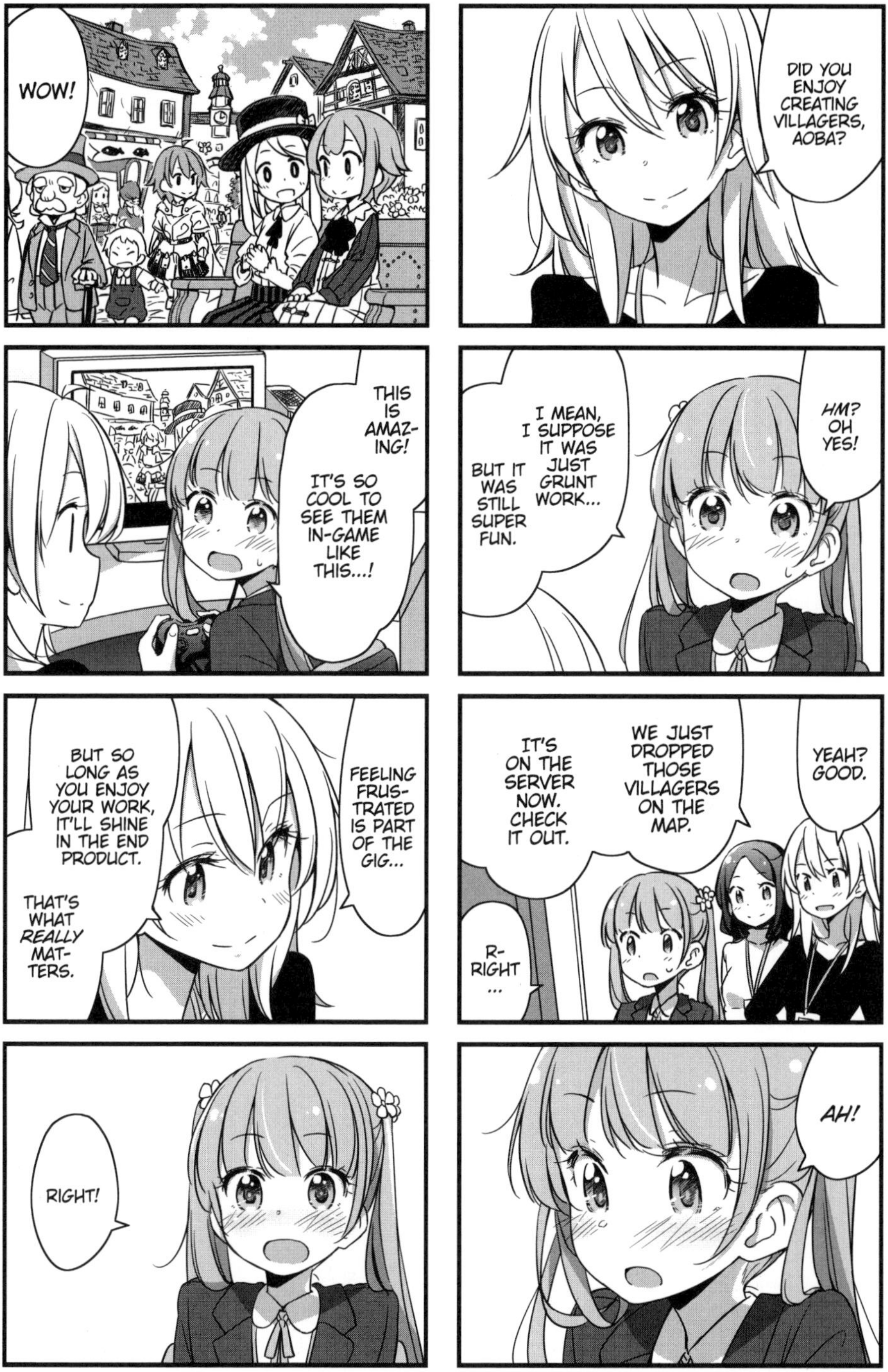
DID YOU ENJOY CREATING VILLAGERS, AOBA?
WOW!
HM? OH YES!
I MEAN, I SUPPOSE IT WAS JUST GRUNT WORK...
BUT IT WAS STILL SUPER FUN.
THIS IS AMAZING!
IT'S SO COOL TO SEE THEM IN-GAME LIKE THIS...!
YEAH? GOOD.
WE JUST DROPPED THOSE VILLAGERS ON THE MAP.
IT'S ON THE SERVER NOW. CHECK IT OUT.
R-RIGHT...
FEELING FRUSTRATED IS PART OF THE GIG...
BUT SO LONG AS YOU ENJOY YOUR WORK, IT'LL SHINE IN THE END PRODUCT.
THAT'S WHAT *REALLY* MATTERS.
AH!
RIGHT!

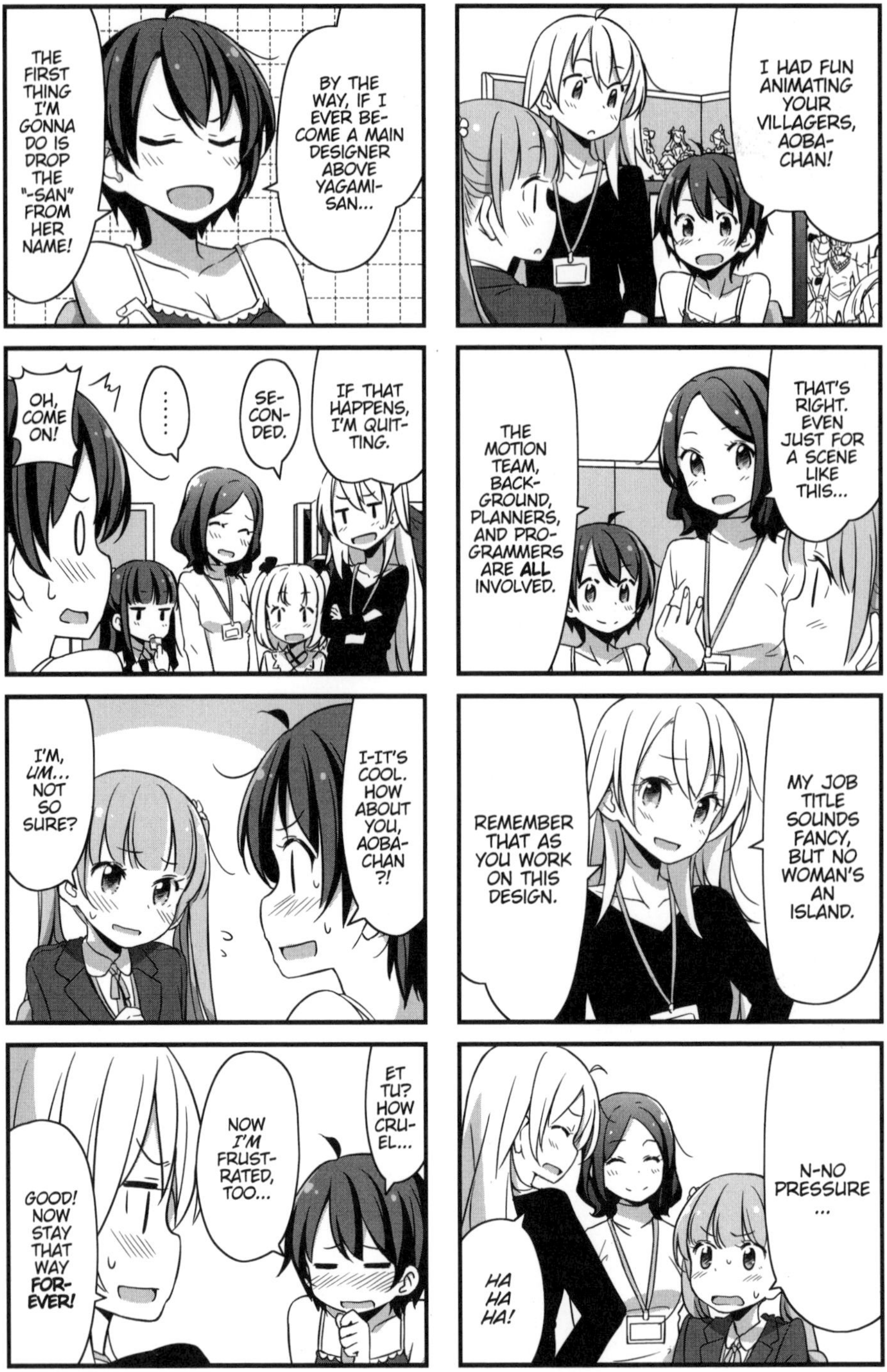
I HAD FUN ANIMATING YOUR VILLAGERS, AOBA-CHAN!
BY THE WAY, IF I EVER BE-COME A MAIN DESIGNER ABOVE YAGAMI-SAN...
THE FIRST THING I'M GONNA DO IS DROP THE "-SAN" FROM HER NAME!
THAT'S RIGHT. EVEN JUST FOR A SCENE LIKE THIS...
THE MOTION TEAM, BACK-GROUND, PLANNERS, AND PRO-GRAMMERS ARE **ALL** INVOLVED.
IF THAT HAPPENS, I'M QUIT-TING.
SE-CON-DED.
......
OH, COME ON!
MY JOB TITLE SOUNDS FANCY, BUT NO WOMAN'S AN ISLAND.
REMEMBER THAT AS YOU WORK ON THIS DESIGN.
I-IT'S COOL. HOW ABOUT YOU, AOBA-CHAN?!
I'M, *UM*... NOT SO SURE?
N-NO PRESSURE ...
HA HA HA!
ET TU? HOW CRU-EL...
NOW *I'M* FRUST-RATED, TOO...
GOOD! NOW STAY THAT WAY **FOR-EVER!**

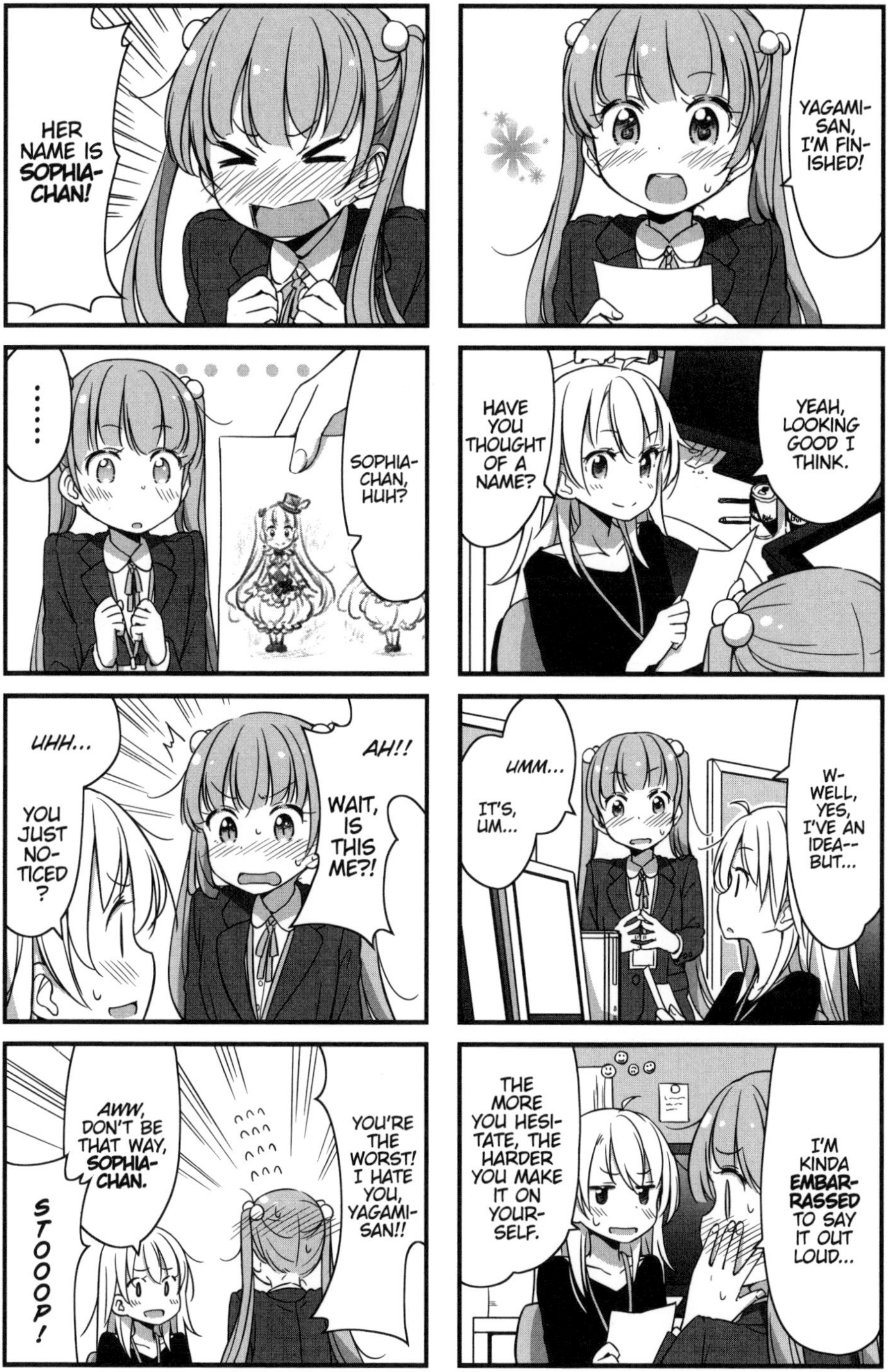
YAGAMI-SAN, I'M FINISHED!
HER NAME IS SOPHIA-CHAN!
YEAH, LOOKING GOOD I THINK.
HAVE YOU THOUGHT OF A NAME?
SOPHIA-CHAN, HUH?
......
W-WELL, YES, I'VE AN IDEA-- BUT...
UMM... IT'S, UM...
AH!! WAIT, IS THIS ME?!
UHH... YOU JUST NOTICED?
I'M KINDA EMBARRASSED TO SAY IT OUT LOUD...
THE MORE YOU HESITATE, THE HARDER YOU MAKE IT ON YOURSELF.
YOU'RE THE WORST! I HATE YOU, YAGAMI-SAN!!
AWW, DON'T BE THAT WAY, SOPHIA-CHAN.
STOOOP!

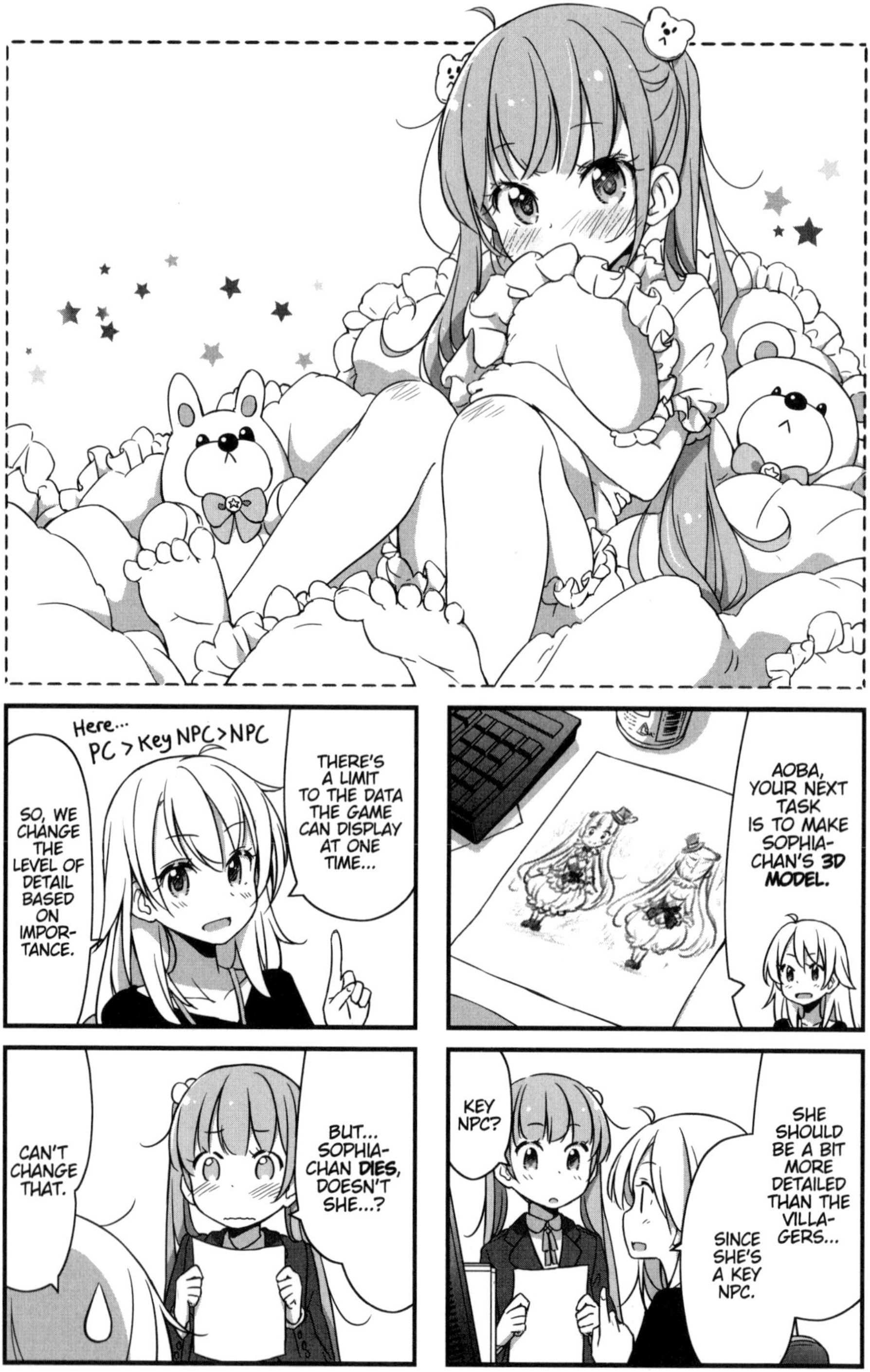
AOBA, YOUR NEXT TASK IS TO MAKE SOPHIA-CHAN'S **3D MODEL.**
THERE'S A LIMIT TO THE DATA THE GAME CAN DISPLAY AT ONE TIME...
Here... PC > Key NPC > NPC
SO, WE CHANGE THE LEVEL OF DETAIL BASED ON IMPOR-TANCE.
SHE SHOULD BE A BIT MORE DETAILED THAN THE VILLA-GERS...
KEY NPC?
SINCE SHE'S A KEY NPC.
BUT... SOPHIA-CHAN **DIES**, DOESN'T SHE...?
CAN'T CHANGE THAT.

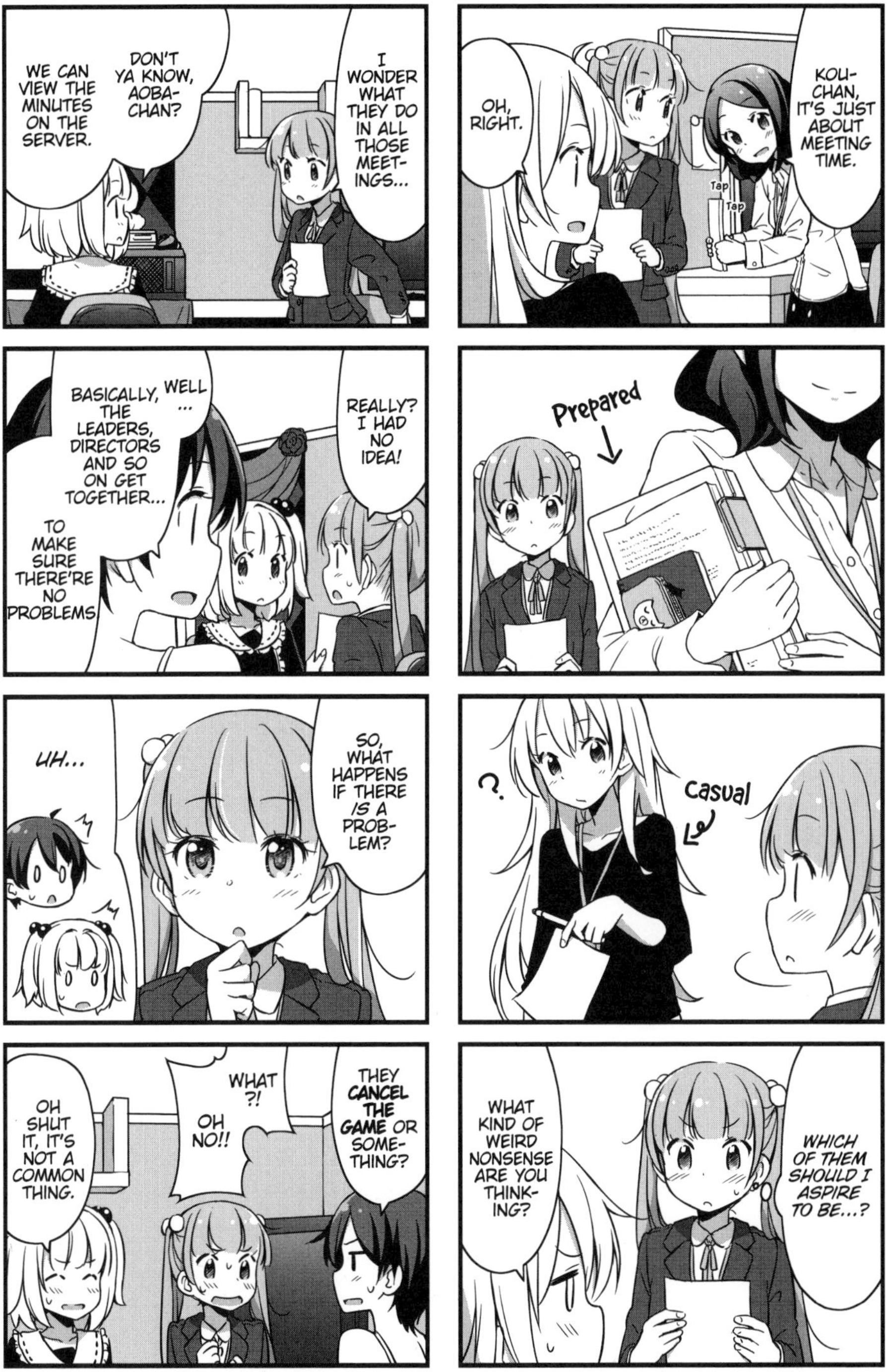
KOU-CHAN, IT'S JUST ABOUT MEETING TIME.
Tap Tap
OH, RIGHT.
Prepared
Casual
?
WHICH OF THEM SHOULD I ASPIRE TO BE...?
WHAT KIND OF WEIRD NONSENSE ARE YOU THINKING?
I WONDER WHAT THEY DO IN ALL THOSE MEETINGS...
DON'T YA KNOW, AOBA-CHAN?
WE CAN VIEW THE MINUTES ON THE SERVER.
REALLY? I HAD NO IDEA!
WELL...
BASICALLY, THE LEADERS, DIRECTORS AND SO ON GET TOGETHER...
TO MAKE SURE THERE'RE NO PROBLEMS.
SO, WHAT HAPPENS IF THERE IS A PROBLEM?
UH...
THEY CANCEL THE GAME OR SOMETHING?
WHAT?!
OH NO!!
OH SHUT IT, IT'S NOT A COMMON THING.

※ It is.

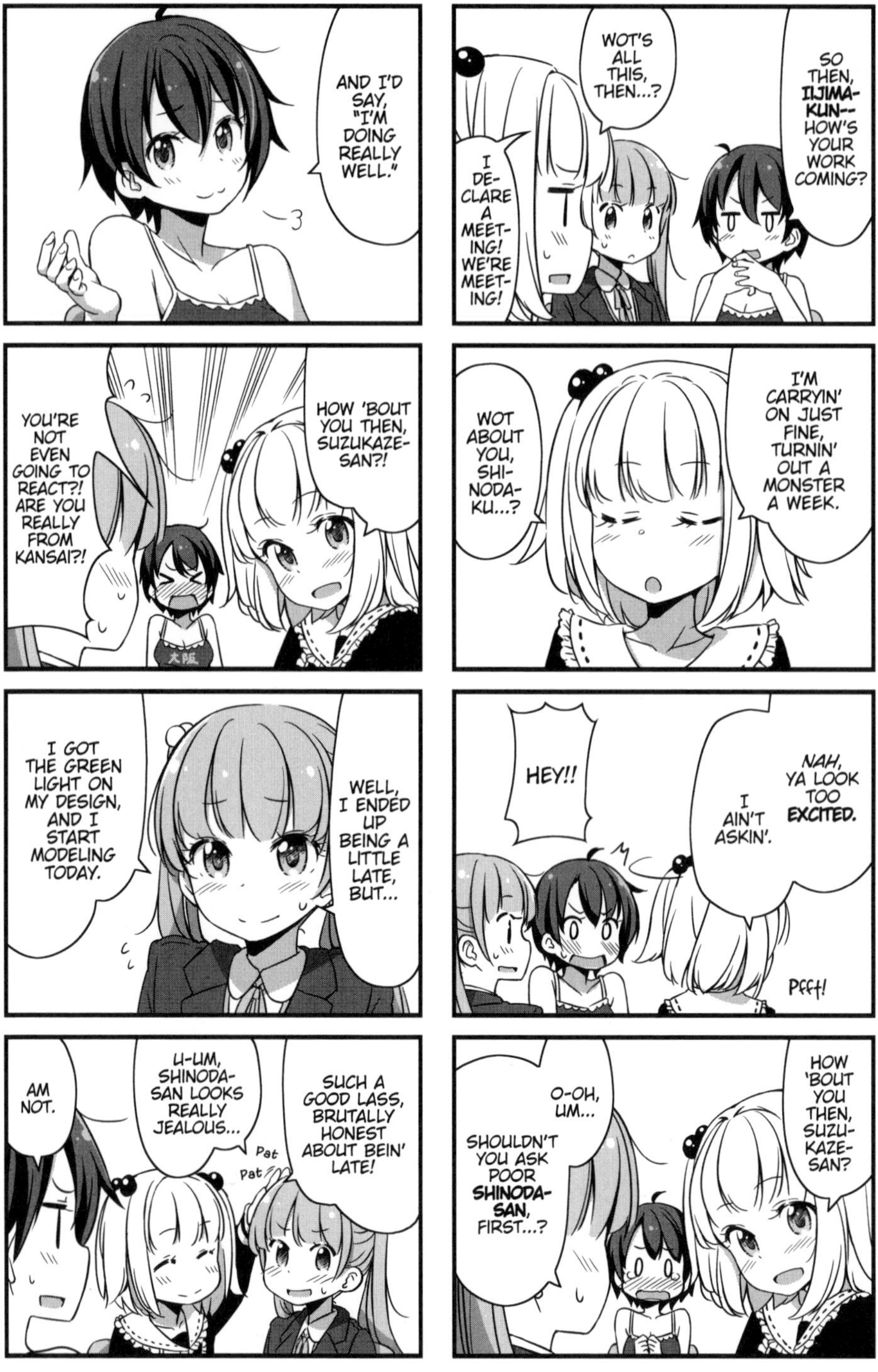
SO THEN, IIJIMA-KUN-- HOW'S YOUR WORK COMING?
WOT'S ALL THIS, THEN...?
I DE-CLARE A MEET-ING! WE'RE MEET-ING!
AND I'D SAY, "I'M DOING REALLY WELL."
I'M CARRYIN' ON JUST FINE, TURNIN' OUT A MONSTER A WEEK.
WOT ABOUT YOU, SHI-NODA-KU...?
HOW 'BOUT YOU THEN, SUZUKAZE-SAN?!
YOU'RE NOT EVEN GOING TO REACT?! ARE YOU REALLY FROM KANSAI?!
NAH, YA LOOK TOO **EXCITED.**
I AIN'T ASKIN'.
HEY!!
Pfft!
WELL, I ENDED UP BEING A LITTLE LATE, BUT...
I GOT THE GREEN LIGHT ON MY DESIGN, AND I START MODELING TODAY.
HOW 'BOUT YOU THEN, SUZU-KAZE-SAN?
O-OH, UM...
SHOULDN'T YOU ASK POOR **SHINODA-SAN**, FIRST...?
SUCH A GOOD LASS, BRUTALLY HONEST ABOUT BEIN' LATE!
U-UM, SHINODA-SAN LOOKS REALLY JEALOUS...
Pat
Pat
AM NOT.

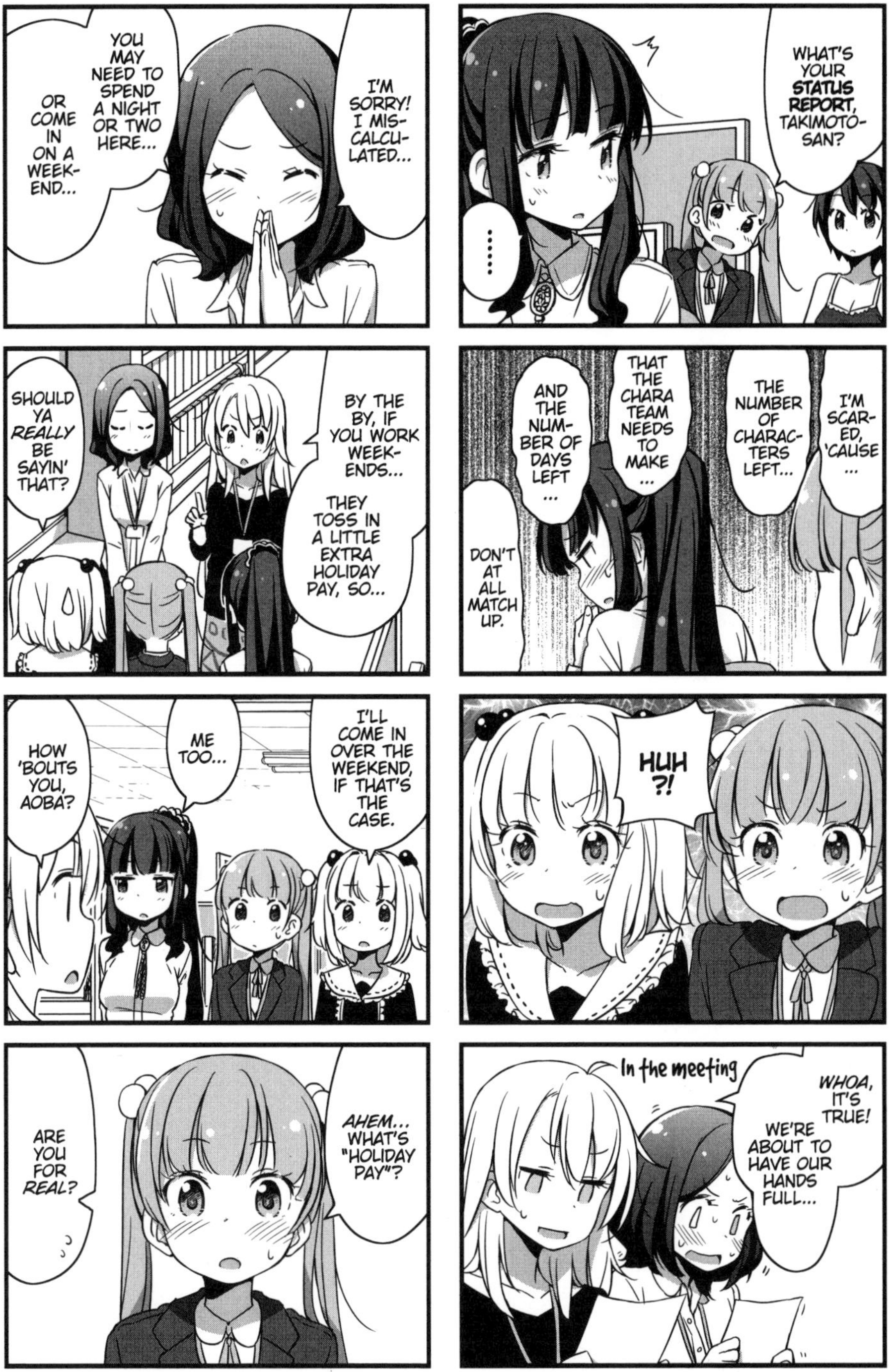

WHAT'S YOUR STATUS REPORT, TAKIMOTO-SAN?
......
I'M SCARED, 'CAUSE...
THE NUMBER OF CHARACTERS LEFT...
THAT THE CHARA TEAM NEEDS TO MAKE...
AND THE NUMBER OF DAYS LEFT...
DON'T AT ALL MATCH UP.
HUH ?!
In the meeting
WHOA, IT'S TRUE!
WE'RE ABOUT TO HAVE OUR HANDS FULL...
I'M SORRY! I MIS-CALCULATED...
YOU MAY NEED TO SPEND A NIGHT OR TWO HERE...
OR COME IN ON A WEEK-END...
BY THE BY, IF YOU WORK WEEK-ENDS...
THEY TOSS IN A LITTLE EXTRA HOLIDAY PAY, SO...
SHOULD YA REALLY BE SAYIN' THAT?
I'LL COME IN OVER THE WEEKEND, IF THAT'S THE CASE.
ME TOO...
HOW 'BOUTS YOU, AOBA?
AHEM... WHAT'S "HOLIDAY PAY"?
ARE YOU FOR REAL?

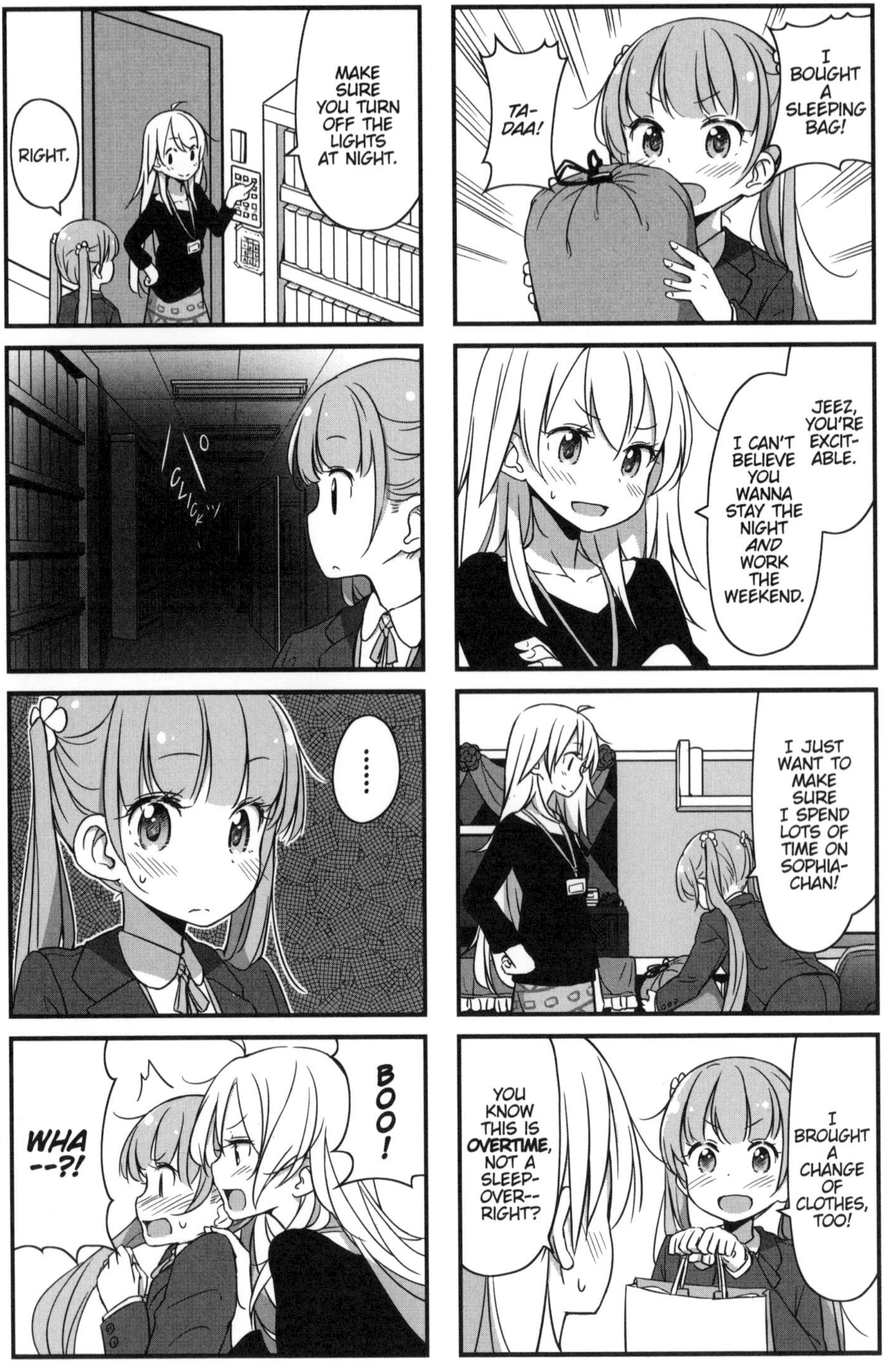
I BOUGHT A SLEEPING BAG!
TA-DAA!
JEEZ, YOU'RE EXCIT-ABLE.
I CAN'T BELIEVE YOU WANNA STAY THE NIGHT *AND* WORK THE WEEKEND.
I JUST WANT TO MAKE SURE I SPEND LOTS OF TIME ON SOPHIA-CHAN!
I BROUGHT A CHANGE OF CLOTHES, TOO!
YOU KNOW THIS IS **OVERTIME**, NOT A SLEEP-OVER--RIGHT?
MAKE SURE YOU TURN OFF THE LIGHTS AT NIGHT.
RIGHT.
CLICK
......
BOO!
WHA--?!

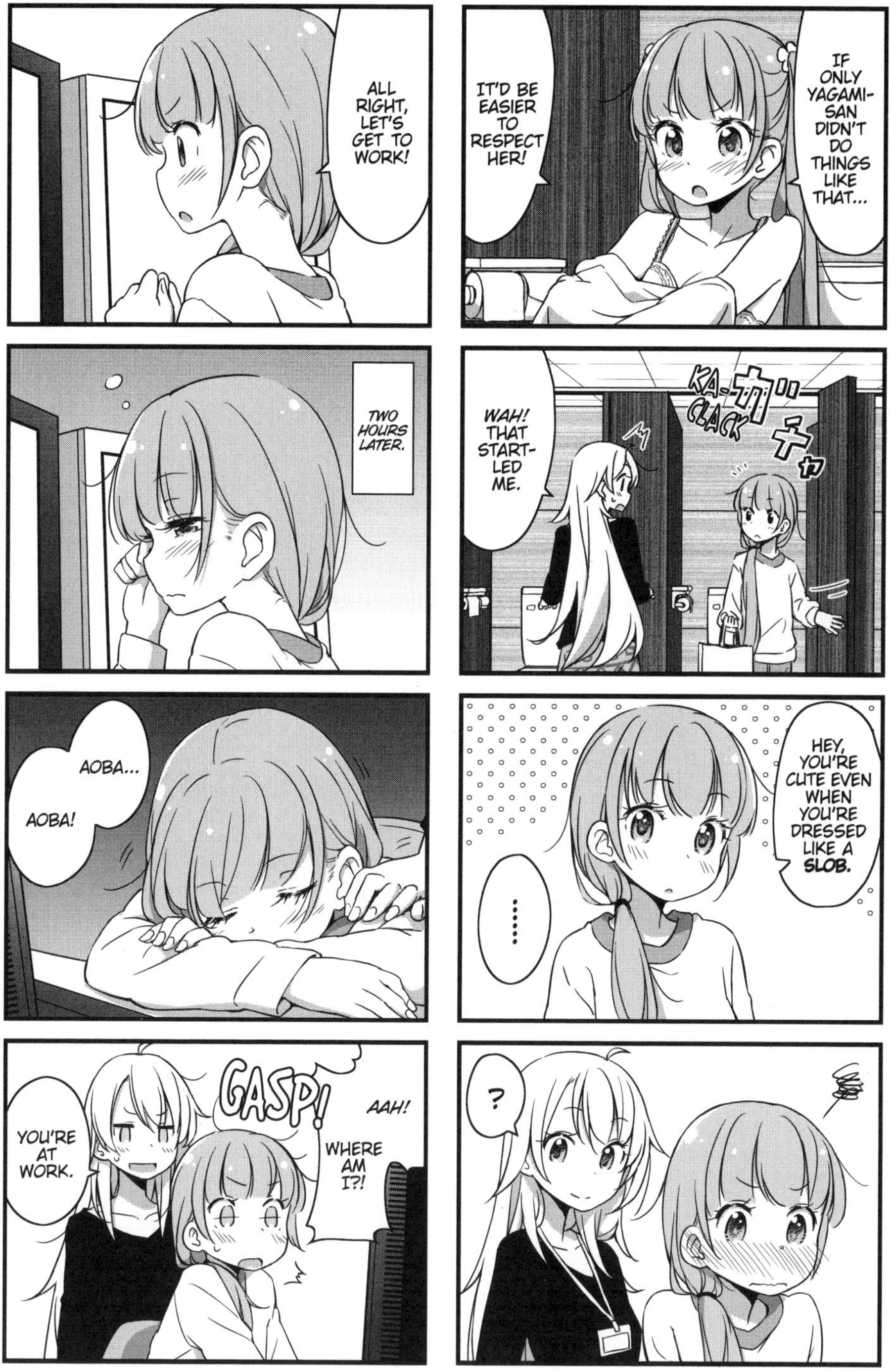
IF ONLY YAGAMI-SAN DIDN'T DO THINGS LIKE THAT...
IT'D BE EASIER TO RESPECT HER!
ALL RIGHT, LET'S GET TO WORK!
KA-CLACK
WAH! THAT START-LED ME.
TWO HOURS LATER.
HEY, YOU'RE CUTE EVEN WHEN YOU'RE DRESSED LIKE A **SLOB.**
......
AOBA...
AOBA!
?
GASP!
AAH!
WHERE AM I?!
YOU'RE AT WORK.

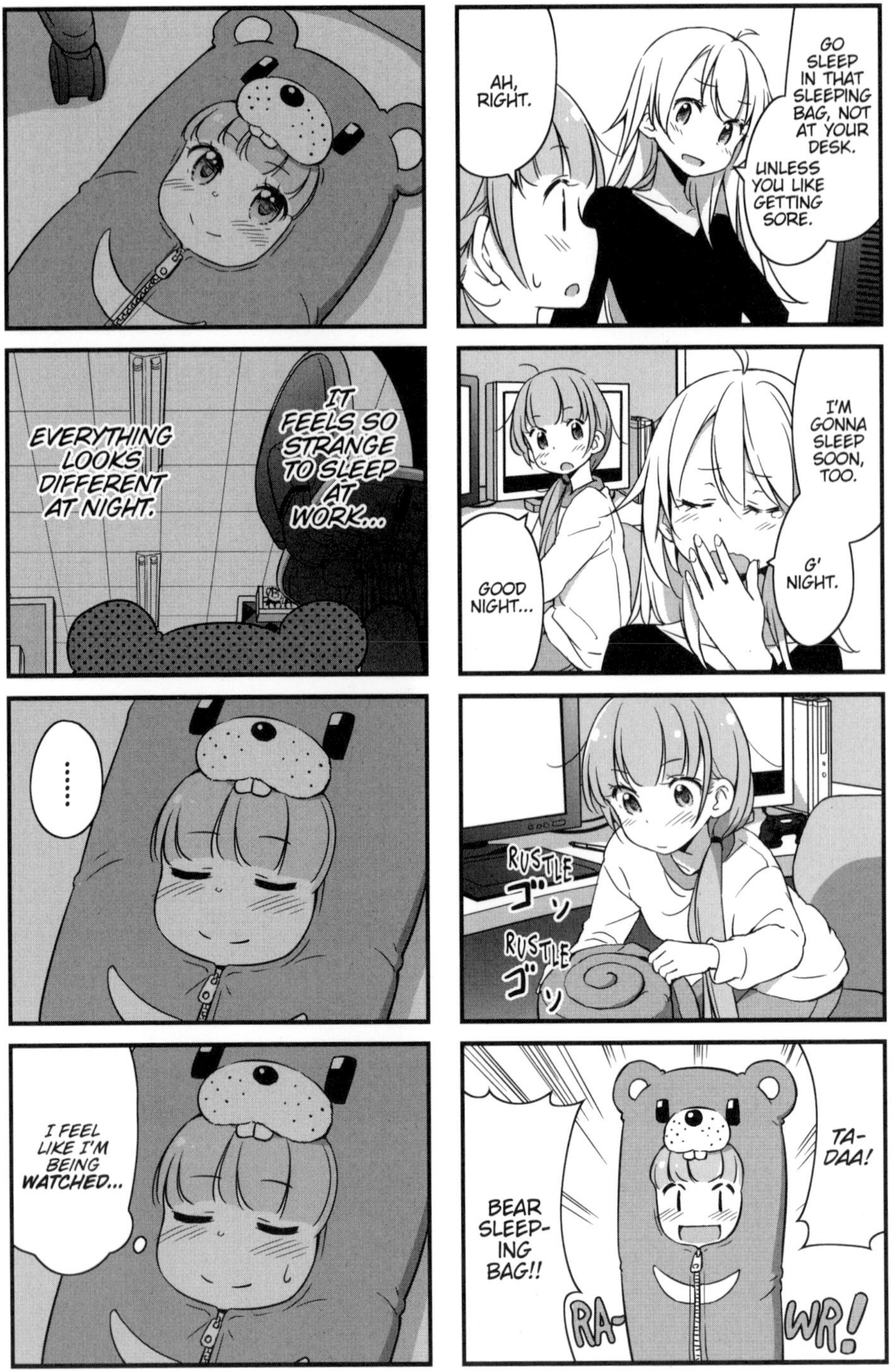
GO SLEEP IN THAT SLEEPING BAG, NOT AT YOUR DESK.
UNLESS YOU LIKE GETTING SORE.
AH, RIGHT.
I'M GONNA SLEEP SOON, TOO.
G' NIGHT.
GOOD NIGHT...
RUSTLE ゴソ
RUSTLE ゴソ
TA-DAA!
BEAR SLEEPING-BAG!!
RA-WR!
IT FEELS SO STRANGE TO SLEEP AT WORK...
EVERYTHING LOOKS DIFFERENT AT NIGHT.
......
I FEEL LIKE I'M BEING WATCHED...

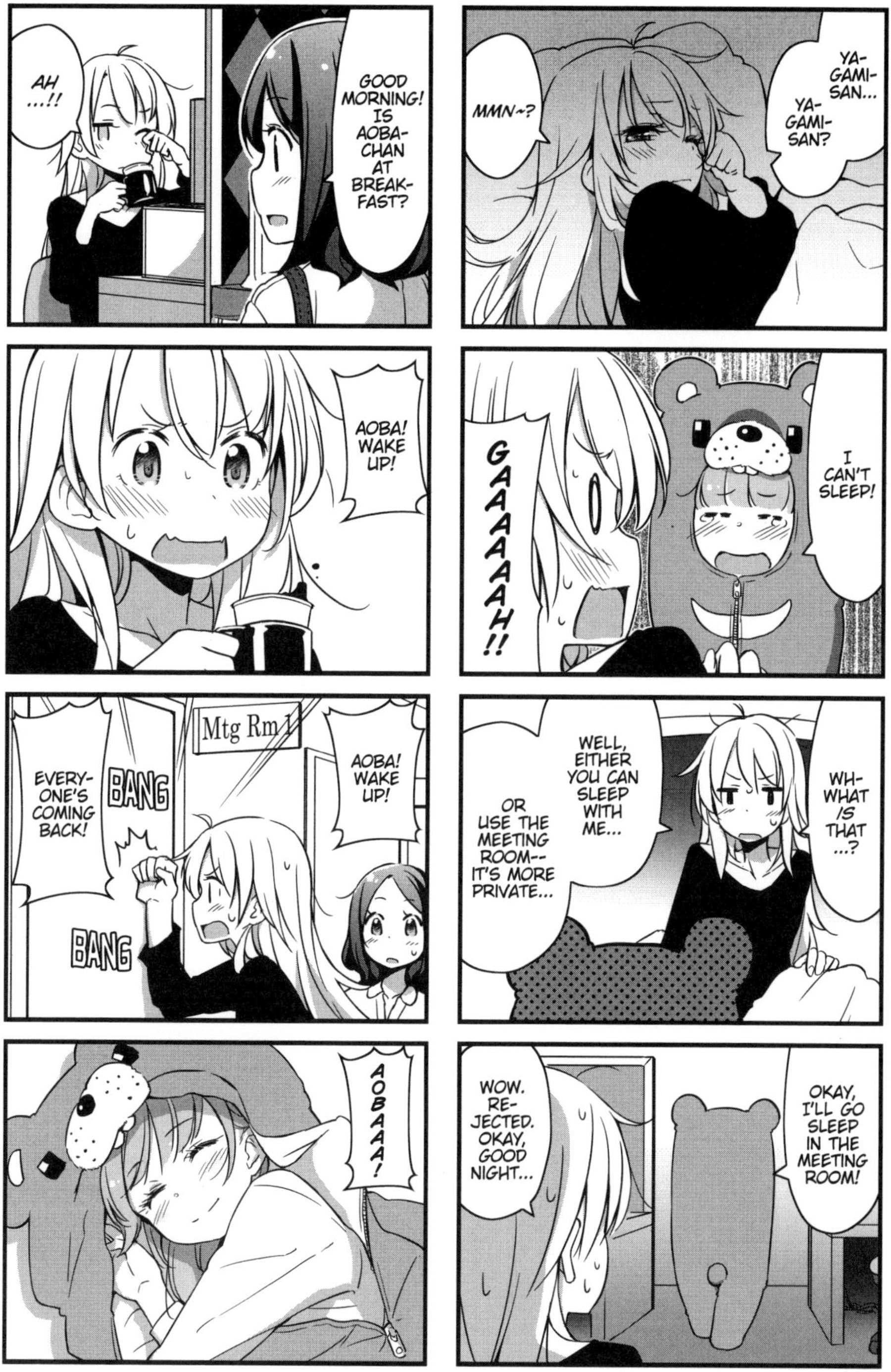
YA-GAMI-SAN...
YA-GAMI-SAN?
MMN~?
I CAN'T SLEEP!
GAAAAAAAH!!
WH-WHAT IS THAT...?
WELL, EITHER YOU CAN SLEEP WITH ME...
OR USE THE MEETING ROOM--IT'S MORE PRIVATE...
OKAY, I'LL GO SLEEP IN THE MEETING ROOM!
WOW. RE-JECTED. OKAY, GOOD NIGHT...
GOOD MORNING! IS AOBA-CHAN AT BREAK-FAST?
AH ...!!
AOBA! WAKE UP!
Mtg Rm 1
AOBA! WAKE UP!
BANG
EVERY-ONE'S COMING BACK!
BANG
AOBAAAA!

NEW GAME!

NEW GAME!

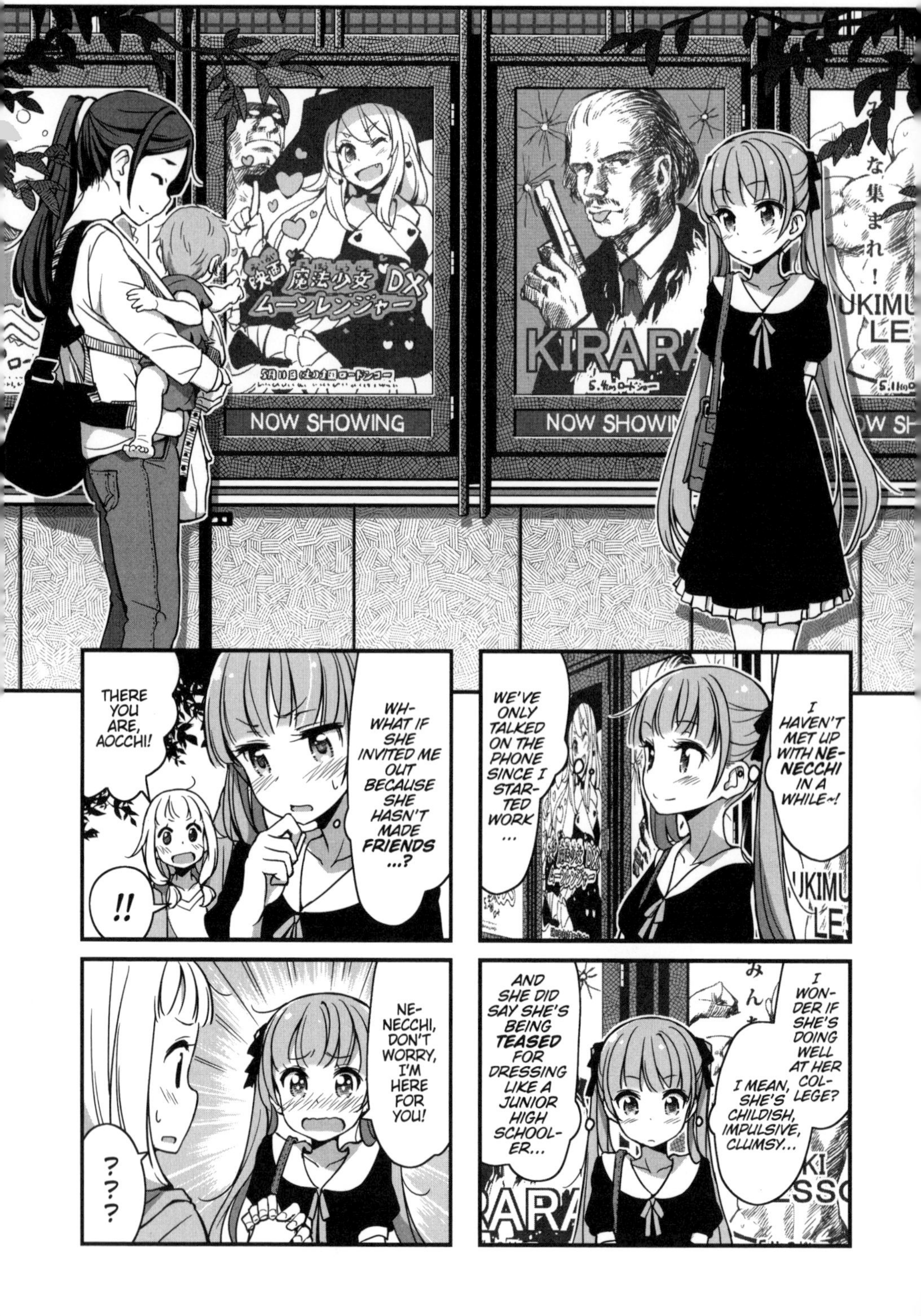
映画 魔法少女DX ムーンレンジャー
NOW SHOWING
KIRARA
NOW SHOWIN
みんな集まれ！
UKIMU
LE
I HAVEN'T MET UP WITH NENECCHI IN A WHILE~!
WE'VE ONLY TALKED ON THE PHONE SINCE I STARTED WORK...
WH-WHAT IF SHE INVITED ME OUT BECAUSE SHE HASN'T MADE FRIENDS...?
THERE YOU ARE, AOCCHI!
!!
I WONDER IF SHE'S DOING WELL AT HER COLLEGE?
I MEAN, SHE'S CHILDISH, IMPULSIVE, CLUMSY...
AND SHE DID SAY SHE'S BEING TEASED FOR DRESSING LIKE A JUNIOR HIGH SCHOOLER...
NENECCHI, DON'T WORRY, I'M HERE FOR YOU!
?-?-?

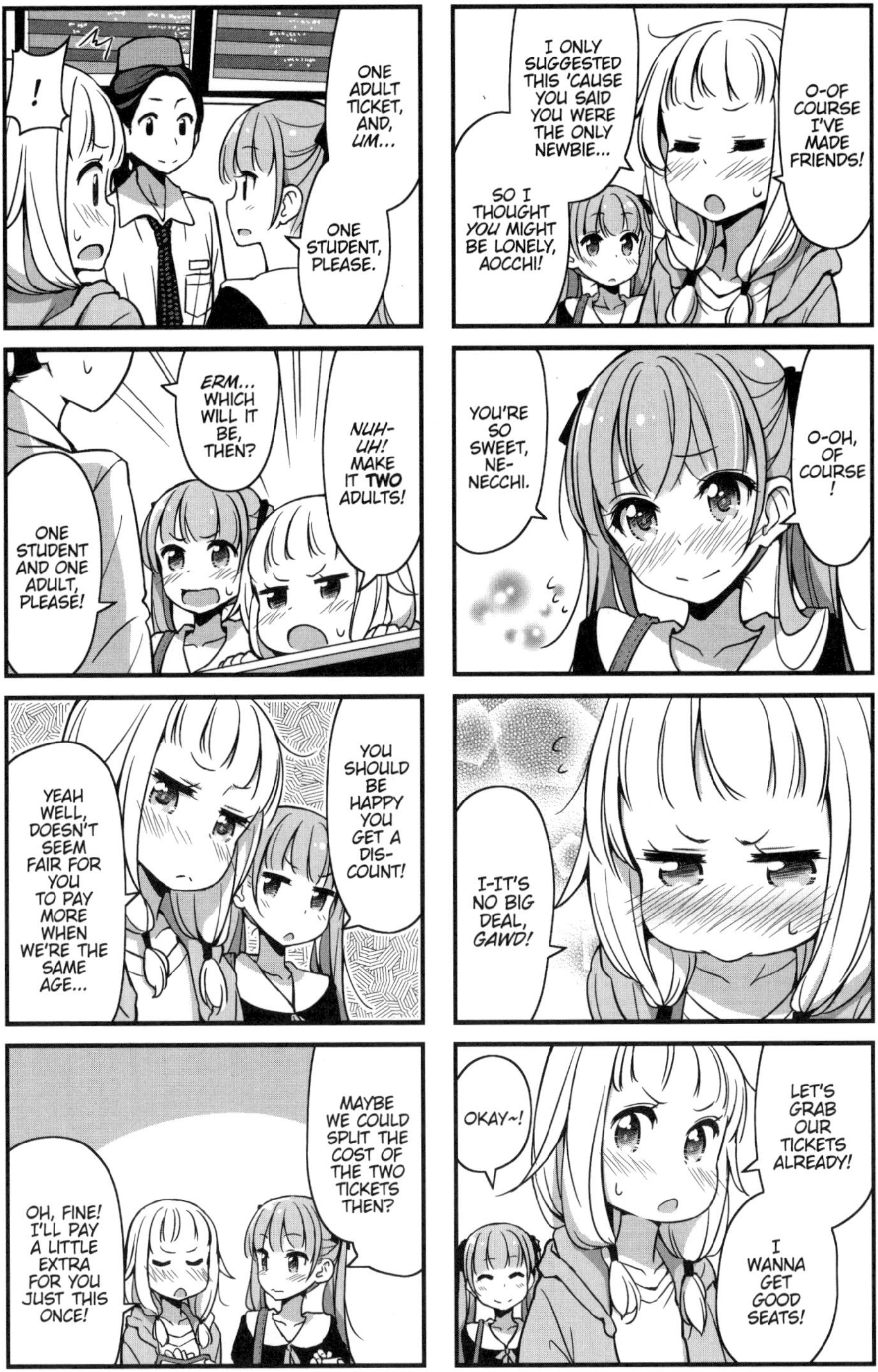
O-OF COURSE I'VE MADE FRIENDS!
I ONLY SUGGESTED THIS 'CAUSE YOU SAID YOU WERE THE ONLY NEWBIE...
SO I THOUGHT *YOU* MIGHT BE LONELY, AOCCHI!
O-OH, OF COURSE!
YOU'RE SO SWEET, NE-NECCHI.
I-IT'S NO BIG DEAL, *GAWD!*
LET'S GRAB OUR TICKETS ALREADY!
OKAY~!
I WANNA GET GOOD SEATS!
ONE ADULT TICKET, AND, *UM...*
ONE STUDENT, PLEASE.
NUH-UH! MAKE IT **TWO** ADULTS!
ERM... WHICH WILL IT BE, THEN?
ONE STUDENT AND ONE ADULT, PLEASE!
YOU SHOULD BE HAPPY YOU GET A DISCOUNT!
YEAH WELL, DOESN'T SEEM FAIR FOR YOU TO PAY MORE WHEN WE'RE THE SAME AGE...
MAYBE WE COULD SPLIT THE COST OF THE TWO TICKETS THEN?
OH, FINE! I'LL PAY A LITTLE EXTRA FOR YOU JUST THIS ONCE!

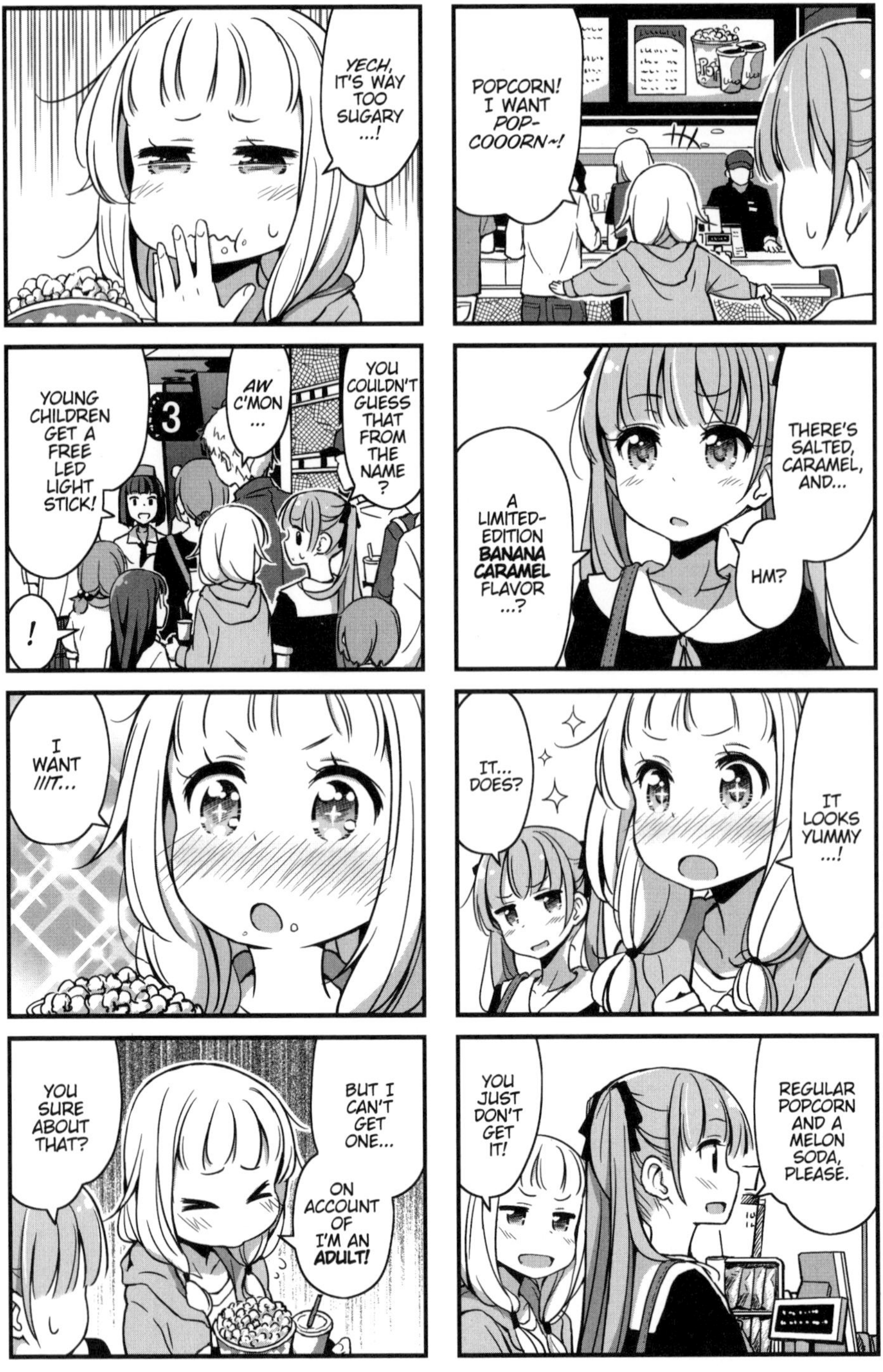
POPCORN! I WANT POP-COOORN~!
YECH, IT'S WAY TOO SUGARY ...!
THERE'S SALTED, CARAMEL, AND...
HM?
A LIMITED-EDITION BANANA CARAMEL FLAVOR ...?
YOU COULDN'T GUESS THAT FROM THE NAME?
AW C'MON ...
YOUNG CHILDREN GET A FREE LED LIGHT STICK!
!
IT LOOKS YUMMY ...!
IT... DOES?
I WANT IIIT...
REGULAR POPCORN AND A MELON SODA, PLEASE.
YOU JUST DON'T GET IT!
BUT I CAN'T GET ONE...
ON ACCOUNT OF I'M AN ADULT!
YOU SURE ABOUT THAT?

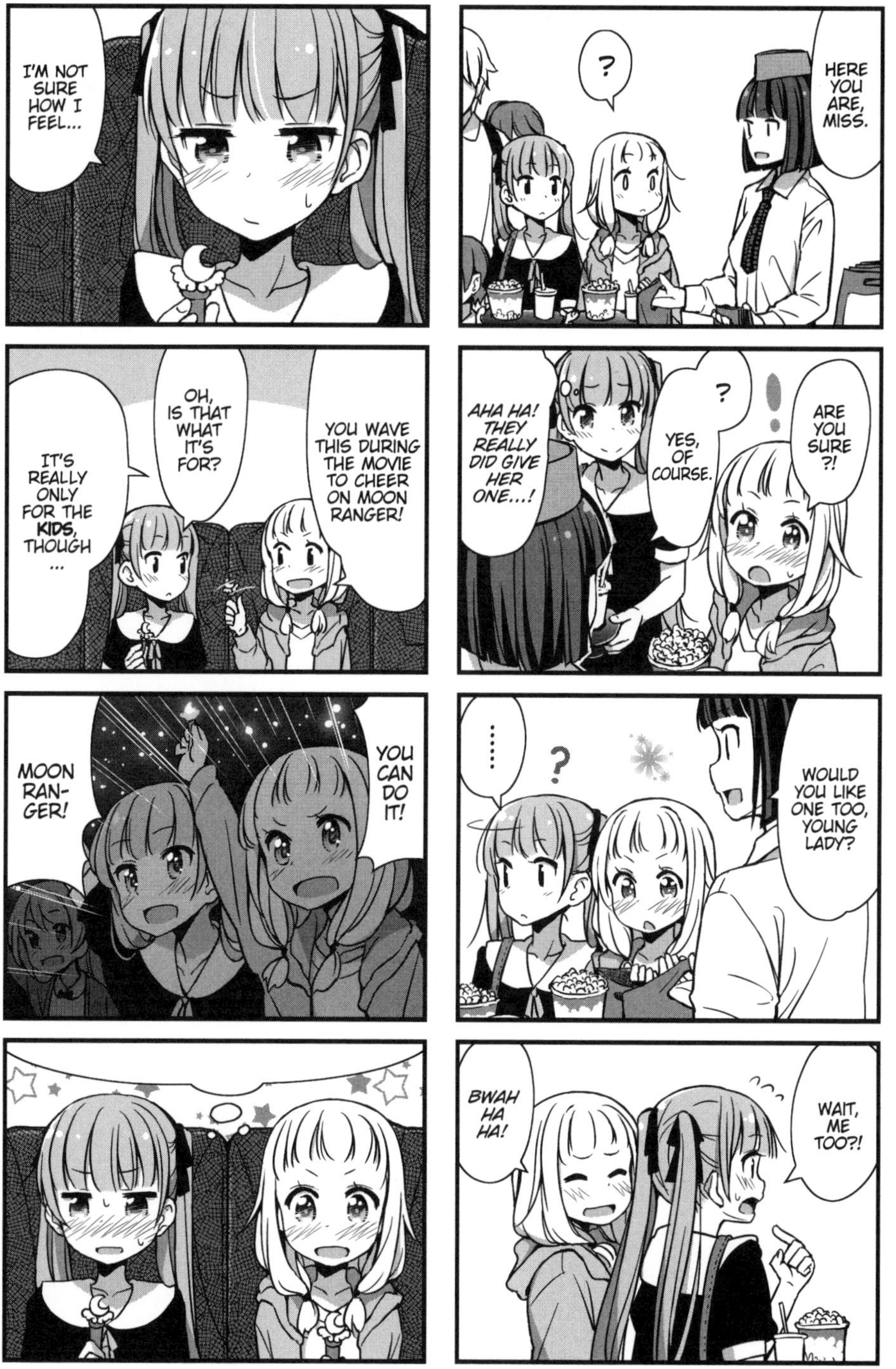
HERE YOU ARE, MISS.
?
ARE YOU SURE?!
YES, OF COURSE.
?
AHA HA! THEY REALLY DID GIVE HER ONE...!
WOULD YOU LIKE ONE TOO, YOUNG LADY?
......
WAIT, ME TOO?!
BWAH HA HA!
I'M NOT SURE HOW I FEEL...
YOU WAVE THIS DURING THE MOVIE TO CHEER ON MOON RANGER!
OH, IS THAT WHAT IT'S FOR?
IT'S REALLY ONLY FOR THE **KIDS**, THOUGH ...
YOU CAN DO IT!
MOON RAN-GER!

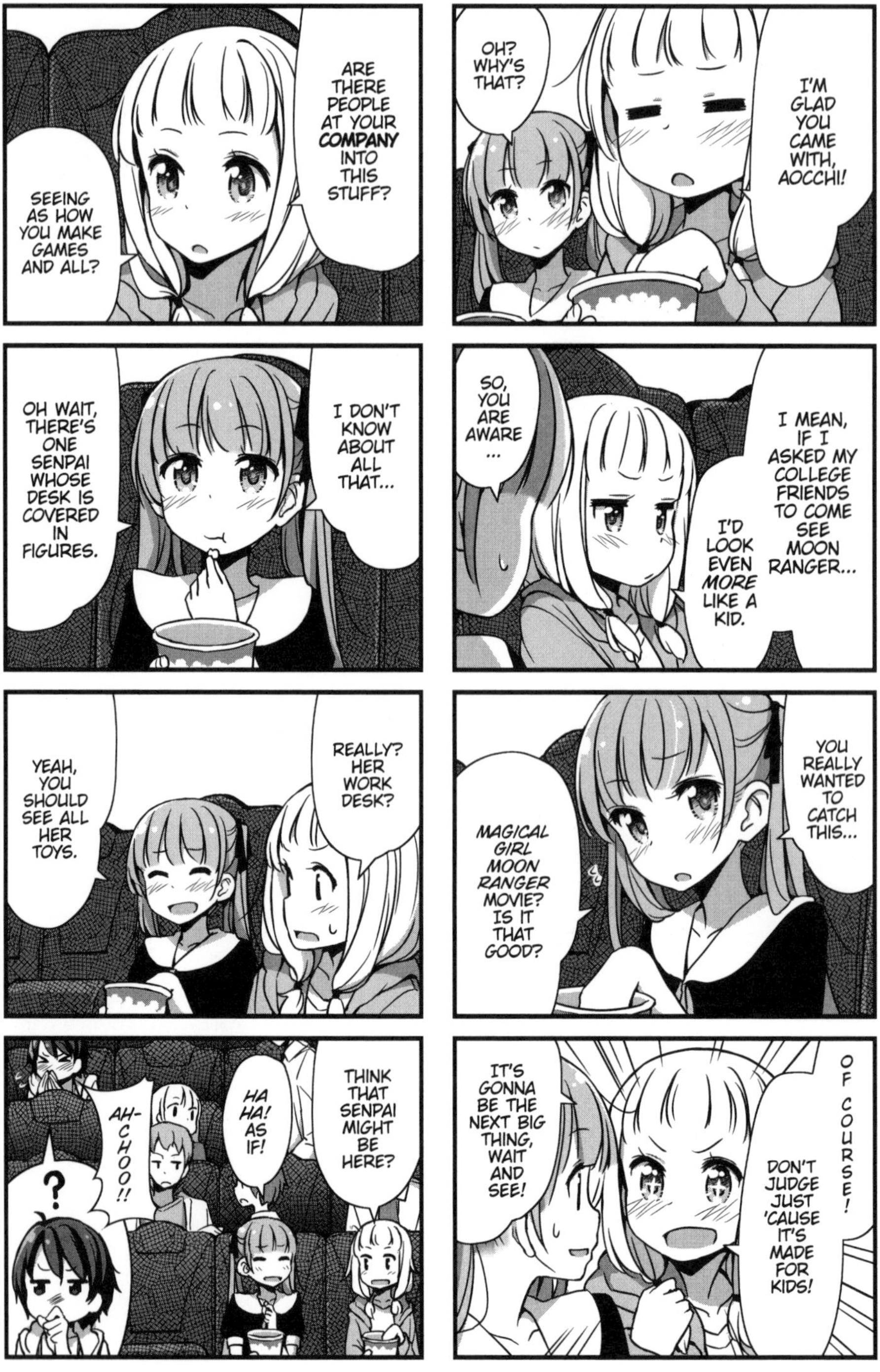
I'M GLAD YOU CAME WITH, AOCCHI!
OH? WHY'S THAT?
ARE THERE PEOPLE AT YOUR **COMPANY** INTO THIS STUFF?
SEEING AS HOW YOU MAKE GAMES AND ALL?
I MEAN, IF I ASKED MY COLLEGE FRIENDS TO COME SEE MOON RANGER...
I'D LOOK EVEN *MORE* LIKE A KID.
SO, YOU ARE AWARE...
I DON'T KNOW ABOUT ALL THAT...
OH WAIT, THERE'S ONE SENPAI WHOSE DESK IS COVERED IN FIGURES.
YOU REALLY WANTED TO CATCH THIS...
MAGICAL GIRL MOON RANGER MOVIE? IS IT THAT GOOD?
REALLY? HER WORK DESK?
YEAH, YOU SHOULD SEE ALL HER TOYS.
OF COURSE!
DON'T JUDGE JUST 'CAUSE IT'S MADE FOR KIDS!
IT'S GONNA BE THE NEXT BIG THING, WAIT AND SEE!
THINK THAT SENPAI MIGHT BE HERE?
HA HA! AS IF!
AH-CHOOO!!
?

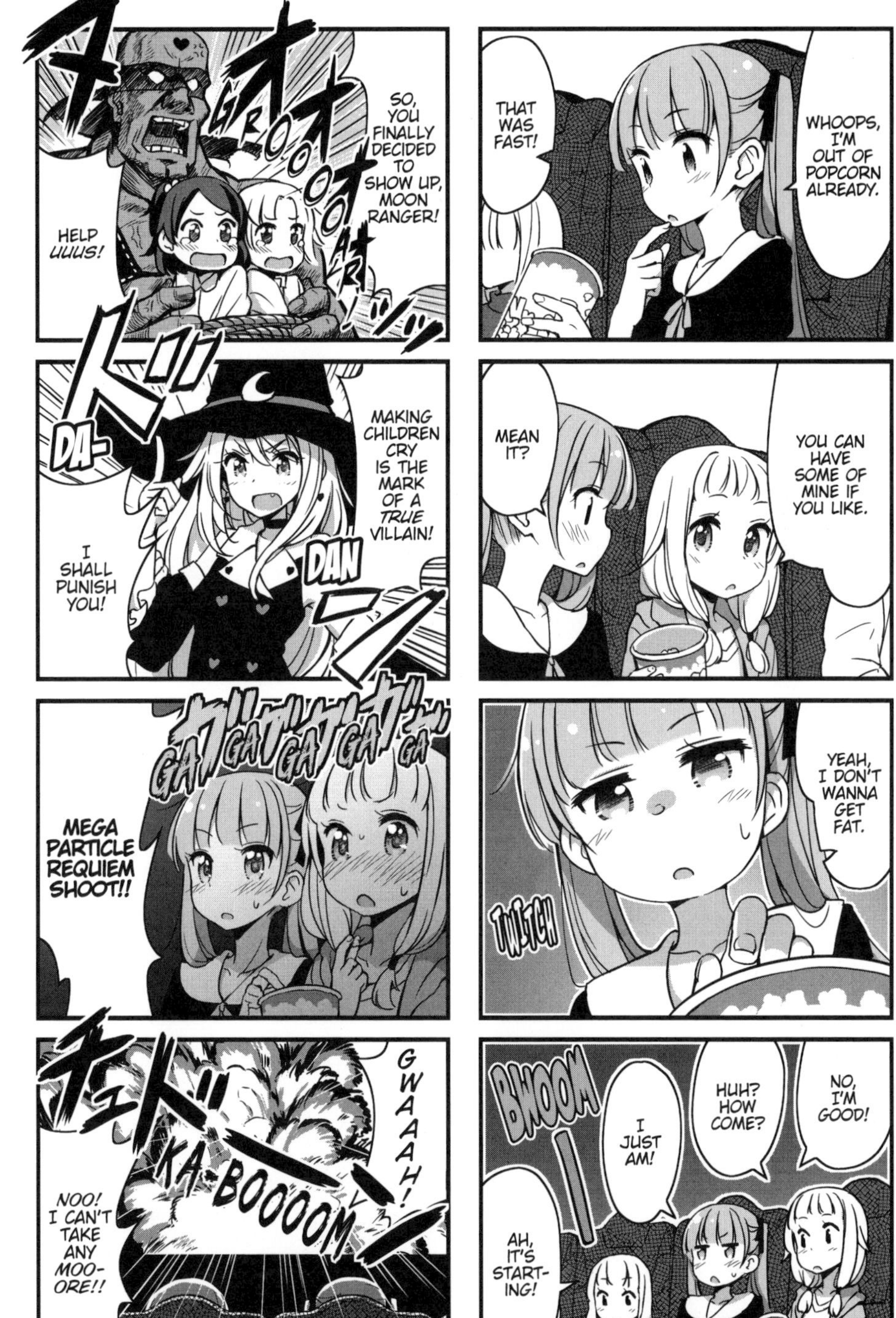

WHOOPS, I'M OUT OF POPCORN ALREADY.
THAT WAS FAST!
YOU CAN HAVE SOME OF MINE IF YOU LIKE.
MEAN IT?
YEAH, I DON'T WANNA GET FAT.
TWITCH
NO, I'M GOOD!
HUH? HOW COME?
I JUST AM!
BWOOM
AH, IT'S START-ING!
SO, YOU FINALLY DECIDED TO SHOW UP, MOON RANGER!
GROOOOOOAR!
HELP UUUS!
MAKING CHILDREN CRY IS THE MARK OF A TRUE VILLAIN!
DA-
I SHALL PUNISH YOU!
DAN
GA GA GA GA GA
MEGA PARTICLE REQUIEM SHOOT!!
GWAAAAH!
KA-BOOOOM
NOO! I CAN'T TAKE ANY MOOO-ORE!!

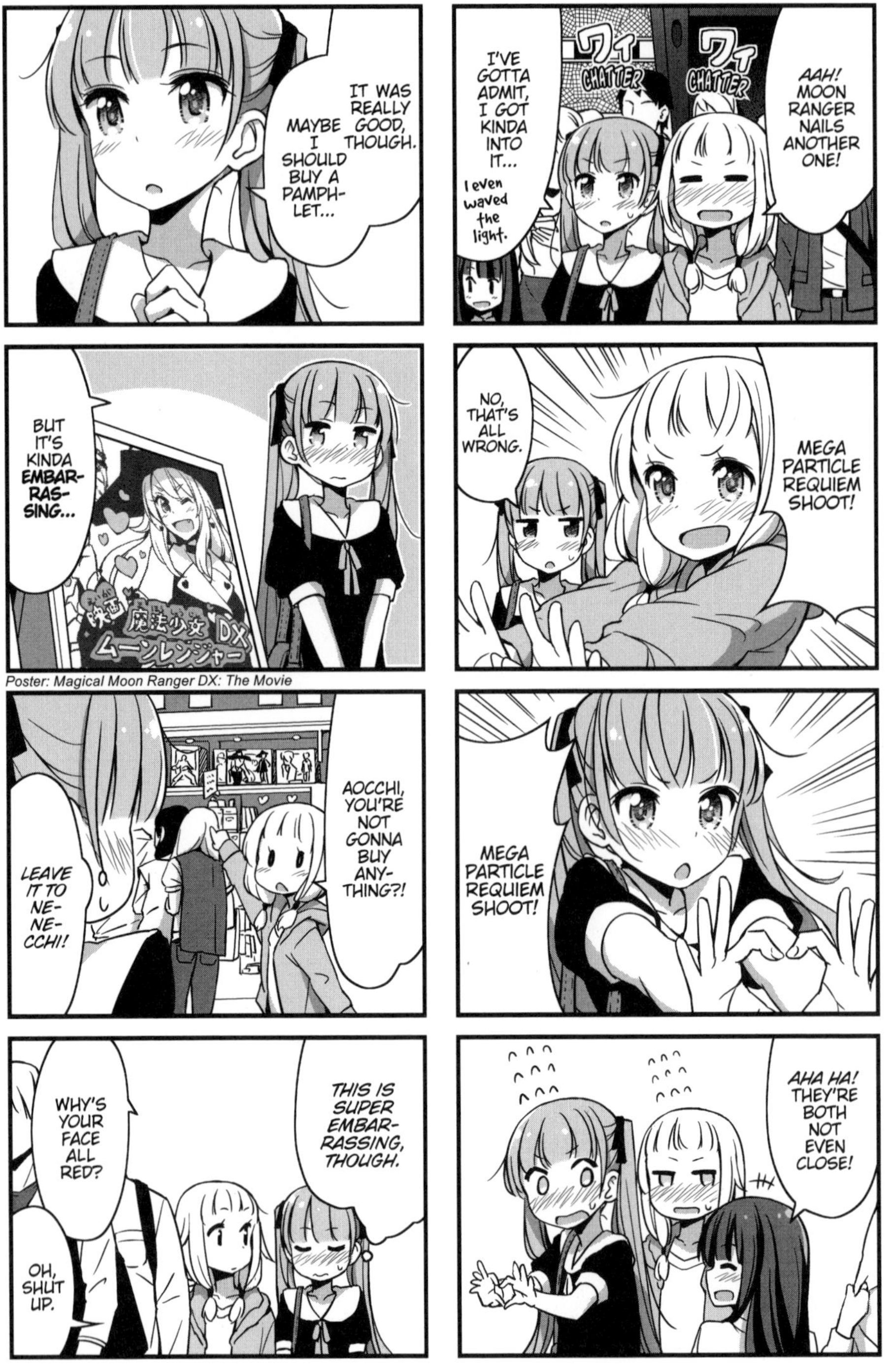
AAH! MOON RANGER NAILS ANOTHER ONE!
ワイ CHATTER
ワイ CHATTER
I'VE GOTTA ADMIT, I GOT KINDA INTO IT...
I even waved the light.
MEGA PARTICLE REQUIEM SHOOT!
NO, THAT'S ALL WRONG.
MEGA PARTICLE REQUIEM SHOOT!
AHA HA! THEY'RE BOTH NOT EVEN CLOSE!
IT WAS REALLY GOOD, THOUGH.
MAYBE I SHOULD BUY A PAMPHLET...
BUT IT'S KINDA EMBARRASSING...
映画 魔法少女DX ムーンレンジャー
AOCCHI, YOU'RE NOT GONNA BUY ANYTHING?!
LEAVE IT TO NENECCHI!
THIS IS SUPER EMBARRASSING, THOUGH.
WHY'S YOUR FACE ALL RED?
OH, SHUT UP.
Poster: Magical Moon Ranger DX: The Movie

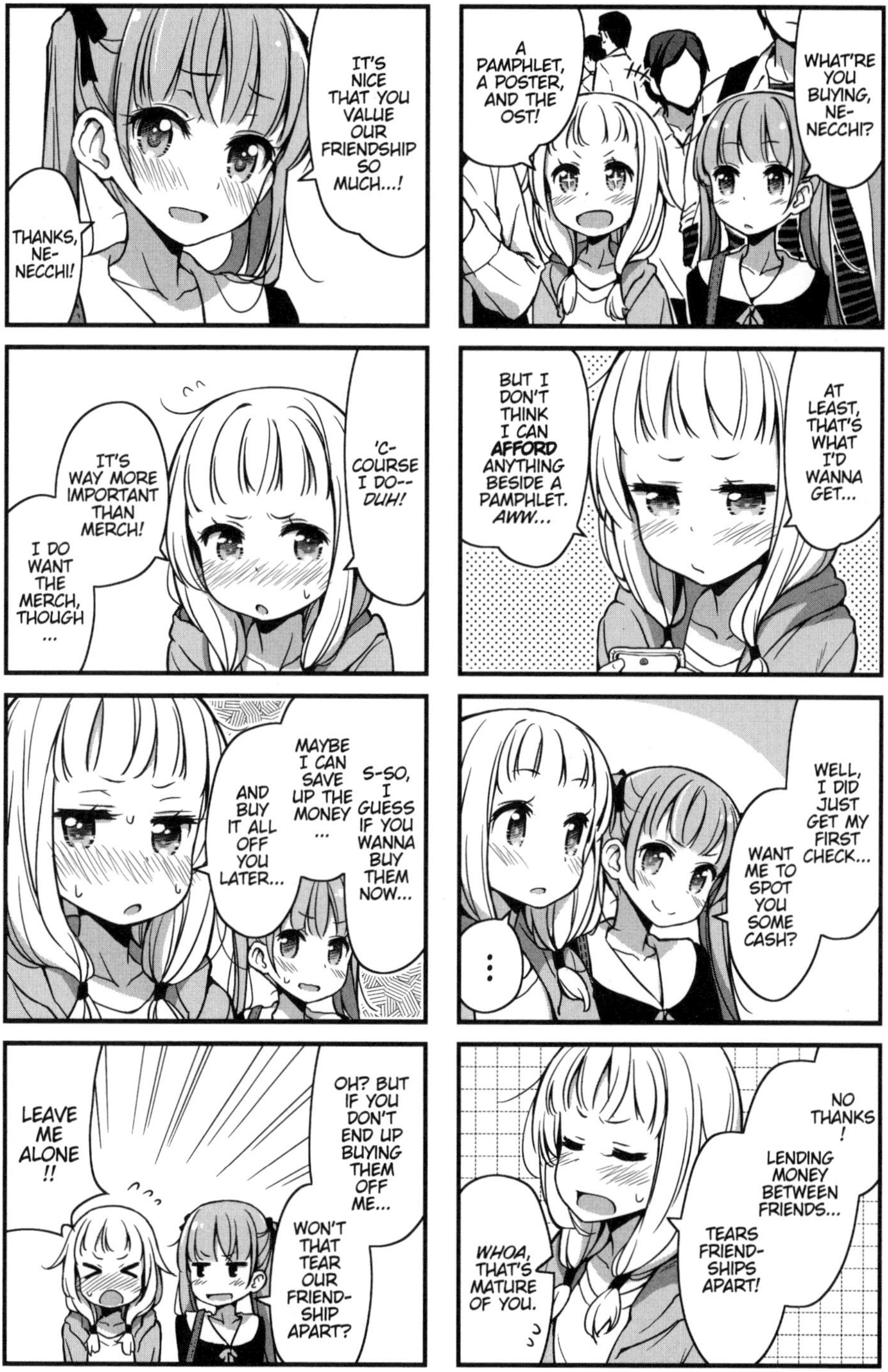
WHAT'RE YOU BUYING, NE-NECCHI?
A PAMPHLET, A POSTER, AND THE OST!
IT'S NICE THAT YOU VALUE OUR FRIENDSHIP SO MUCH...!
THANKS, NE-NECCHI!
AT LEAST, THAT'S WHAT I'D WANNA GET...
BUT I DON'T THINK I CAN **AFFORD** ANYTHING BESIDE A PAMPHLET. *AWW...*
'C-COURSE I DO--*DUH!*
IT'S WAY MORE IMPORTANT THAN MERCH!
I DO WANT THE MERCH, THOUGH...
WELL, I DID JUST GET MY FIRST CHECK...
WANT ME TO SPOT YOU SOME CASH?
...
S-SO, I GUESS IF YOU WANNA BUY THEM NOW...
MAYBE I CAN SAVE UP THE MONEY...
AND BUY IT ALL OFF YOU LATER...
NO THANKS!
LENDING MONEY BETWEEN FRIENDS...
TEARS FRIENDSHIPS APART!
WHOA, THAT'S MATURE OF YOU.
OH? BUT IF YOU DON'T END UP BUYING THEM OFF ME...
WON'T THAT TEAR OUR FRIENDSHIP APART?
LEAVE ME ALONE!!

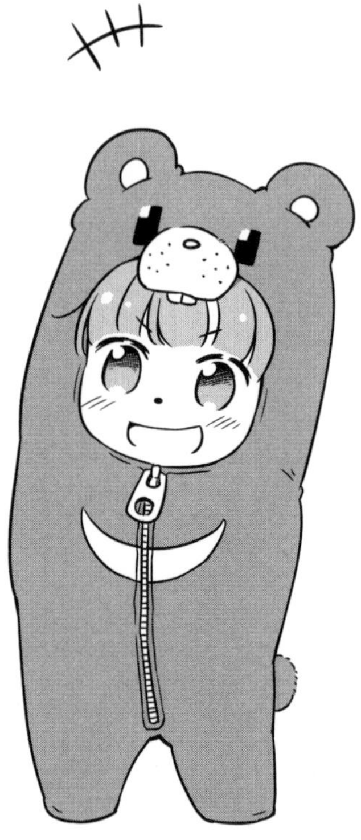

Aoba's Day Off

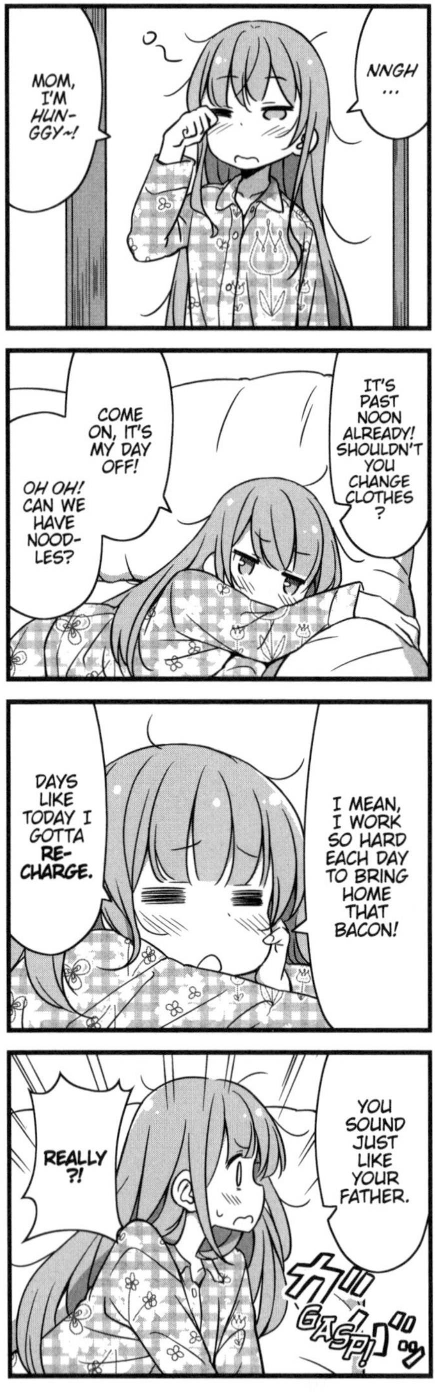
NNGH ...
MOM, I'M HUN-GGY~!
IT'S PAST NOON ALREADY! SHOULDN'T YOU CHANGE CLOTHES?
COME ON, IT'S MY DAY OFF!
OH OH! CAN WE HAVE NOODLES?
I MEAN, I WORK SO HARD EACH DAY TO BRING HOME THAT BACON!
DAYS LIKE TODAY I GOTTA **RE-CHARGE.**
YOU SOUND JUST LIKE YOUR FATHER.
REALLY ?!
GASP!

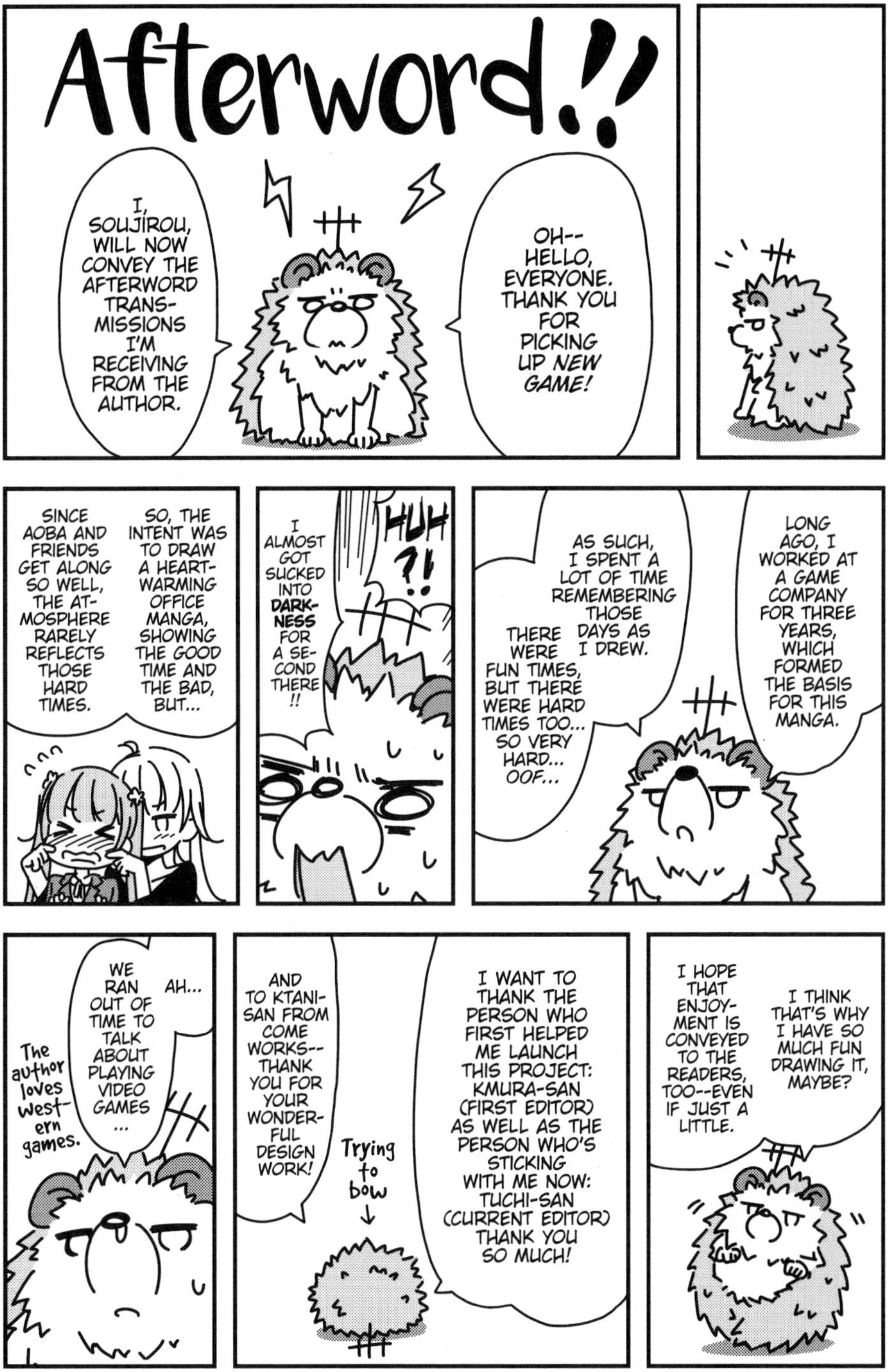
Afterword!!
OH-- HELLO, EVERYONE. THANK YOU FOR PICKING UP *NEW GAME!*
I, SOUJIROU, WILL NOW CONVEY THE AFTERWORD TRANSMISSIONS I'M RECEIVING FROM THE AUTHOR.
LONG AGO, I WORKED AT A GAME COMPANY FOR THREE YEARS, WHICH FORMED THE BASIS FOR THIS MANGA.
AS SUCH, I SPENT A LOT OF TIME REMEMBERING THOSE DAYS AS I DREW.
THERE WERE FUN TIMES, BUT THERE WERE HARD TIMES TOO... SO VERY HARD... OOF...
HUH ?!!
I ALMOST GOT SUCKED INTO DARKNESS FOR A SECOND THERE!!
SO, THE INTENT WAS TO DRAW A HEARTWARMING OFFICE MANGA, SHOWING THE GOOD TIME AND THE BAD, BUT...
SINCE AOBA AND FRIENDS GET ALONG SO WELL, THE ATMOSPHERE RARELY REFLECTS THOSE HARD TIMES.
I THINK THAT'S WHY I HAVE SO MUCH FUN DRAWING IT, MAYBE?
I HOPE THAT ENJOYMENT IS CONVEYED TO THE READERS, TOO--EVEN IF JUST A LITTLE.
I WANT TO THANK THE PERSON WHO FIRST HELPED ME LAUNCH THIS PROJECT: KMURA-SAN (FIRST EDITOR) AS WELL AS THE PERSON WHO'S STICKING WITH ME NOW: TUCHI-SAN (CURRENT EDITOR) THANK YOU SO MUCH!
AND TO KTANI-SAN FROM COME WORKS--THANK YOU FOR YOUR WONDERFUL DESIGN WORK!
Trying to bow ↓
AH...
WE RAN OUT OF TIME TO TALK ABOUT PLAYING VIDEO GAMES...
The author loves western games.

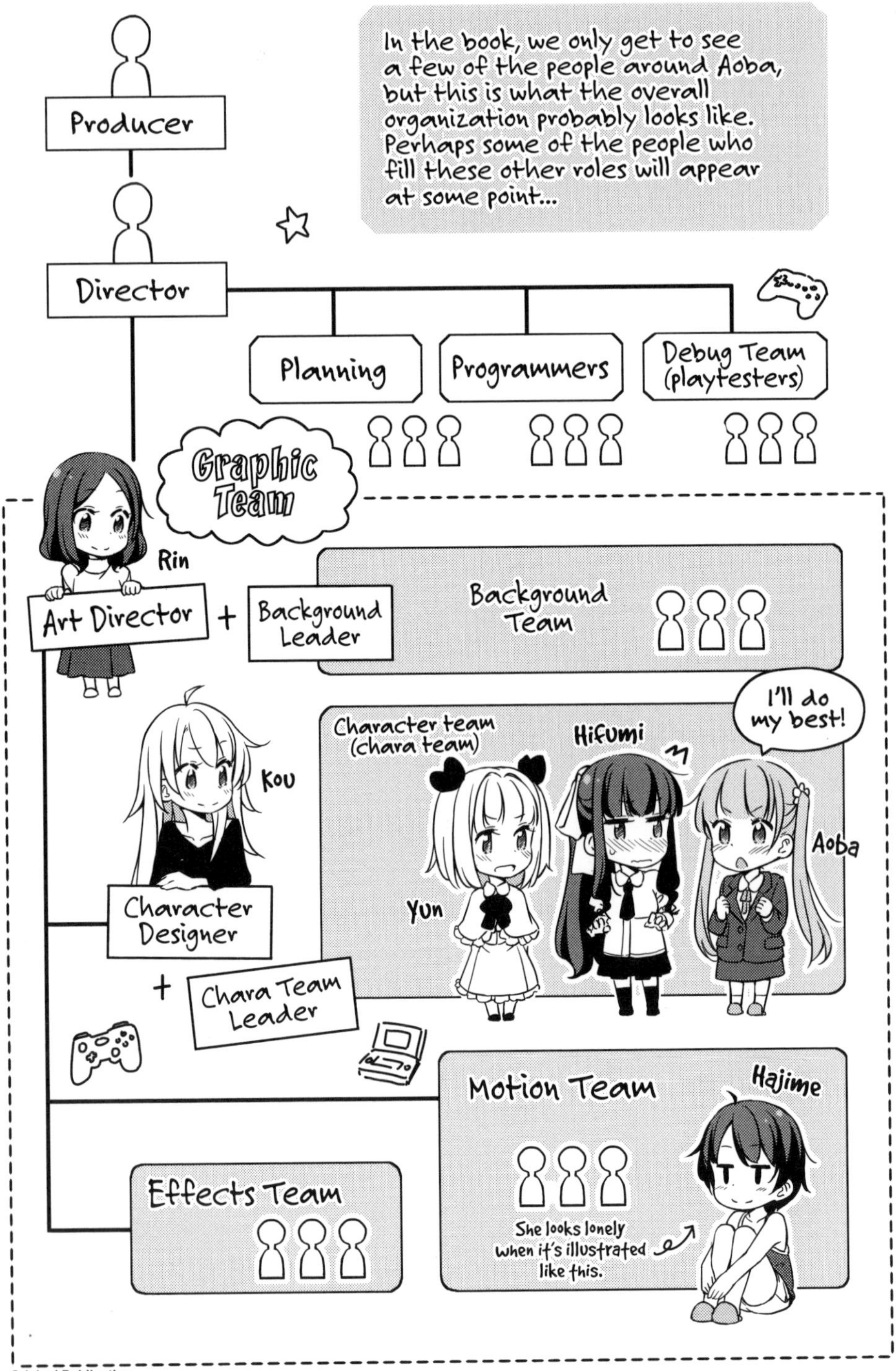
In the book, we only get to see a few of the people around Aoba, but this is what the overall organization probably looks like. Perhaps some of the people who fill these other roles will appear at some point...
Producer
Director
Planning
Programmers
Debug Team (playtesters)
Graphic Team
Rin
Art Director
+
Background Leader
Background Team
Kou
Character Designer
+
Chara Team Leader
Character team (chara team)
Hifumi
I'll do my best!
Aoba
Yun
Motion Team
Hajime
She looks lonely when it's illustrated like this.
Effects Team

Original Publication
This book collects work from the following:
• *Manga Time Kirara Carat* H25/March ~H25/May .H25/July ~H26/February
• *Manga Time Kirara Carat* 100th Issue Commemoration Website "Countdown 100" Work drawn specifically for this volume.

Employment Interview ①

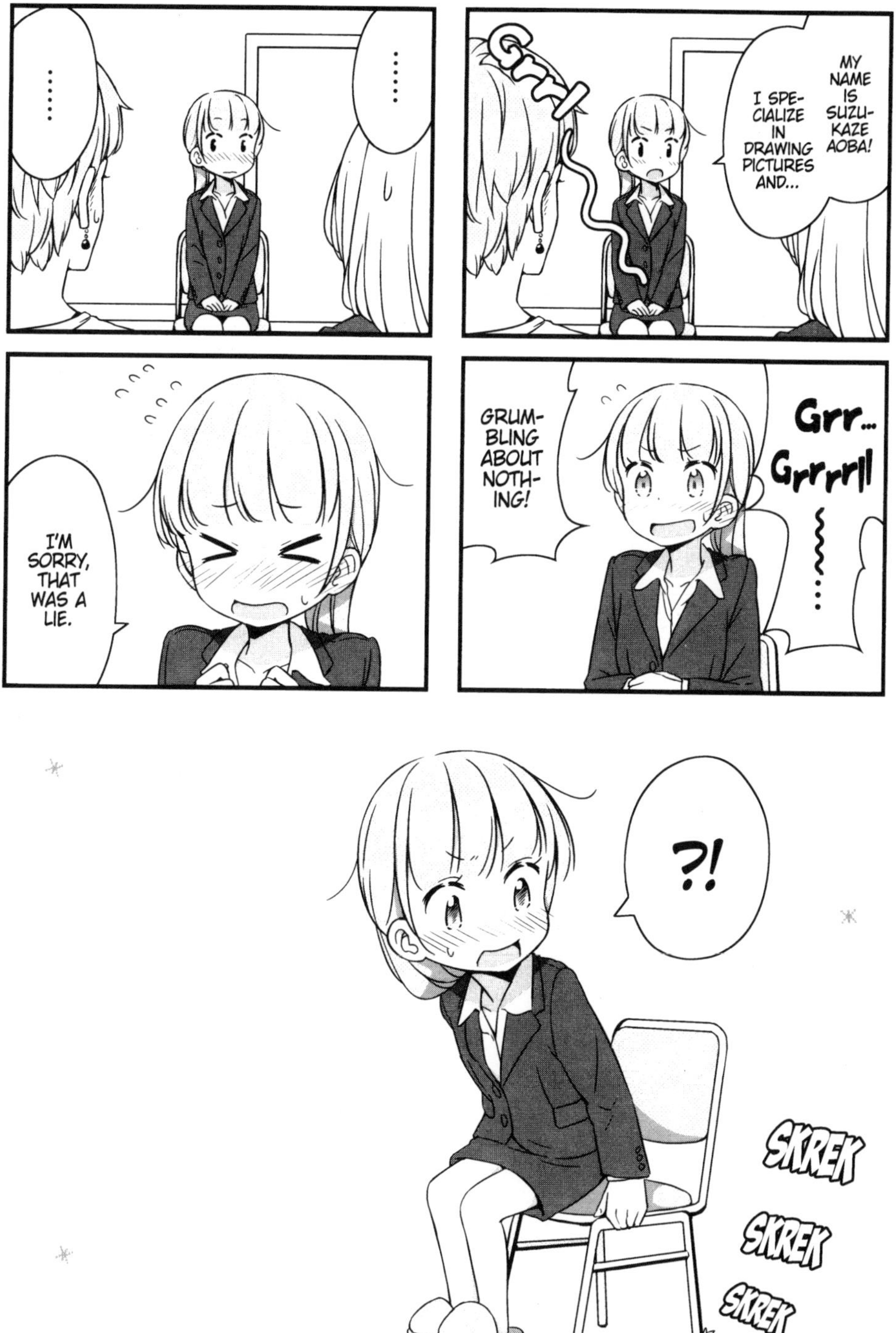
MY NAME IS SUZUKAZE AOBA!
I SPECIALIZE IN DRAWING PICTURES AND...
Grrl
......
......
Grr... Grrrrl
GRUMBLING ABOUT NOTHING!
I'M SORRY, THAT WAS A LIE.
?!
SKREK
SKREK
SKREK